Bonoure and Buxum

Sue Niebrzydowski

Bonoure and Buxum

A Study of Wives in
Late Medieval
English Literature

PETER LANG
Oxford · Bern · Berlin · Bruxelles · Frankfurt am Main · New York · Wien

Bibliographic information published by Die Deutsche Bibliothek
Die Deutsche Bibliothek lists this publication in the Deutsche
Nationalbibliografie; detailed bibliographic data is available on
the Internet at ‹http://dnb.ddb.de›.

British Library and Library of Congress Cataloguing-in-Publication Data:
A catalogue record for this book is available from The British Library,
Great Britain, and from The Library of Congress, USA

Cover illustration: Misericords (fifteenth century), St Laurence's Church, Ludlow.
Reproduced by kind permission of the Rector and church wardens.
Photo: Sue Niebrzydowski.

ISBN 3-03910-727-5
US-ISBN 0-8204-7990-X

© Peter Lang AG, International Academic Publishers, Bern 2006
Hochfeldstrasse 32, Postfach 746, CH-3000 Bern 9, Switzerland
info@peterlang.com, www.peterlang.com, www.peterlang.net

All rights reserved.
All parts of this publication are protected by copyright.
Any utilisation outside the strict limits of the copyright law, without the
permission of the publisher, is forbidden and liable to prosecution.
This applies in particular to reproductions, translations, microfilming,
and storage and processing in electronic retrieval systems.

Printed in Germany

Contents

Acknowledgements		7
Abbreviations		9
Introduction		11
Chapter One	Eligibility, Contract and Choice	29
Chapter Two	Ceremonies and Feasts	61
Chapter Three	'Bonoure & buxum in bed & at borde'	91
Chapter Four	The Drama of Childbirth and Motherhood	141
Chapter Five	Hardworking Housewife and Garrulous Shrew	177
Conclusion		211
Bibliography		219
Index		235

Acknowledgements

There are many good friends and scholars who have offered support and advice on this project and it is my pleasure to thank them. I am indebted to my former supervisor, Jane B. Stevenson, who has been a source of encouragement and scholarly insight from the project's inception to its realization. I am grateful to my colleagues at Warwick, Peter Mack, Lynne Long and Amanda Hopkins, who read chapters and offered many valuable insights and much practical advice. Special thanks are due to Christiania Whitehead; for her scrupulous and perceptive comments and for being such a supportive friend. I should also like to thank Mair Evans whose enthusiasm for the project has never flagged. In addition, thanks are due to Alexis Kirschbaum at Peter Lang AG for her patience, helpfulness and efficiency and Alan G. Mauro for his invaluable help with the preparation of the manuscript. All errors of fact and judgement remain my own.

An incalculable debt of gratitude is due to my partner, Bryan Poultney, who has displayed the patience of Job during many visits to cathedrals, churches and castles in search of medieval wives. It is to him and to my parents, Lorna and Mateusz Niebrzydowski, that this book is dedicated.

A version of Chapter Two appeared as 'Encouraging Marriage IN FACIE ECCLESIAE: The Mary Play 'Betrothal' and the Sarum *Ordo ad faciendum Sponsalia*', *Medieval English Theatre*, 24 (2002), 44–61 and appears by kind permission of the editorial board. Sections of the chapter exploring the sex life of the Wife of Bath feature in 'So wel koude he me glose': The Wife of Bath and the Eroticism of Touch' in *The Erotic in Medieval Britain*, eds., Amanda Hopkins and Cory Rushton (Woodbridge: Boydell and Brewer, forthcoming). It appears by kind permission of the editors.

Abbreviations

EETS	Early English Text Society; volume numbers in the Original Series are prefixed OS, in the Extra Series by ES, and those in the Supplementary Series by SS
HMSO	His/Her Majesty's Stationery Office
MED	*Middle English Dictionary*, ed. by S. M. Kuhn (Ann Arbor: The University of Michigan Press, 1963)

Introduction

> Yblessed be God that I have wedded fyve! [...]
> Welcome the sixte, whan that evere he shal.
> (*Wife of Bath's Prologue*, 43, 45)

Chaucer's Wife of Bath is one of the few medieval women – fictional or actual – to be remembered primarily as a wife. First married at the age of twelve, she has participated in not one but five wedding ceremonies, enjoyed an active sex-life, and experienced both marital bliss and strife in the shifting power relations of her successive co-habitations.[1] She is, without doubt, the most infamous wife of late medieval English literature and because she eagerly anticipates husband number six, she is a useful introduction to this study of wives in English literature of the later Middle Ages.

Young and old, rich and poor, chaste and wanton, married women populate courtly romance, fabliau, cycle drama, life-writing, lyrics and hagiography of the fourteenth and fifteenth centuries. During the 1990s the academy embraced queer theory and set about exploring alternative sexualities.[2] Under the influence of post modern critical practices that explore marginal lives, late twentieth century medievalism focuses upon the virgin and the widow, and continues to interrogate lifestyles and sexualities other than normative, married heterosexuality. Historians have made medieval marriage *per se* the subject of frequent investigation and recovered women's testimony of their matrimonial

---

[1] *The Riverside Chaucer*, ed. by L. D. Benson (Oxford: Oxford University Press, 1988), p.105. All quotations from Chaucer are taken from this edition.

[2] For studies of widowhood see *Wife and Widow in Medieval England*, ed. by S. Sheridan Walker (Ann Arbor, Michigan: The University of Michigan Press, 1993) and *Medieval London Widows 1300–1500*, ed. by C. M. Barron and A. F. Sutton (London: Hambledon Press, 1994). Virginity has been most recently explored in *Medieval Virginities*, ed. by A. Bernau, S. Salih and R. Evans (Cardiff: University of Wales Press, 2003).

experiences: literary scholars have not been so forthcoming.[3] There are some exceptions. Neil Cartlidge's study of marriage in early medieval literature is invaluable, but his *terminus post quem* is 1300.[4] The edited collections of Eve Salisbury and Conor McCarthy demonstrate the breadth of medieval interest in marriage and make available less well-known works, but analysis of their contents is not their primary purpose.[5] When Conor McCarthy does examine medieval literature, his work draws on examples ranging from the Anglo-Saxon period to the later Middle Ages, and is succinct in its focus on the influence of ecclesiastical and secular marriage law on selected literary examples.[6] Frances Minetti Biscoglio focuses on those wives in Chaucer's *Canterbury Tales* who exemplify the *mulier fortis* or valiant woman of Proverbs 31.[7] While any discussion of late medieval literary wives

3   For detailed studies of the canon law governing marriage see J. A. Brundage, *Law, Sex and Christian Society in Medieval Europe* (Chicago: University of Chicago Press, 1987) and *Medieval Canon Law* (London: Longman, 1995), *Sexual Practices and the Medieval Church*, ed. by J. Brundage and V. L. Bullough (Buffalo, NY: Prometheus Books, 1982). On the importance of consent in marriage formation see A. Cosgrove, 'Consent, consummation and indissolubility: some evidence from medieval ecclesiastical courts', *Downside Review*, 109 (1991), 94–104 and P. L. Reynolds, 'Marriage, Sacramental and Indissoluble: Sources of the Catholic Doctrine', *Downside Review*, 109 (1991), 105–50. On the impact of marriage on social and household structures see P. Fleming, *Family and Household in Medieval England* (Basingstoke: Palgrave, 2001). Examples of women's marital experiences are revealed in *Women in England c. 1275–1525: Documentary Sources*, trans. and ed. by P. J. P. Goldberg (Manchester: Manchester University Press, 1995). A fascinating insight into the marital strife of a couple from York is given in F. Pedersen, *Romeo and Juliet of Stonegate: a medieval marriage in crisis*, Paper 87 (York: Borthwick Institute of Historical Research, University of York, 1995).
4   N. Cartlidge, *Medieval Marriage: Literary Approaches 1100–1300* (Cambridge: D. S. Brewer, 1997).
5   *The Trials and Joys of Marriage*, ed. by E. Salisbury, TEAMS Middle English Text Series (Kalamazoo, Michigan: Medieval Institute Publications, 2002); *Love, Sex and Marriage in the Middle Ages: A Sourcebook*, ed. by C. McCarthy (London: Routledge, 2004).
6   C. McCarthy, *Marriage in Medieval England: Law, Literature and Practice* (Woodbridge: The Boydell Press, 2004).
7   F. M. Biscoglio, *The Wives of the Canterbury Tales and The Tradition of the Valiant Woman of Proverbs 31: 10–31* (San Francisco: Mellen Research Uni-

would be incomplete without a consideration of Chaucer's fictive creations, this one included, wives have a presence in many texts in addition to those of Richard II's Clerk of Works.

This book seeks to direct the spotlight on a literary figure whose role is considered so familiar and so well understood that it has excited little exploration. In this enquiry, virginity features in as much as it is normally a prerequisite in first-time brides. Widowhood *per se* has been excluded, but widows on the point of remarriage are included as their path to marriage reveals the variety of experience between being wooed and wed on a first and on a subsequent occasion. This volume examines peasant, bourgeois and noble wives in a selection of English vernacular texts that describe one or more (but unfortunately never all) of the defining moments in a wife's lifetime. Commencing with how a woman becomes a wife, chapters are devoted to her wedding ceremony, becoming a mother and living as a wife of many years' standing. Some wives included are happily wed, others not so fortunate in their marital relationships.

How to interrogate and interpret such diversity is suggested in a scene towards the close of the Wife of Bath's prologue in which Jankyn reads aloud from his compilation of cautionary *exempla* of wicked wives. Suffering what Priscilla Martin calls 'ordeal by literature'[8] Alisoun recognises that her representation as a wife, and Jankyn's understanding and expectation of this role, is in dialogue with contemporary textual discourses that define and attempt to construct appropriate wifely conduct. This the Wife of Bath shares with all the wives included in this volume. The list is long of the discourses that seek to influence when and how a woman becomes a wife, the nature of her wedding ceremony and the conduct of her life as a married woman. Canon and

versity Press, 1993). For other studies of Chaucerian wives see H. A. Kelly, *Love and Marriage in the Age of Chaucer* (Ithaca, NY: Cornell University Press, 1975), C. Brook, *The Medieval Idea of Marriage* (Oxford: Clarendon Press, 1989), P. Martin, *Chaucer's Women: Nuns, Wives and Amazons* (London: Macmillan, 1990, reprint 1996), M. Hallissy, *Clean Maids, True Wives, Steadfast Widows: Chaucer's Women and Medieval Codes of Conduct* (Westport: Greenwood Press, 1993) and K. Jacobs, *Marriage Contracts from Chaucer to the Renaissance Stage* (Gainesville: University Press of Florida, 2001).

8   Martin, *Chaucer's Women*, p.6.

secular law, the marriage liturgy, medical treatises on the female body, sermons, manuals of spiritual instruction, biblical paradigms, conduct books and misogamous writings all endeavour to define and regulate being a wife. Their influence can be detected in the representation of wives in late medieval literature. Each chapter in this volume opens with an examination of the texts that seek to determine a particular moment in the career of a wife and explores the way in which the literary text engages with such material.

From Jankyn's perspective Alisoun is found wanting in comparison with the good wifely paradigms and has all too much in common with the bad. When she asks 'Who peyntede the leon, tel me who?' (*Wife of Bath's Prologue*, 692), Alisoun recognises the importance of point of view or situatedness of the creators of these discourses. Alisoun argues that had women written about wives, their views would have been different from those of the celibate clerics who were largely responsible for the discourses that frame wifehood. In this work every effort has been made to present the point of view of the lion. Hearing women's voices within the predominantly male-authored literature of the Middle Ages is indubitably problematic. This applies as much to Alisoun of Bath as to any other female fictive character. Although dynamic, engaging and plausible Chaucer's creation is, nonetheless, as Anne Laskaya points out, 'the masquerade of the female voice'.[9] E. Jane Burns faces this same dilemma when listening for female voices in Old French literature.[10] Burns advocates an interpretative strategy that examines female characters' speech or 'bodytalk', 'however constructed it may admittedly be listening for something other than the dominant discourse that medieval heroines' bodies and voices were designed to convey.[11] Burns argues that in listening to this 'bodytalk' one can hear 'how female voices, fashioned by a male author to represent misogynous fantasies of female corporeality, can also be heard

---

9   A. Laskaya, *Chaucer's Approach to Gender in the Canterbury Tales* (Cambridge: D. S. Brewer, 1995), p.166.
10 E. J. Burns, *Bodytalk: When Women Speak in Old French Literature* (Philadelphia: University of Pennsylvania Press, 1993), p.xii.
11 Burns, *Bodytalk*, pp.xii, 7.

to rewrite the tales in which they appear'.[12] On listening to the wives included in this volume, as they speak within and against the dominant male discourses that sought to influence wifedom, one can hear the paradigm of the ideal wife, male anxiety about and expectation of inappropriate wifely conduct and women's attitudes toward these parameters. These married women's actions demonstrate the possibility of manoeuvring within them. The attitudes expressed by literary wives are supplemented along the way by what the Wife of Bath might call the discourse of lived experience. The words and histories of real wives found preserved in church and manorial court records, in their wills and in their writings provide testimony of the attitudes held and strategies practised by the real women whom these discourses were designed to regulate.

By the later Middle Ages the nature and status of a wife had long been subject to debate and ambivalent response. Beginning with Eve, the archetype of wifely disobedience, the Old Testament contains numerous examples of behaviour that give wives a poor press. Adam's decision to listen to his wife and eat the fruit earns hard labour for himself and all successive men (Genesis 3. 17–19). God's punishment of Eve and all successive wives is painful childbirth and subordination to her husband (Genesis 3. 16). In addition to disobedience and lust Old Testament writers accuse wives of anger, garrulity and audacity:

> *nequitia mulieris inmutat faciem eius et obcaecabit vultum suum tamquam ursus, et quasi saccum ostendit in medio proximorum eius et audiens suspirabit modicum brevis malitia super malitiam mulieris sors peccatorum cadat super illam ascensus harenosus in pedibus veterani sic mulier linguata homini quieto ne respicias in mulieris speciem et non concupiscas mulierem in specie mulieris ira et inreverentia et confusio magna mulier si primatum habeat contraria est viro suo.*
>
> [The wickedness of a woman changeth her face; and she darkeneth her countenance as a bear: and showeth it like sack-cloth. In the midst of her neighbours, her husband groaned, and hearing he sighed a little. All malice is short to the malice of a woman, let the lot of the sinner fall upon her. As the climbing of a sandy way is to the feet of the aged, so is a wife full of tongue to a quiet man. Look not upon a woman's beauty, and desire not a woman for beauty. A woman's

---

12   Ibid., p.7.

> anger, and impudence, and confusion is great. A woman, if she have superiority, is contrary to her husband].
> (Ecclesiasticus 25. 24–30)[13]

The author of Ecclesiasticus has heard far too many wives loudly remonstrate their way to the upper hand. This view is countered, however, by the writer of Proverbs 31. 10–31.[14] A wife is trustworthy and able to manage her time well. Her husband profits materially through her industry (spinning, weaving, gathering food) and property development. She is physically strong, charitable, optimistic, dignified, wise, kindly spoken and fertile. The writer of Proverbs acknowledges that such wives are hard to find.

Early Christian writers reveal a similar ambivalence towards wives (and husbands) since some of the Church Fathers considered those who married to be less spiritual than those who did not. Paul's often quoted dictum, '*Melius est enim nubere quam uri*' [It is better to marry than to burn] (I Corinthians 7. 9), that remained so influential in medieval thought, succeeded in damning marriage with faint praise. Although Paul offered this as advice to the early Christians at Corinth *against* abandoning marriage in favour of celibacy, this is not how it was interpreted by later ages. Peter Brown notes how this argument 'slid perceptibly into an attitude that viewed marriage itself as no more than

---

13 All quotations from the Vulgate are taken from R. Weber, et al., eds., *Biblia Sacra iuxta Vulgatam Versionem*, 2 vols (Stuttgart: Württembergische Bibelanstalt, 1969). The translation can be found in *Woman Defamed and Woman Defended*, ed. by A. Blamires (Oxford: Clarendon Press, 1992), p.35.

14 The Latin reads: *Mulierem fortem quis inveniet procul et de ultimis finibus pretium eius confidit in ea cor viri sui et spoliis non indigebit reddet ei bonum et non malum omnibus diebus vitae suae quaesivit lanam et linum et operata est consilio manuum suarum facta est quasi navis institoris de longe portat panem suum et de nocte surrexit deditque praedam domesticis suis et cibaria ancillis suis consideravit agrum et emit eum de fructu manuum suarum plantavit vineam accinxit fortitudine lumbos suos et roboravit brachium suum gustavit quia bona est negotiatio eius non extinguetur in nocte lucerna illius manum suam misit ad fortia et digiti eius adprehenderunt fusum manum suam aperuit inopi et palmas suas extendit ad pauperem non timebit domui suae a frigoribus nivis omnes enim domestici eius vestiti duplicibus stragulam vestem fecit sibi bysus et purpura indumentum eius nobilis in portis vir eius quando sederit cum senatoribus terrae.*

a defence against desire'.[15] Most famously, concern about the deleterious effects of sex upon the soul prompted Jerome, in around 393, to write in his treatise *Adversus Jovinianum* (Jovinian having written in defence of marriage) of the relative spiritual value of being a virgin, wife and widow. In the next life, Jerome argues, virgins will reap a hundredfold reward, chaste widows a sixtyfold and the married a mere thirtyfold.[16] Being a spouse and sexually active in this world was believed, by some, to militate against one's reward in the next.

Although Jerome advocated celibacy as the better way of living, St Paul had formulated the concept of the marital debt or sexual intercourse on demand. This he makes clear is the both the right and the duty of either spouse to demand and give (I Corinthians 7. 1–3). Paul strongly encourages widows and widowers to remain single after the death of their spouse (I Corinthians 7. 40) but recognises that some will want to remarry. He stipulates that if her husband dies, a woman is free to marry whom she will '*si dormierit vir eius liberata est cui vult nubat tantum in Domino*' [if her husband dies, she is freed. Let her marry whom she will in the Lord] (I Corinthians 7. 39). Later St Augustine was to argue that marriage was made in Paradise with the union of Adam and Eve[17] and in his *De Bono Conjugali* (*c.* 401) that marriage contains three goods or benefits.[18] These are *fides* (friendship

15 P. Brown, *The Body and Society. Men, Women and Sexual Renunciation in Early Christianity* (New York: Columbia University Press, 1988), p.55.
16 Selections from the *Adversus Jovinianum* can be found translated in Blamires, *Woman Defamed*, pp.63–74.
17 In Book I of the *De genesis contra Manichaeos* (written in the late 380s) Augustine contended that Adam and Eve's marriage in Paradise was created by God as a spiritual, non-carnal relationship in which they would have reproduced asexually. Augustine's more mature view, as expressed in Book IX of the *De Genesi ad litteram* (first decade of the fifth century), was that God created Eve for the means of sexual procreation within marriage. For a detailed analysis of the progression of Augustine's attitude to marriage see P. L. Reynolds, *Marriage in the Western Church: The Christianisation of Marriage During the Patristic and Early Medieval Periods* (Leiden: E. J. Brill, 1994), Chapter Eleven, 'Augustine on Marriage as Spiritual Union'.
18 Augustine adhered to the patristic honouring of virginity over marriage when he stated that 'marriage and continence are two goods whereof the second is the better', *De Bono Conjugali: The Good of Marriage*, translated by C. L. Cornish

and fidelity), *proles* (the bearing and rearing of children) and *sacramentum*. The latter was the sacramental quality or character of marriage that unites the participants with Christ's union with the Church and extends to them some form of sacramental grace if both are baptised.[19] From its inception Christian marital discourse did not allow divorce and advised against, but did not forbid, second marriages on the death of a spouse.[20]

Rooted in the teachings of some of the early Church Fathers, monogamous attitudes blossom in the Middle Ages into gender-specific attacks against the person of the wife. Katherine Wilson and Elizabeth Makowski demonstrate how anti-marriage literature, of which they define three main strands, re-emerged in the twelfth century to proliferate in the cities and bourgeois culture of the thirteenth century.[21] Ascetic misogamy, a direct descendant of the views expressed by Jerome, advocated the avoidance of marriage in the expectation of imminent apocalypse and heavenly reward. Philosophic misogamy advocated celibacy for philosophers and scholars because family life distracted from the more important tasks of religion and learning. Heloise (1101–64) encapsulates this attitude in her comment to her erstwhile husband, Abelard (1079–1142),

> *Que enim conventio scolarium ad paedissequas, scriptoriorum ad cunabula, librorum sive tabularum ad colos, stilorum sive calamorum ad fusos? Quis denique sacris vel philosophicis meditationibus intentus, pueriles vagitus, nutriacum que hos mittigant nenias, tumultuosam familie tam in viris quam in feminis turbam sustinere poterit?*
>
> [What harmony can there be between pupils and nursemaids, desks and cradles, books or tablets and distaffs, pen or stylus and spindles? Who can concentrate on thoughts of Scripture or philosophy and be able to endure babies crying, nurses

---

in *A Select Library of the Nicene and Post-Nicene Fathers of the Christian Church*, ed. by P. Schaff, II, *St Augustine* (Michigan: Wm. B. Eerdmans, reprint 1978), p. 401. See also Reynolds, 'Marriage, Sacramental and Indissoluble', p.116.

19   Reynolds, *Marriage in the Western Church*, p.xxi.
20   Brundage, *Law, Sex and Christian Society*, p.61.
21   K. M. Wilson and E. M. Makowski, *Wykked Wyves and the Woes of Marriage: Misogamous Literature from Juvenal to Chaucer* (Albany, NY: State University of New York, 1990), p.160.

soothing them with lullabies, and all the noisy coming and going of men and women about the house?].[22]

Both ascetic and philosophic misogamy was expressed in texts written in Latin for an educated audience. The third strand, that Wilson and Makowski term general misogamy, is most pertinent to this study. Characterised in its delivery by an indignant persona who catalogues the misdeeds of wicked wives, this branch of misogamous literature, much of which is written in or translated into the vernacular, was directed at Everyman.[23] Often wryly humorous in tone, this strand argued that marriage is madness and hell for the poor, victimised husband whose goods and energies are drained by a wife who is sexually voracious and prone to adultery. It is a literary tradition that remained in vogue throughout the Middle Ages, as illustrated by the immense popularity of *De Coniuge non Ducenda* [Against Marrying] or *De Poena Coniugii* [The punishment of Marriage], composed *c.* 1225–50, and still being translated in the fifteenth century when it was falsely attributed to Walter Map.[24] In it wives are criticised for using any excuse to leave the house for sexual dalliance:

> Of ther nature they gretly hem delite
> With holy face fayned for the nones
> In seyntuaries ther frends to visite,
> More then for relikkes or any seyntis bones,
> Though they be closed under precious stones,
> To gete hem pardon like there olde usages,
> To kys no shrynes but lusty yong images.[25]

---

22 *Historia Calamitatum: The Story of His Misfortunes* in B. Radice, ed, and trans., *The Letters of Abelard and Heloise* (Harmondsworth: Penguin, 1973), p.73. For the Latin see *Abélard: Historia Calamitatum* ed. by J. Monfrin (Paris: Librarie Philosophique J. Vrin, 1959), p.70.

23 Wilson and Makowski, *Wykked Wyves*, p.161.

24 A. G. Rigg, *A Glastonbury Miscellany of the Fifteenth Century: A Descriptive Index of Trinity College, Cambridge MS. O. 9. 38* (Oxford: Oxford University Press, 1968), p.41. Map is identified as the author in the *explicit*: Explicit Magister *Walterus Mape de Pena Coniugii.*

25 *The Payne and Sorowe of Evyll Maryage*, Oxford, Bodleian Library, MS Digby, No. 181, fol. 7 in *The Latin Poems commonly attributed to Walter Mapes*, ed. by T. Wright (London: The Camden Society, 1841), pp.295–99 (p.298).

Such sentiments occurred in lyrics that outline the trials of marriage and advised men against hasty marriage,

> Know or thow knytte [marry]; Prove or thow preyse yt.
> 3yf þou knyt er þou knowe, Than yt ys to late.
> Ther-fore Avyse þe er þou þe knot knytte [tie the knot in marriage],
> Ffor 'had y wyst' commeth to late for to lowse yt.[26]

The Wife of Bath is no stranger to such texts and their sentiments. The book read night and day and with much amusement by Jankyn, is a compilation of '[...] Valerie and Theofraste, / [...] Seinte Jerome, / [...] Tertulan, [...] and Helowys' (*Wife of Bath's Prologue*, 671, 674, 677). Valerius, Theofrastus, St Jerome, Tertullian and Heloise; the Wife of Bath is familiar with names of the writers of misogamous literature from the classical period until the early Middle Ages.[27] As we shall see, misogamist vilification was only one textual influence upon the representation of wives in late medieval literature.

A more positive attitude towards wives was encouraged by the affirmation of marriage that occurred in the twelfth and thirteenth centuries. During the twelfth century those who married were offered protection by canon law, devised notably by Gratian (*fl. c.* 1140), Peter Lombard (*c.* 1095–1160) and Hugh of St Victor (d. 1141). In this period marriage liturgies were developed to celebrate the union.[28] By the thirteenth century marriage was included among the seven sacraments of

---

26 *Secular Lyrics of the XIVth and XVth Centuries*, ed. by R. H. Robbins (Oxford: Clarendon Press, 1952, reprint 1961), number 40, p.37.

27 'Valerie' is Walter Map's *The Dissuasio Valerii ad Rufinum philosophum, ne uxorem ducat*, probably composed in the 1170s. This work circulated independently before being incorporated into Map's *De Nugis Curialium*, Distinction IV, C. 3. See *Walter Map De Nugis Curialium: Courtiers Trifles*, ed. and trans. by M. R. James (Oxford: Clarendon Press, 1983), pp.288–311. 'Theofraste' is conceivably the work of Theophrastus (*c.* 373–288 BC) and Jerome's 'book agayn Jovinian' is the *Adversus Jovinianum* composed 393. For a translation and examination of these works see *Jankyn's Book of Wikked Wyves. Volume I: The Primary Texts*, ed. by R. Hanna III and T. Lawler (Athens: The University of Georgia Press, 1997).

28 K. Stevenson, *Nuptial Blessing: A Study of Christian Marriage Rites* (New York: Oxford University Press, 1983) and *Medieval Liturgy: A Book of Essays*, ed. by L. Larson-Miller (New York: Garland Publishing, 1997).

the New Covenant and if between baptised Christians, was believed to confer grace and to be spiritually efficacious to those who participated in it.[29] Only fifty years after the death of Heloise, the Fourth Lateran Council (1215) declared that 'not only virgins and the celibate but also married persons find favour with God by right faith and good actions and deserve to attain eternal blessedness'.[30] The fourteenth-century spiritual manual, *The Book of the Vices and Virtues*, considered marriage, faithfully kept, was to be praised,

> For it is a state of grete autorite. God sett it and made it [in] paradis terrestre [Eden] in þe state of innocence, to-fore þat euer any man dide synne. And þerfore schulde men kepe it holiliche for God, þt ordeyned it, and for þe stede þat it was made ynne. After, it is a state of grete worþinesse. For God himself, wolde be bore of a wif [...] After, men schulde kepe it holiliche, for it is a sacrament of holy chirche, and bitwex God and þe soule [...].[31]

With this cultural shift in attitude towards marriage can be detected a change in outlook toward women in general. Alcuin Blamires observes how in the twelfth and thirteenth centuries *topoi* stating the case in defence of women draw together and stabilise.[32] Typically,

29 Thomas Aquinas explained why in his *Summa contra Gentiles* (1259–64): And because the sacraments effect what they signify it must be believed that through this sacrament a grace is conferred on those who marry by means of which they may conform [*pertineant*] to the union between Christ and the Church. This is most necessary for them, in order that they should so attend to carnal and earthly things that they are not separated from Christ and the Church. As quoted in Reynolds, 'Marriage, Sacramental and Indissoluble', p.138. The view that marriage conferred grace and was one of the Seven Sacraments had been accepted in England at the First Council of Salisbury (1217–19). It was adopted as dogmatic truth by the Council of Florence (1431–46) and the Council of Trent (1546–63) ultimately condemned contrary views as heresy, Brundage, *Law, Sex and Christian Society*, p.433.
30 *Decrees of the Ecumenical Councils. Volume I (Nicaeai–Lateran V)*, ed. by N. P. Tanner (London: Sheed & Ward; Washington: Georgetown University Press, 1990), pp.250–51.
31 *The Book of Vices and Virtues: A Fourteenth century English Translation of the Somme Le Roi of Lorens d'Orleans*, ed. by W. N. Francis, EETS OS 217 (London: Oxford University Press, 1942, reprint 1968), pp.245–46.
32 A. Blamires, *The Case for Women in Culture* (Oxford: Clarendon Press, 1997), p.9.

these include recognition of women's powerful interventions in history, beginning with the Virgin Mary, and of women's greater capacity for moral rectitude.[33] By the fourteenth century the case for women was supported further by the acknowledgement that they excelled in nursing, healing, and running households, that they brought men joy and repose, could transform men's behaviour and that they are, if physically weak, more praiseworthy for their moral strength.[34] This complement of virtues is extolled in the lyric, 'In Praise of Women',

> To onpreyse wemen yt were a shame,
> For a woman was thy dame;
> Our blessyd lady beryth the name
> of all women wher that they goo.
> A woman ys a worthy thyng-
> they do the washe and do the wrynge [out clothes];
> 'lullay, lullay,' she dothe the synge,
> And yet she hath but care and woo.
> A woman ys a worthy wyght,
> she seruyth a man both daye and nyght,
> therto she puttyth all her myght,
> And yet she hathe bot care and woo.[35]

The attitudinal change toward marriage and women is significant for the literary representation of wives. Frances Minetti Biscoglio demonstrates the popularity in the writings of Chaucer of presentations of wives based on the *mulier fortis*.[36] The appearance of the *mulier fortis* and her sisters in the literature of the later Middle Ages occurred in a period that extolled the virtues of the good wife as well as the failings of the bad and ugly. Some wives literally were saintly since, by this period, sanctity was no longer the preserve of the virgin martyrs. This change is illustrated by comparison of Christina of Markyate and St Anne, the mother of the Virgin Mary. In early female saints' lives marriage is presented as something to be avoided, often in the face of great physical torment or obstacles that would deter lesser mortals. This

---

33 Ibid., p.9.
34 Ibid., pp.60–61.
35 Robbins, *Secular Lyrics*, number 34, p.31.
36 Biscoglio, *Wives of the Canterbury Tales*, p.7.

is the case for Christina of Markyate (*c.* 1096–98 – *c.* 1155–66). She was married to Burthred against her will but preserved her virginity despite her parents' ruse of letting Burthred into her room while she was asleep in order that he might rape her.[37] Christina dealt with the situation by sitting on her bed with him and relating the story of St Cecilia and her husband Valerian who lived together in chastity (a tale told later in the *Canterbury Tales* by the Second Nun). Christina endeavoured to teach Burthred that marriage at best was a severe burden to be endured while maintaining one's chastity. This proved to be the case since Burthred tried on two further occasions to consummate their marriage. On the first Christina was hidden miraculously behind a wall hanging and, believing the room empty, Burthred departed. On the second occasion, as Burthred entered her room, Christina fled through another door and leaped an impossibly high spiked fence to escape her husband.[38] Her angry father stripped Christina of her clothes leaving her only her shift and threatened to throw her naked from the house while her mother persecuted her with what the *vita* writer calls '*nunc occultis nunc apertis insidiis iniuriisque persecuta est*' [unheard-of cruelty, sometimes openly, at other times secretly] (*The Life of Christina of Markyate*, p.72). Burthred finally released Christina from her marriage vows after he received a vision of the Virgin Mary who harshly reproached him for persecuting his wife.[39]

By the thirteenth century the sea-change in attitude towards marriage affected the sanctity acknowledged to married women. Marc Glasser identifies one outcome of what he terms 'the new view of the healthiness and holiness of Christian marriage' as hagiographers' willingness to find model lives for all Christendom in the careers of married women and men.[40] Later medieval England venerated a saintly

37 *The Life of Christina of Markyate: A Twelfth Century Recluse*, ed. by C. H. Talbot (Oxford: Clarendon Press, 1959), p.50. The Latin reads '[…] *Si forte dormientem virginem reperiret: repente oppresse illuderet*'.
38 Ibid., p.53.
39 Talbot, *Life of Christina of Markyate* , p.109.
40 M. Glasser, 'Marriage in Medieval Hagiography', *Studies in Medieval and Renaissance History*, 4 (1987), 3–34 (p.23). Clarissa Atkinson notes how between the thirteenth and fifteenth centuries there is a new appreciation of marriage, family and motherhood that offered an alternative route towards female sanctity,

23

wife, St Anne, the mother of the Virgin Mary. In his fourteenth-century sermon for Anne's feast day (26 July) in the *Festial* (c. 1400), John Myrc instructed people to,

> Knele adowne, and pray Saynt Anne to pray to her holy doghtyr, oure lady, þat scho pray to her sonne þat he ȝeue you hele yn body and yn sowle, and grace to kepe your ordyr of wedlok, and gete such chyldryn þat byn plesant and trew seruandys to God, and soo com to þe blys þat Saynt Anne ys yn.[41]

Anne was perceived as a saintly exemplar precisely because she was understood to have married on no fewer than three occasions and produced a holy dynasty of daughters and grandsons.

Information concerning Anne's multiple marriages (sometimes called the *Trinubium*) was disseminated through Middle English translations of the *Legenda Aurea*,[42] the Latin collection of saints' lives written between the 1260s and 1290 by the Dominican, Jacobus de Voragine. In his entry for the Nativity of Mary (8 September) Voragine tells how Anne was married three times; first to Ioachim from which marriage Mary was born, next to Joseph's brother, Cleophas with whom she produced Mary Cleophas and finally to Salomas by whom she bore Mary Salomas. Each Mary produced significant figures in God's salvific schema; the Virgin Mary bore Christ, Mary Cleophas James the Less, Simon, Joseph (or Barnabas) and Jude, Mary Salome James the Greater and John the Evangelist.[43] The purpose of the genealogical

---

The Oldest Vocation: Christian Motherhood in the Middle Ages (Ithaca: Cornell University Press, 1991), p.144.

41 *Myrc's Festial: a Collection of Homilies by Johannes Myrcus (John Myrc), Part I*, ed. by T. Erbe, EETS 96 (London: Kegan Paul, Trench, Trübner, 1905), p.216.

42 Jacobus de Voragine, *Legenda aurea vulgo historia lombardica dicta*, ed. by J. G. T. Graesse (Arnold: Leipzig, 1846).

43 *Anna solet dici tres concepisse Marias, / Quas genuere viri Joachim, Cleophas, Salomeque. / Has duxere viri Joseph, Alpheus, Zebedaeus. / Prima parit Christum, Jacobum secunda minorem, / Et Joseph justum peperit cum Simone Judam, / Tertia majorem Jacobum volucremque Joannem.* [Anna is usually said to have conceived three Marys, / Whom [her] husbands, Joachim, Cleophas, and Salome, begot. / The Marys were taken in marriage by Joseph, Alpheus, Zebedee. / The first Mary bore Christ, the second, James the Less, / Joseph the Just with Simon and Jude, / the third, James the Greater and John the Wingèd.] *Jacobus de*

detail of Anne's three marriages was to safeguard the perpetual virginity of Mary from the troublesome existence of Jesus' brothers and sisters mentioned in Matthew 12. 46, Mark 3. 31 and Luke 19. 21. These children are explained away as the offspring of Anne's daughters from her second and third marriages and are thus Jesus' cousins.

Although arousing controversy in the twelfth century primarily because it was considered a challenge to the growing belief in Anne's immaculate conception of Mary,[44] by the later Middle Ages Anne's multiple marriages and the wide kinship group that they produced was celebrated in written word and plastic arts. A Middle English *Life of Anne* records the details of Anne's multiple marriages whose complexity it makes no attempt to disguise, exhorting its audience, 'To here and to lere of thyng that is good.'[45] The annotator of the N-Town plays attempted to represent visually the relationships in the margin of the plays' manuscript. Pamela Sheingorn identifies two English Psalters, the *Imola Psalter* and the *Queen Mary Psalter*, that 'juxtapose such a clearly female genealogy with the patriarchal Tree of Jesse by placing the two genealogies on consecutive or facing pages [...]'.[46] Eamon Duffy interprets the late fifteenth-century painted images on the north screen of Houghton St Giles as 'a complete image of abundant fruitfulness – Emeria [Anne's sister], Mary Salome, Mary Cleophas, the Blessed Virgin, Elizabeth, Anne, and all their holy children'.[47] Pre-Reformation England boasts also a number of stained glass windows depicting the Holy families arising from Anne's multiple marriages, a configuration that is often called *The Holy Kinship*. Panels in the south

Voragine: The Golden Legend. Readings on the Saints, trans. by W. G. Ryan, 2 vols (Princeton, NJ: Princeton University Press, 1993), 2, p.150, note 3.

[44] *The Dogma of the Immaculate Conception: History and Significance*, ed. by E. D. O'Connor (Notre Dame, Indiana: University of Notre Dame Press, 1958).

[45] *The Middle English Stanzaic Versions of the Life of St Anne*, ed. by R. E. Parker EETS OS 174 (London: Oxford University Press, 1928), p.xxvi.

[46] P. Sheingorn, 'Appropriating the Holy Kinship', in *Interpreting Cultural Symbols: Saint Anne in Late Medieval Society*, ed. by K. Ashley and P. Sheingorn (Athens: The University of Georgia Press, 1990), pp.169–98 (p.171).

[47] E. Duffy, 'Holy Maydens, Holy Wyfes: The Cult of Women Saints in Fifteenth- and Sixteenth-Century England', *Studies in Church History*, 27 (1990), 175–96 (p.193).

window of the Saville chapel of Thornhill church (West Yorkshire) dating from around 1447 portray the three Holy families with the window donors. In around 1470, Holy Trinity Goodramgate in York was given a window with a separate panel for each of the families of Mary Salome, Mary Cleophas and the Virgin Mary. By the later Middle Ages Anne's multiple marriages were a matter for veneration.

Perhaps most persuasive of the rise in the esteem of the married woman is the interest in this period in representing the Virgin Mary as a holy housewife. Representations of Mary's wedding ceremony appear in the image-rich environment of England from the thirteenth century onwards, proliferating in the fourteenth and fifteenth centuries. Included among the series pictures on the south wall in All Saint's Church Croughton, Northamptonshire, dated by Tristram and James to around 1300,[48] is Mary's marriage to Joseph. Although most of Mary has been effaced, the priest can clearly be seen joining Mary and Joseph's hands in a wedding ceremony. Similar images are to be located in church windows, on walls and vestments. Lives of the Virgin and sermons recounted the fact of Mary and Joseph's marriage and offered reasons for their union. Drama re-enacted the wedding and spiritual guides counselled their readers/listeners to replicate Mary and Joseph's example as husband and wife.

In its structure this volume follows the life cycle of a wife. Not every text in which a wife appears details her betrothal, wedding ceremony, and life as a spouse. The literary texts included have been deliberately chosen because each describes one or more of the steps along the road of wifedom. Those works in which a woman's married status is incidental or allegorical, as is the case with Lady Meed in *Piers Plowman*, are excluded.[49] Chaucer provides examples of women as they are courted and become wives. Chapter One analyses the manner in which Alisoun of Bath, Custance, Griselda and May become wives,

---

48 A detailed illustrated study of these wall paintings is to be found in E. W. Tristram and M. R. James, 'Wall-paintings in Croughton Church, Northamptonshire', *Archaeologia*, 76 (1926–7), 179–204.
49 Lady Meed's marriage occurs in Passus 2–4 in all versions. Its significance is interrogated by M. T. Tavormina in *Kindly Similitude: Marriage and Family in Piers Plowman* (Woodbridge: D. S. Brewer, 1995).

exploring to what degree these fictive creations are in dialogue with the canon law and secular custom that exerted a significant and competing influence over when and who a woman married. A woman's transition from maiden to wife is marked usually by some kind of ceremony, detailed descriptions of which are rare in the surviving literature of the later Middle Ages. All too often we meet the couple after the event has taken place. We are fortunate that Chaucer describes a little of May and Januarie's wedding and, even more so, that a detailed performance of a ceremony has come down to us: the marriage of the Virgin Mary and Joseph in the *Mary Play*. Chapter Two examines how these portrayals of wedding ceremonies were influenced by the Church's desire, not always satisfied, for a public, witnessed ceremony whose irrefutable existence could not be challenged at a later date. For the majority of women living as a wife was intimately bound up with sex. Chapter Three investigates the dialogue between male-authored texts defining women's sexuality and the sex-lives of May, Alisoun of Bath and Margery Kempe. Margery Kempe differs from the other literary wives included in this study in that her *Book* is life-writing rather than fiction. Her *Book* merits inclusion since Margery's perception of her wifehood is as much in dialogue with those texts that demonise women's sexuality as are any of the fictional wives. Margery's representation of herself is testimony to the power of sexual/textual politics in influencing the lives of real medieval women. The representation of May, Alisoun and Margery reveal that, in as much as canon law and cultural productions had an attitude towards women's sexuality, so women had an attitude towards these texts. In the Middle Ages the result of coitus was usually pregnancy. The process of parturition is another aspect of being a wife that, all too frequently, literature reports rather than describes, for example the births of Griselda's children. In Chapter Four the volume returns to the Virgin Mary and examines how her childbearing and motherhood, as presented in the Nativity and Purification plays found in civic cycle drama, engaged with patriarchal assumptions and religious custom regarding the parturient body. The book closes with an exploration of good wifely conduct and its converse, as defined in sermons and conduct books, and its impact on the anonymous wives in *The Wright's Chaste Wife* by Adam of Cobsam (*fl.* 1462) and *Ballad of a Tyrannical Husband*, and the notorious Mrs Noah of the cycle plays.

    Bonoure and Buxum contends that the literature of the later Middle Ages pays significant attention to wives and their experiences. This occurs in a historical moment awash with conflicting and competing discourses about ideal wifely conduct, and the bad behaviour to which women were prone, and out of which they were to be educated. This instructive material was made available and reinforced in a variety of ways; from the pulpit, built into the fabric of the churches in which people worshipped, through the play performances that they attended and the literature that they either read or heard read aloud. At the same time that literary wives render visible cultural anxieties concerning inappropriate behaviour and promote a paradigm of the ideal wife, they reveal that as much as this material had an attitude to women, so women had an attitude to it.

Chapter One
Eligibility, Contract and Choice

The Canon Law of Eligibility

Although the Wife of Bath eagerly anticipates becoming a wife for the sixth time, at the time of her pilgrimage to Canterbury she is not currently married and her representation initiates discussion of how literature presents the path to wifehood. During the Middle Ages getting married was, as Philip Reynolds comments, 'a process rather than a simple act'[1] regulated by canon law developed during the twelfth and thirteenth centuries. Underpinning this legislation was an awareness of marriage as a personal relationship and a move to make unions easier to contract and more difficult to dissolve.[2]

Canon law stipulated who could and could not marry. Both parties had to have reached *adolescentia* or the age of puberty: twelve for girls and fourteen for boys and each had to freely consent to the union.[3] One could not marry if one had a living spouse, was below the prescribed age, was in holy orders, had taken a vow of chastity or was insane.[4] Marriage was prohibited between those considered too closely

---

[1] Reynolds, *Marriage in the Western Church*, p.315.
[2] Brundage, *Law, Sex and Christian Society*, p.333.
[3] Cosgrove, 'Consent, Consummation and Indissolubility', p.95. D. T. Kline identifies *adolescentia* (adolescence) as the last of three stages that defined childhood in the Middle Ages, those preceding it being *infantia* [infancy] and *pueritia* [childhood] in 'Female childhoods', in *The Cambridge Companion to Medieval Women's Writing*, ed. by Carolyn Dinshaw and David Wallace (Cambridge: Cambridge University Press, 2003), pp.13–20 (p.13).
[4] Brundage, *Law, Sex and Christian Society*, p.195. Since St Paul had defined the conjugal debt whereby each spouse might legitimately ask the other for sex because the wife's body belonged to the husband and *vice versa* (I Corinthians 7. 3–6), the Church insisted that any vow of continence made by married couples should be mutual and freely given. Once given this vow, whether for

related by blood, termed consanguinity. Marriage was forbidden also between those considered to have a tie of affinity: a bond created between an unwed individual and the close relatives of the partner with whom he or she has sex. A tie of spiritual affinity existed between those individuals who acted as godparents to a child at baptism or sponsors at his or her confirmation which prevented them from subsequently contracting a marriage with any member of the child's family. The Fourth Lateran Council (1215) forbade marriage between those related by way of consanguinity or affinity within four degrees.[5] Those who married within the prohibited degree of relationship or someone with whom they had a bond of affinity had either to secure papal dispensation or accept the risk that their marriage might be annulled.[6] Digamy was permitted and although some canon lawyers expressed reservation about the propriety of remarriage,[7] in his twelfth-century *Decretum* that became the seminal textbook in medieval canon law, Gratian concluded that remarriage was not to be condemned.[8] Canon law required that consent be freely given but marriages that began through force (such as an act of rape or abduction) were rec-

    continence within marriage or with the intention of entering a monastery/convent, could not be rescinded. M. McGlynn and R. J. Moll, 'Chaste Marriage in the Middle Ages: "It Were to Hire a Greet Merite"', in *Handbook of Medieval Sexuality*, ed. by V. L. Bullough and J. A. Brundage (New York: Garland Publishing, 1996), pp.103–22 (p.109).

5   Marriage was forbidden within seven degrees of relationship but this was reduced to four at the Fourth Lateran Council: *Prohibitio quoque copulae coniugalis quartum consanguinitatis et affinitatis gradum de caetero non excedat, quoniam in ulterioribus gradibus iam non potest absque gravi dispendio huiusmodi prohibitio generaliter observari.* [Moreover the prohibition against marriage shall not in future go beyond the fourth degree of consanguinity and of affinity, since the prohibition cannot now generally be observed to further degrees without grave harm]. Tanner, *Decrees*, p.257. Although the decree states that the reduction was done to avoid 'grave harm' it seems likely that people simply did not know or could not remember who was related to who at such far remove and so a more easily computable degree of relationship was instituted.

6   Brundage, *Law, Sex and Christian Society*, p.356.

7   J. A. Brundage, 'Widows and Remarriage: Moral Conflicts and Their Resolution in Classical Canon Law', in Walker, *Wife and Widow*, pp.17–31 (p.19).

8   Ibid., p.19.

ognised as licit if consummation by consent followed. Once a licit marriage had been made it could be rendered null, that is, a legal fiction was created that no marriage existed on the grounds of an *impedimentum dirimens*; relationship within the forbidden degrees of consanguinity, relationship by way of spiritual affinity, existence of a prior contract, one of the parties is in holy orders or insane, the infancy of the parties or male impotence that having lasted for three years is presumed permanent.[9] For those couples who simply did not get along, all that was available was divorce *a mensa et thoro* (from bed and table) that discharged them from living together but left them as husband and wife.

The canon law of eligibility was reinforced via the pulpit. In the section of his *De Septem Sacramentis* devoted to *De Matrimonio*[10] William of Shoreham, Vicar of Chart-Sutton in Kent (1320), explained to his congregation the prohibited degrees of consanguineous relationship, 'Þe sibbe mowe to-gadere nauȝt / Þe foerþe grees wyþ-inne' (stanza 274, 1912–13) and the relationship of affinity created through intercourse,

    ȝef þou myd word of þet hys novþe
    Aryȝt bi-treuþest one–
    Oþer þaȝ þet [þou] bi-treuþy hy nauȝt–
    And hast flesches mone,
      By lawe
    Alle here sybbe affinite
    To þe for þan schel drawe.
    (Stanza 275, 1919–25)

---

9   H. Jewell, *Women in Medieval England* (Manchester: Manchester University Press, 1996), p.126. The three year period stipulation for the presumption of permanent impotence that justified annulment with the right to remarriage is found in Alexander of Hales, *Glossae in sententiae* 4.34.5 and William of Pagula, *Summa Summarum* 4. 13, as quoted in Brundage, *Law, Sex and Christian Society*, p.457, note 202.
10   *The Poems of William of Shoreham. Part I. Preface, Introduction, Text and Notes*, ed. by M. Konrath, EETS ES 86 (London: Kegan Paul, Trench, Trübner, 1902).

He described too how a relationship of spiritual affinity was created between godparents and godchildren (stanza 266), and reiterated the importance that consent be freely given:

> Ne no treuþing stonde ne schel
> Wyþ strenþe ymaked ine mone,
> Bote þer folȝy by assent
> Ryȝt flesch y-mone ine dede.
> (Stanza 250, 1744–48)

Shoreham pointed out that if marriage was exacted by 'strenþe' (force) it was invalid unless consummation by consent followed. History provides testimony to coercion and force having been employed in making a match. Perhaps the best known case is recorded in the letters of the wealthy Paston family. In 1449, Agnes Paston found a suitable suitor for her twenty-year old daughter, Elizabeth. The man in question was one Stephen Scrope, a widower of about fifty who had suffered a lengthy illness that had left him permanently disfigured.[11] While accepted by his future mother-in-law, Scrope was refused by his prospective bride. In an attempt to force her consent, Elizabeth was shut away and severely beaten, 'son Esterne þe most part be betyn onys in þe weke or twyes, and som tyme twys on o day, and hir hed broken in to or thre places'.[12] Elizabeth did not give in and her mother gave up. But history also provides evidence that marriages contracted by force did become valid. Corinne Saunders cites the late fourteenth-century example of Eleanor, daughter of the knight Sir Thomas West, who is said to have been 'feloniously ravished [abducted] and deflowered [raped]' by one Nicholas Clifton, after which she married her abductor.[13] It is possible that Eleanor was complicit from the outset in her abduction by a man whose wife she secretly wished to be. Further, if a woman was found to consent to the union, canon law upheld her decision even in the face of continued opposition from her

11   A. S. Haskell, 'The Paston Women on Marriage in Fifteenth-Century England', *Viator*, 4 (1973), 458–71 (pp.466–67).
12   *Paston Letters and Papers of the Fifteenth Century*, ed. by N. Davis, 2 parts, EETS SS 20 and 21 (Oxford: Oxford University Press, 2004), 2, letter 446.
13   C. Saunders, *Rape and Ravishment in the Literature of Medieval England* (Woodbridge: D. S. Brewer, 2001), p.62.

family. This Sir Thomas West found out to his cost when he brought a law suit to annul the marriage, and the Commons found against the family.[14] As William of Shoreham informed his parishioners, canon law would recognise a marriage as valid even if it began with force as long as it ended with consensual consummation. Shoreham confirmed also the permanent nature of a licit union and how impotence was grounds for annulment, as long as the incapacity existed before the marriage (stanza 281). Should it occur during the marriage to those who are 'bewitched' so that when they come together they 'myȝte don ryȝgt nauȝt' (stanza 282, 1970–71), as stated in canon law the couple must wait three years before they could separate.

Conduct books advised a woman how to behave should she receive a marriage proposal. *How the Good Wijf Tauȝte hir Douȝtir*,[15] a work possibly composed in the early fourteenth century and that remained in circulation until the close of the fifteenth,[16] was written for an urban audience of girls in service or other employment, by a male, and perhaps, clerical author. The work warned a prospective bride to make known any offer of marriage that she receives,

> If ony man biddiþ þe worschip, and wolde wedd þee,
> Loke þat þou scorne him not, what-so-euer he be,
> But schewe it to þi freendis, & for-hile [conceal] þou it nouȝt:
> Sitte not bi him, neiþer stoonde, þere synne myȝte be wrouȝt,
> For a sclaundre reisid ille

---

14 Saunders, *Rape and Ravishment*, p.62.
15 *The Babees Book*, ed. by F. J. Furnivall, EETS OS 32 (London: Trübner, 1868), pp.36–47. See also F. Riddy, 'Mother Knows Best: Reading Social Change in a Courtesy Text', *Speculum*, 71 (1996), 66–86.
16 Goldberg, *Women in England*, p.97, argues for a mid fourteenth-century date of composition whereas Riddy suggests that the poem itself pre-dates the Black Death and so can be dated to the first half of the fourteenth century, Riddy, 'Mother Knows Best', p.70. Both Goldberg (p.97) and Riddy (p.72) believe that the work was a product of the urban environment into which teenage girls had moved.

> Is yuel for to stille,
> Mi leue childe.
> (32–38)

No offer should be scorned outright and any proposal should be made known to friends and/or relatives. Once an offer had been made a woman should not be in the man's company in such a way as to encourage gossip and damage, either to her reputation or that of the employers under whose roof she was currently living. Worse still, was fear of an offer of marriage that might lead to pregnancy without its ever being honoured, as is expressed in the lyric, 'A Forsaken Maiden's Lament':

> He seyde to me he wolde be trewe,
> & change me for non oþur newe;
> now y sykke & am pale of hewe,
> for he is far.
>   Wer it vndo þat is y-do
>   I wolde be-war.
>
> he seide his sawus [promises] he wolde fulfille,
> þerfore y lat him haue al his wille;
> now y sykke & morne stille.
> For he is far.
>   Wer it vndo &c.[17]

Social, public occasions, of which religious ceremonies were the focus, provided opportunity for the survey of potential partners. According to Barbara Hanawalt, village rituals, such as May Day celebrations, carolling and dancing, encouraged 'institutionalized flirtatious behaviour' among the peasantry.[18] This much is suggested in another lyric, 'A Midsummer Day's Dance', in which the narrator has sex with 'Iak, oure haly watur clerk' at the celebration after which she discovers that she is pregnant, 'my gurdul a-ros, my wombe wax out'.[19] Kim Phillips' research into the existence of Maidens' Guilds and their

---

17 Robbins, *Secular Lyrics*, number 23, pp.17–18.
18 B. Hanawalt, *The Ties that Bound: Peasant Families in Medieval England* (Oxford: Oxford University Press, 1986), p.193.
19 Robbins, *Secular Lyrics*, number 28, p.24.

attendance at May Day festivities suggests that women of other social classes also participated in public gatherings.[20] Margery Kempe, the burgher's daughter born in Bishop's (now Kings) Lynn in around 1373 and married at around the age of twenty to John Kempe, experienced attempted seduction by her neighbour during her church's patronal festival. He propositioned her 'on Seynt Margaretys Evyn befor evynsong, that for anythyng he wold ly be hir and have hys lust of hys body' (*Book*, Chapter 4, 435–37).[21] Such opportunity to go courting may have been available to women whose daily working lives permitted some degree of freedom to move within the public sphere in their daily working lives: for the aristocracy, especially if unmarried, such opportunities cannot have so readily presented themselves.

Contract

Throughout the Middle Ages, arranged marriages persisted, especially among the nobility for whom matrimony was, as Peter Coss stresses, 'largely a matter of family strategy in which material concerns were uppermost'.[22] When a wealthy woman became a bride she brought with her to the union her dowry (money and, if wealthy enough, land) to a value that reflected her parents' financial status. In turn, the father of the bridegroom or the groom himself settled a jointure on the couple (formerly the dower).[23] Peter Fleming explains the change from

---

20   K. M. Phillips, *Medieval Maidens: Young Women and gender in England, 1270–1540* (Manchester: Manchester University Press, 2003), pp.186–91.

21   *The Book of Margery Kempe*, ed. by B. A. Windeatt (London: Pearson Education Limited, 2000), pp.67–8. All quotations are taken from this edition.

22   P. Coss, *The Medieval Lady in England 1000–1500* (Stroud: Sutton Publishing, 1998), p.87.

23   Mary Carruthers notes that by the fourteenth century dower was being replaced by jointure, property settled on the wife by the husband usually as a condition of the marriage contract but sometimes at a later point in the marriage, 'The Wife of Bath and the painting of lions', in *Feminist Readings in Middle English Literature: The Wyf of Bath and all her Sect*, ed. by R. Evans and L. Johnson

dower to jointure arose from a perceived disadvantage to wives in the system of dower. Two kinds of dower were recognised in common law; nominated (*dos nominate*) and reasonable (*dos rationabilis*). The former was allocated to the bride at the time of her marriage and could not exceed one third of the property held by the groom at the time of the marriage. This was problematic to his widow since it took no account should the husband's wealth increase during the marriage. In the 1275 revision of Magna Carta it was assumed that widows of all men who owned land had a right to a reasonable share of all lands held by the husband at the time of his death and reasonable dower had superseded nominated dower by the fourteenth century. Serious weaknesses in reasonable dower existed, however; the widow had to claim it from her husband's heirs, she might lose it should her husband's lands be forfeit for treason or her husband predecease his father and so never come into his inheritance. Also, if at the time of their marriage her husband was merely enfeoffed to the use of his land rather than owning it, the land could not be claimed by his widow as reasonable dower. The answer to these predicaments came in 'jointure': land and/or property granted by the groom's family to the couple, held jointly by them throughout their lives and which automatically came solely to the wife on her husband's death without the need to sue any heirs for it and in which she retained a life interest.[24] This arrangement was recorded in some form of nuptial contract (the *dos* or *dotalium*).

The negotiations over jointure might become protracted, as demonstrated in the wrangling between the Pastons and the Brews over the marriage of John Paston III to the Brews' daughter, Margery. Draft memoranda of the pre-nuptial agreement were drawn up by John Paston, and submitted to Sir Thomas for adoption as the terms by which he would give his daughter in marriage. Everything seems to have depended upon Margaret Paston's contribution to her son's

(London: Routledge, 1994), pp.22–38 (p.25). For a detailed explanation of thirteenth century widow's rights see F. Pollock and F. Maitland, *History of English Law Before the Time of Edward I*, 2nd edn (Cambridge: Cambridge University Press, 1911), Book II, Chapter VII.

24 Fleming, *Family and Household*, pp.38–41.

jointure.[25] If Margaret offered the couple the profits from the Paston manor of Sweynsthorpe but no more than ten marks from those of their manor at Sparham, Sir Thomas would either contribute 200 marks and give the couple free board and lodging for two or three years, or would give them 300 marks without board, payable at fifty marks annually until the full 300 are paid. Should Margaret agree to let John and Margery take all of the profits from Sparham and Sweynsthorpe 'for terme of ther two lyves and the longest of theym leveing', Sir Thomas should contribute 400 marks, payable as fifty pounds on the day of their marriage and fifty pounds annually until the full 400 marks are paid.

The wealthy were not the only ones to make use of a pre-nuptial agreement. Barbara Hanawalt's research into the lives of peasant families reveals how money was put down towards a future match,

> John Love, [...] wanted to take up a vacant holding, but could not afford the entry fee of £3. Agnes Bentley offered to pay the fine if he married her daughter Alice. [...] Another woman, Agnes Smith, was so desirable a marriage match that John Tolle gave her 24*s*. to reserve herself for marriage to him.[26]

Agnes Bentley was willing to pay to secure her daughter a good catch while other women might be 'bought'. Perhaps Agnes Smith was desirable because she had been left money with which to marry by a recently deceased benefactor. The wealthy left sums of money in their wills specifically to help poor women to marry. In 1415 Thomas Walwayn of Much Marcle in Herefordshire bequeathed one sixth of the sale money on some land for this purpose, and in 1428 John Toker, a vinter of London, bequeathed 'to the mariage of onest and poure maidens [...] xiiii l*i*. vj*s*.'[27] In addition to any money paid out to secure a bride, a peasant was required to pay a merchet fine to the lord of the manor, for licence to marry. Ranging between 3*d*. and 4*s*., this tax was applied to those villein girls who could afford to pay and was

---

25 Davis, *Paston Letters*, I, letter 376.
26 Hanawalt, *Ties that Bound*, p.199.
27 *The Fifty Earliest English Wills in the Court of Probate, London 1387–1439*, ed. by F. J. Furnivall, EETS OS 78 (London: Oxford University Press, 1882, reprint 1964), pp.23, 79.

a combination of a marriage tax and a transfer fee for land transferred at marriage. Ramsey Abbey's *Liber Gersumarum* (1398–1458), records that out of 426 merchet cases, the bride's father paid in thirty-three per cent of the cases, the bridegroom in twenty-six per cent and another person (such as the bride's mother) in eight percent.[28] This tax was gradually phased out during the fifteenth century.[29]

A wealthy woman might bring with her a trousseau of jewels, clothes and other belongings, again reflective of her family's wealth. The size of a girl's dowry depended on the number of daughters to be provisioned for, and the demands made by potential sons-in-law trading on their value as a good catch. This is illustrated also in the negotiations between the Pastons and the Brews over John Paston III's proposed marriage to Margery. A flurry of letters were exchanged during February and March 1477 between John, his elder brother John II and their mother; between John, Margery and her mother; between John II and Margery's father; between the mothers, Margaret Paston and Dame Elizabeth Brews, and between John III and the Brews' secretary, Thomas Kela, over the size of Margery's dowry. Margery was very conscious that the £100 pounds and fifty marks that her father was offering (pleading the strain of finding money for dowries since he had already set aside £100 for the marriage of a younger daughter), was insufficient for John.[30] Thomas Kela promised that the Brews were actually offering 200 marks along with her personal items and clothes to the value of 100 marks.[31] In turn, John's mother, Margaret, complained that she too was under pressure from John's siblings over the size of jointure that she had promised him, telling Elizabeth Brews that she had 'to purvey for more of my chylder then hym, of whiche some be of that age that they can tell me well j-now that I dele not evenly with theym, to geve John Paston so large and theym so lytyll'.[32] All turned out well, for the couple were eventually married in August

---

28   Hanawalt, *Ties that Bound*, p.200.
29   Ibid., p.202.
30   Davis, *Paston Letters*, I, letters 374–79 for the Paston family letters and II, letters 789–91 for those from Margery Brews.
31   Davis, *Paston Letters*, II, letter 792.
32   Davis, *Paston Letters*, I, letter 378.

1477. Margery was pregnant by December with their first son, Christopher, who was born in 1478.

The Pastons were astute regarding nuptial contracts. In as much as Elizabeth Paston was reluctant to marry the widowed Stephen Scrope because of his age and disfigurement, she was also concerned about how a man with a living daughter envisaged making provision for a second wife and heir(s). Her concern is apparent in Elizabeth Clere's explanation to John Paston I of his sister's hesitation,

> And Scrop seith to me, if he be maried and have an eyre, his dowter [that is married] schal have of his liflode [inheritance] L [fifty] mark and no more; [...] And sche [Elizabeth Paston] seith if [ȝe] may se by his evydences þat his childern and hire may enheryten, and sche to have resonable joynture, sche hath herd so mech of his birth and his condicions þat, and ȝe will, sche will have hym, whethir that hir moder wil or wil not, notwythstandyng it is tolde hir his persone is symple [sickly and deformed].[33]

Elizabeth was wise to be cautious. Should the husband predecease the wife, the nuptial contract agreed at the time of her marriage might make the wife a wealthy widow. The material desires of surviving heirs, especially if they were the product of a previous marriage, might prove problematic, A widow was entitled to any freehold land that she held in her own right, use for life of the jointure settled on her at the time of or during the marriage, and any other gifts bequeathed to her in her husband's will. Elizabeth appears to have exacted a promise from Scrope that, as his second wife, she would be well provisioned for.

For the wealthy, a church wedding was crucial since claims to dower and dowry would not be considered in secular courts unless the marriage had received the degree of publicity that solemnisation before witnesses provided.[34] Wedding ceremonies might begin with reading aloud of the contract at the church door, thus making its contents known to, and witnessed by, all those present at the wedding.[35] Even so, nuptial contracts could and did end up as a matter of

---

33 Davis, *Paston Letters*, II, letter 446.
34 Fleming, *Family and Household*, p.52.
35 Marriage liturgies that make provision for the reading of the contract are; the *Pontifical of Anianus* (Bishop of Bangor) 1268–1304, the *Parish Missal of Hanley Castle*, Worcestershire (thirteenth century), the *Liber Evesham* (end of

dispute in the secular courts where heirs and the groom's family tried to deny the widow what had been set aside as provision for her widowhood. This is evidenced by the numbers of widows suing for their dower before the London court of common pleas and elsewhere in England.[36]

Choice

In the choice of a bride and groom the Church simply required that a prospective spouse be free of any impediment as defined by canon law. The marriage sermon in John Myrc's *Festial* advised that in choosing a spouse a man should select 'a wyf lyke of age, lyk of condicions, and lyk of burth; for þereos þese ben acordyng, it is lyk to fare wel, and ellys not' (*Sermo de Nupcijs*, folio 117a). Although Kim Phillips identifies an English held preference for companionate marriage,[37] that is, marriage based upon an affective relationship, for the aristocracy breeding potential, wealth and advantageous political alliance continued to be sought after qualities in a bride. A pretty face and figure were not a necessity but an added bonus, as Anne Crawford wryly observes, in medieval royal matchmaking where any royal bride was considered who brought with her diplomatic advantages 'provided she was not known to be simple-minded, cross-eyed or hump-backed'.[38] In the marriages of royalty particularly, as is the case for Custance and the Sultan in the *Man of Law's Tale* and for the upper

thirteenth, beginning of fourteenth century), the *Pontifical of the Abbot of Westminster* (fourteenth century), London, British Museum MS Harley 2860 (early fifteenth century) as discussed in *The Publications of the Surtees Society*, 63 (1874), Appendix 4.

36 Fleming, *Family and Household*, pp.88–89.
37 K. Phillips, 'Margery Kempe and the Ages of Woman', in J. H. Arnold and K. J. Lewis, eds., *A Companion to the Book of Margery Kempe* (Cambridge: D. S. Brewer, 2004), pp.17–34 (p.25).
38 *Letters of the Queens of England*, ed. by A. Crawford (Stroud: Sutton Publishing, 1994), p.4.

echelons of society as with May and Januarie in the *Merchant's Tale*, the couple may not have met before negotiations have been completed and a treaty signed. As well as being governed by canon law becoming a bride could be influenced by the wishes of parents wanting to make a politically and financially expedient match. In contrast, as an older, independent woman, Alisoun of Bath is able to seek a husband for herself in her second and subsequent marriages. As a businesswoman, Alisoun is well aware that to sell one's goods one has to display them, and if one is no longer in the first bloom of youth, the marketing must be more aggressive and the packaging that much more eye-catching. She puts herself out into the market place and goes into the company of 'lusty folk'; at visits, holy vigils, processions, at miracle plays and weddings (551–59) and of course, on pilgrimages, where she can look for a prospective husband. She remains, however, subject to canon law.

Chaucer's interest in marriage has been long recognised and, as observed by Helen Cooper and Peter Beidler, is detectable in many more of the *Canterbury Tales* than those first identified as the 'Marriage Group' by George Lyman Kittredge.[39] Priscilla Martin suggests expansion of Kittredge's list of the Wife of Bath, the Clerk, the Merchant and the Franklin to include the Knight, the Shipman, the Miller and the Manciple as tellers for whom marriage is the subject of discussion.[40] Our focus here falls on those women about whom Chaucer provides detail of their marriage negotiations and the level of choice in her life-partner that each exercises. In his representation of the Wife

---

39 G. L. Kittredge, 'Chaucer's discussion of marriage' in *Modern Philology*, 9 (1912), 435–67. For a history and review of the identification of the marriage group see J. Bronfman, *Chaucer's Clerk's Tale: The Griselda Story Received, Rewritten, Illustrated* (New York: Garland Publishing, 1994), Chapter Two. Helen Cooper's analysis of the *Clerk's Tale* and its position in manuscripts of the *Canterbury Tales* raises doubt that Chaucer conceived of a schema based on a distinct marriage group, H. Cooper, *Oxford Guides to Chaucer: The Canterbury Tales* (Oxford: Oxford University Press, 1989), p.186. Peter Beidler advises against seeing the group as a deliberately constructed, discrete unit in *Geoffrey Chaucer: The Wife of Bath*, ed. by P. Beidler (Boston: Bedford Books, 1996), p.16.

40 Martin, *Chaucer's Women*, pp.122–23.

of Bath, May, Custance and Griselda Chaucer explores the first step towards wifehood and reveals the influence of canon law and secular custom upon the process. In the words or body talk of these brides can be heard a female perspective on becoming a wife and on those discourses that sought to regulate this event.

Eligibility and the marriages of Alisoun of Bath

In her first three marriages Alisoun of Bath uses canon law designed for her spiritual protection to her financial benefit. In her fourth and fifth, her choice of life partner is constrained by the far reaching influence of canon law's rules of eligibility. Alisoun's first marriage takes place when she is twelve (*Wife of Bath's Prologue*, 4), the minimum age permissible under canon law. In complying with this requirement Alisoun is no different from many young women. Kim Phillips finds that underage marriage is far from the norm, even amongst the nobility[41] for whom childhood betrothals were made for financial or political expediency. It must be assumed that Alisoun's family arranged her first marriage. For the Pastons match-making was certainly a family affair. We have seen already that, in 1449, John Paston I became involved in the marriage negotiations between his sister Elizabeth and Stephen Scrope.

On the death of each of her spouses Alisoun understands that she can remarry with impunity according to canon law. Aware of the history of ambivalence toward digamy, 'Why sholde men thanne speke of it vileynye?' (34), she is correct in her pragmatic assessment of serial marriage, 'Yet herde I nevere tellen in myn age / Upon this nombre diffinicioun' (24–25). Alisoun's experience of multiple marriages is little different in number and duration from other women of her own class. Peter Fleming cites the example of Thomasine Bonaventure who survives three husbands (one a mayor of London).[42] Married very

41 Phillips, *Medieval Maidens*, p.36.
42 Fleming, *Family and Household*, p.97.

young to men significantly older than her Alisoun outlives husbands one to three and continues childless with four and five. The Wife of Bath's marital history illustrates perfectly the findings of Shulamith Shahar that in the High and Later Middle Ages, especially among the prosperous of society, the early age at which women married, the age gap between them and their spouses, and their remaining childless caused many wives to outlive their husbands.[43]

According to canon law eligibility was impeded if a relationship of consanguinity, affinity or spiritual affinity could be proven to exist between the prospective bride and groom. Alisoun's multiple marriages potentially generate complex relational ties. Her choice of husbands four and five reveals the difficulty in finding a husband from your own social circle, in a relatively small community, if one has been much married before.

Social history indicates that in their quest for a second spouse women of all classes were more likely to seek out a man from their own social group and locality.[44] Alisoun does indeed replicate this *modus operandi* with husbands one, two and three who are similarly rich, old men. In her choice of husbands four and five Alisoun suddenly breaks this pattern, selecting a 'revelour' (453) who keeps a mistress and a 'clerk of Oxenford' (527). Having been so attentive to her first three husbands' financial status, Priscilla Martin explains the absence of comment about four's wealth is indicative of his not bringing this to their marriage.[45] Such a reading is supported in that it is Alisoun who funds his funeral procession, coffin and tomb beneath the crucifix that usually hung in the nave. This was a much sought-after and preferred site as revealed in fifteenth century wills.[46] Its location recalls the funerary arrangements of John Baret, wealthy clothier and property owner of Bury St Edmunds, who died in 1467. In his will Baret stipulated that he was to be buried by the altar of St Mary in St Mary's

---

43   S. Shahar, *Growing Old in the Middle Ages* (London: Routledge, 1997), p.35.
44   J. T. Rosenthal, 'Fifteenth-Century Widows and Widowhood: Bereavement, Reintegration, and Life Choices', in Walker, *Wife and Widow*, pp.33–58, (p.38).
45   Martin, *Chaucer's Women*, p.99.
46   P. Ariès, *The Hour of Our Death*, trans. by Helen Weaver (Harmondsworth: Penguin, 1981), pp.80–81.

Church in Bury, 'the body put in as neer vndyr my grave as be withoute hurt of the seid grave', the building of which tomb commenced before his death.[47] Alisoun's fourth husband appears to have lacked the money to embark on such a structure in his lifetime and Alisoun balks at paying for a grandiose, decorated tomb considering it 'nys but wast to burye hym preciously' (500). In so doing she indulges in a little post mortem revenge on her fourth and unfaithful spouse.

Husband number five also brings no money to their marriage. Mary Carruthers suggests that calling Jankyn a clerk indicates that he is a local young man who has gone to university for some time but did not complete any sort of degree.[48] Many students failed to graduate from Oxford, abandoning their studies at an early stage because they lacked the means to do so.[49] Jankyn is to be understood as no exception. The appeal of husbands four and five lies in their 'nether purs' (44b) rather than in their money bags. Alisoun admits physical attraction for husband number four and choosing Jankyn for his legs. She now seeks the sex appeal so conspicuously absent from her first three husbands about which more shall be said later. Why does she look for a sexy husband among less wealthy men? Is Chaucer wryly commenting on the dearth of potential husbands with sex appeal among the Bath bourgeoisie?

Alisoun's contemporaries would have understood canon law to exercise a limiting effect on her choice of spouse, her age, gapped teeth and large hips not withstanding. An impediment of consanguinity would bar her from marrying among the descendants of her great-great-grandparents (her brothers, uncles, brothers and first, second and third cousins). That of affinity would prevent her from contracting with the widowed uncles, brothers and first, second and third cousins of each of her five husbands[50] and with the 'oother compaignye in youthe' and their blood relatives (*General Prologue*, 461) over whom the narrator

---

47 G. McMurray Gibson, *The Theater of Devotion: East Anglian Drama and Society in the Late Middle Ages* (Chicago: The University of Chicago Press, 1989), p.73.
48 Carruthers, 'The Wife of Bath and the painting of lions', p.33.
49 *The History of the University of Oxford*, ed. by J. I. Catto & R. Evans, 4 vols, 2: Late Medieval Oxford (Oxford: Clarendon Press, 1992), p.500.
50 Cosgrove, 'Consent, Consummation and Indissolubility', p.95.

draws a discreet veil. Canon law prohibited Alisoun from marrying a considerable number of men from within her social circle and she would be caught within a net of kinship, wide enough to encourage what Peter Fleming terms 'marital exogamy, that is [...] marriage beyond one's neighbourhood, or, perhaps, socio-economic rank'.[51]

Had Chaucer wished, he might have portrayed Alisoun marrying at least once within the prohibited degrees of relationship since dispensation for such was available. Through situations similar to that which Alisoun's multiple marriages and the ensuing relational ties potentially generate, Judith Ward finds that the nobility was highly interrelated and sought dispensation to marry within forbidden degrees with some frequency.[52] In 1323, at King Edward II's request, a dispensation to marry was issued to John, the son of the earl of Kildare, and Joan, the daughter of Hugh le Despenser the younger, who are related in the fourth degree.[53] Alternatively Alisoun might have married within the prohibited degrees of relationship without dispensation and concealed this fact, as did William de Hypsconys and Maud Swyninton, alias Pesal, whose marital adventures are revealed in a papal letter to the Bishop of Lichfield, dated 1391.[54] This couple tried to side step the fact that they were related on both sides in the third degree of kindred by marrying in a private chapel and without publishing their banns. This was discovered and their punishment was excommunication. At the petition of the Bishop of Lichfield and King Richard II no less, this was downgraded to separation for a time and then permission to remarry, with past and future offspring declared legitimate but with the caveat that whichever of the two survive, the other will remain perpetually unmarried.

Alisoun is neither royalty nor aristocracy. The secrecy required in breaking canon law would be inconsistent with a woman in whose characterisation everything is open and public, from the details of her five weddings that Lee Patterson imagines to have been 'fully and even

---

51   Fleming, *Family and Household*, p.15.
52   J. C. Ward, *English Noblewomen in the Later Middle Ages* (London: Longman, 1992), p.13.
53   Ibid., p.13.
54   Goldberg, *Women in England*, p.125.

ostentatiously legitimate'[55] to those of her sex-life. The potential public humiliation upon discovery of contravening canon law and the penalty of excommunication would be at odds also with Alisoun's consciousness of her own public persona and status, jealously guarding her position as first at the offering of the Mass (*General Prologue*, 449–52). Nor would this serial wife have appreciated a ruling that legitimated an illegal marriage but in the process forbade her from ever remarrying. The discrepancy in social background between her first three husbands from that of her last two is not a comment on the paucity of attractive men among the Bath bourgeoisie but the effect of Alisoun's attempt to find a pair of legs to which she is attracted and to whose owner she is not in any way related according to canon law. Alisoun casts her net wider than her own social group and with very mixed results.

The Marriage Contracts of Custance, the Wife of Bath and May

The *Canterbury Tales* includes description of marriage contracts. In the *Man of Law's Tale* Custance's marriage negotiations replicate that of royalty and demonstrate what can be staked in the marriage game. Subject to the assent of her father and a wider group of men that includes the pope, the Church and the nobility (*Man of Law's Tale*, 234–35), it is with them that the matter is first broached. The Man of Law tells us that this process is brought about, 'by tretys and embassadrie, / And by the popes mediacioun, / And al the chirche, and al the chivalrie' (233–35). This union is to cement future diplomatic advantages between Syria and Rome, bring about the conversion to Christianity of the Syrian court and maintain trade with Syrian merchants in

---

55   L. Patterson, '"Experience woot well it is noght so": Marriage and the Pursuit of Happiness in the Wife of Bath's Prologue and Tale', in Beidler, *Geoffrey Chaucer*, pp.133–54 (p.144).

> [...] Spicerye,
> Clothes of gold, and satyns riche of hewe.
> Hir chaffare was so thrifty and so newe
> That every wight hath deyntee to chaffare
> With hem, and eek to sellen hem hire ware.
> (136–40)

Her father offers as Custance's dowry gold the quantity of which the Man of Law is uncertain (242) and the prestige of royal blood. Custance consents to the union, 'for I shall to Surrye, / [...] "Allas, unto the Barbre nacioun / I moste anoon, syn that it is youre wille"' (279, 281–82) but in a manner that Jill Mann describes as 'without protest, but also without enthusiasm'.[56] Her agreement to a union for which she lacks enthusiasm reveals the tension that could exist between parental desires and those of a daughter. Although canon law stipulated that consent to the union had to be freely given and that parental consent was not essential to marriage formation,[57] for wealthy women like Custance the prospective bride's family had what Ann Haskell calls 'all the rights of persuasion'.[58] The political nature of Custance's marriage negotiations and the wealth that it accrues recalls the marriage of Eleanor of Castile and Edward I in 1254. Eleanor was chosen with a view to protecting English interests in southern France, the couple were married as a result of a peace treaty between England and Castile, and Eleanor's dowry was the county of Ponthieu, in northern France, inherited from her mother.[59] For all its ceremony and the participation of her father and the pope in drawing up the prenuptial contract, the Syrian marriage ends in disaster with the groom's murder and the bride being set adrift in a boat to die. When her family discovers this, the personal relationship between Custance and the Sultan becomes lost in the wider political fallout. Custance's rights as the Sultan's widow receive no mention in the Europeans' zeal to burn and kill the Syrians, primarily for their slaughter of Christians and only secondarily, for the dishonour shown to Custance (954–65).

---

56   J. Mann, *Geoffrey Chaucer* (London: Harvester Wheatsheaf, 1991), p.128.
57   Brundage, *Law, Sex and Christian Society*, p.183.
58   Haskell, 'The Paston Women on Marriage', p.467.
59   Crawford, *Letters of the Queens of England*, p.68.

Chaucer's description of Alisoun of Bath's first three marriages reveals how a late medieval bride, whose wedding did not cause ramifications in the wider political sphere, might manipulate and live to benefit enormously from a nuptial contract agreed prior to her marriage. When Alisoun speaks of her weddings she emphasises that each takes place at 'at chirche dore' (*General Prologue*, 460, *Wife of Bath's Prologue*, 6), the location in which the *dos* is read aloud. Alisoun employs the nuptial contract to amass great wealth. This enables her to remain a successful player in the marriage market long after her wheat has turned to bran and 'age, allas, that al wole envenyme, / Hath me biraft my beautee and my pith' (*Wife of Bath's Prologue*, 474–75). Sheila Delany notes how this excellent businesswoman demonstrates that marriage is as much a market place as any in which she might trade her cloth and similarly one in which, like cloth, a bride has a price and economic value.[60] Alisoun understands that her initial capital outlay – her youth and potential fertility – is subject to depreciation as she ages, and that she can no longer rely upon youth and beauty to attract a husband. Alisoun re-packages herself as a good financial catch, thanks to her previous marital history through which, by marrying and outliving wealthy, old men, she has been left a very wealthy woman. In 1435 Anne Stafford was possibly the wealthiest woman in England, having amassed her fortune through successive marriages; to two Stafford brothers and Sir William Bouchier, Count of Eu, by whom she bore sons.[61] Alisoun, however, has no children with whom she would have to split the money or who might contest her right to or their part of the family wealth. From each of her first three marriages Alisoun tells us that her good, old rich husbands have given her 'hir lond and hir tresoor' (204). In addition, Alisoun acquires further wealth in a *quid pro quo* exchange of sex for movables,

> I wolde no lenger in the bed abyde,
> If that I felte his arm over my syde,
> Til he had maad his raunson unto me;

---

[60] S. Delany, 'Sexual economics, Chaucer's Wife of Bath and *The Book of Margery Kempe*', in Evans and Johnson, *Feminist Readings*, pp.72–87 (p.73).
[61] Jewell, *Women in Medieval England*, pp.122, 143.

> Thanne wolde I suffre hym do his nycetee.
> (409–12)

The 'raunson' (literally 'ransom or penalty') that she exacts and the wealth that this accumulates enables Alisoun to bring a large dowry to any proposed marriage. With only herself to please and without the demands of relatives to meet, Alisoun can bestow herself as she pleases. She can disregard the advice in *How the Good Wijf Tauȝte hir Douȝtir* that a girl make known to her friends and relatives any marriage proposal. Her money permits Alisoun to broker her own marriage deal. She sounds out Jankyn as a prospective husband in number four's absence on business,

> [...] Of my purveiance
> I spak to hym and seyde hym how that he,
> If I were wydwe, sholde wedde me.
> For certeinly– I sey for no bobance–
> Yet was I nevere withouten purveiance
> Of mariage, n'of othere thynges eek.
> (566–71)

She is wise enough to do so, as Kathryn Jacobs points out,[62] with her friend, Alice, as witness. Jankyn knows a good investment when he sees one. The Paston correspondence confirms that a wealthy widow, from the trade in which Alisoun is involved, was a real find. Edmund Paston II writes to his brother, William Paston III, at some point after 1480,

> Here is lately fallyn a wydow in Woorstede whyche was wyff to on Boolt, a worstede marchant, and worth a m li., [thousand pounds] and gaff to hys wyff a c marke in mony, stuff of howsold and plate to þe valew of an c marke, and x li. be ȝere in land. She is callyd a fayre iantylwoman.[63]

The woman's looks were secondary to the wealth that she possessed. Through successive marriages that have remained childless the Wife of Bath has become very wealthy and it is this wealth that sustains her

---

62 Jacobs, *Marriage Contracts*, p.60.
63 Davis, *Paston Letters*, I, letter 398.

attraction in older age and, as we shall see, her repeated efforts to find Mr Right.

In the *Merchant's Tale* Chaucer depicts a marriage in which the bride is from a lower social group than the groom. History reveals that social mis-matches did happen. On the death of her first husband, the Earl of Gloucester, Joan of Acre (1272–1307), daughter of Eleanor of Castile and Edward I, married one of his squires. Of this second union Joan is said to have commented, 'it is neither shameful nor disgraceful for a great earl to marry a poor and simple woman; nor is it blameworthy or too strange that a countess should thus promote a likely youth'.[64] May is acquired by negotiations from which she is absent, replicating those carried out customarily by either the father or male relatives where women were young and under the control of their elders.[65] Chaucer tells us that these negotiations comprise

> [...] Sly and wys tretee, / [...]
> [...] Every scrit and bond
> By which that she was feffed in his lond,
> Or for to herknen of hir riche array.
> (*Merchant's Tale*, 1692, 1697–99)

The terms 'tretee', 'scrit' and 'bond' describe the legally binding, pre-nuptial contract in which May is very well provided for as Januarie enfeoffs to her his land. This term is capable of meaning not only granting a life interest but also the modern sense of convey,[66] the latter of which is surely intended here. Like a trainee Wife of Bath, May consents to marriage to a man very much her senior, to whom she is not physically attracted and is likely to outlive. Before marrying a pre-nuptial contract assures that May has already gained much financially and in terms of social rank, and will gain further on being widowed.

---

64   J. C. Parsons, 'Mothers, Daughters, Marriage, Power: Some Plantagenet Evidence, 1150–1500', in *Medieval Queenship*, ed. by J. C. Parsons (Stroud: Sutton, 1994), pp.63–78 (p.76).
65   Fleming, *Family and Household*, p.36.
66   Ibid., p.40.

Choosing the Ideal Wife

In the choice of a bride, the Church simply required a woman to be free of any impediment as defined by canon law and to freely consent to the union while custom, particularly amongst the wealthy, might demand breeding potential and wealth as prime qualities. In the marriages of royalty particularly, and as is the case for Custance, the couple may not have met before negotiations have been completed and a treaty signed.

The *Canterbury Tales* reveal the pervasive attraction of the *mulier fortis* of Proverbs 31 in choosing a wife. The wife of Proverbs is far more precious than jewels and is trustworthy, industrious, physically strong, charitable, optimistic, dignified, wise, kindly spoken, fertile and obedient. The Sultan desires Custance as his bride because of the animated hearsay of his merchants and common opinion that,

> In hire is heigh beautee, withoute pride,
> Yowthe, withoute grenehede or folye;
> To alle hire werkes vertu is hir gyde;
> Humblesse hath slayn in hire al tirannye.
> She is mirour of all curteisye;
> Hir herte is verray chambre of hoolynesse,
> Hir hand, ministre of fredam for almesse.
> (*Man of Law's Tale*, 162–68)

The Man of Law affirms the truth of this report. In addition to the status that she brings as the only daughter and heir of the Emperor of Rome, Custance is very beautiful, young but not immature, virtuous and chaste, humble, well-mannered and generous to the poor. Her virtue combines the beauty of a typical courtly heroine with the humility, holiness and almsgiving of a saint. She is physically attractive and potentially fertile, wise, tractable, and someone who will enhance her husband's reputation. The Sultan is not disappointed.

While we might think that Custance's virtues are exceptional, in the *Clerk's Tale* Walter also seeks similar qualities in a wife. Walter accepts Griselda without either a dowry or mention of the merchet to which, as her lord, he would have been entitled. Griselda brings to her marriage her potential fertility that allays the people's fear of Walter's dying childless and ensuing political upheaval:

> Delivere us out of al this bisy drede,
> And taak a wyf, for hye Goddes sake!
> For if it so bifelle, as God forbede,
> That thurgh youre deeth youre lyne sholde slake,
> And that a straunge successour sholde take
> Youre heritage, O wo were us alyve!
> (134–39)

Walter sees in this peasant girl, a young virgin,

> [...] Of vertuous beautee,
> Thanne was she oon the faireste under sonne; [...]
> No likerous lust was thurgh hire herte yronne. [...]
> She knew wel labour but noon ydel ese.
> But thogh this mayde tendre were of age,
> Yet in the brest of hire virginitee
> Ther was enclosed rype and sad corage.
> (211–20)

Again, the bride-to-be is young, beautiful, virtuous and chaste, wise beyond her years, with a penchant for sobriety and industry illustrated by the work that she does at her father's home. Walter is quite specific about the behaviour that he requires from a wife,

> To al my lust, and that I frely may,
> As me best thynketh, do yow laughe or smerte,
> And nevere ye to grucche it, nyght ne day?
> And eek whan I say 'ye,' ne say nat 'nay,'
> Neither by word ne frownyng contenance?
> (352–56)

Walter demands absolute obedience, delivered with a fixed smile of the sort that when told to jump inquires how high, no matter how he chooses to treat his wife. Griselda never disappoints him. As if this is not enough, Griselda is replete not only with 'al the feet of wyfly hoomlinesse' (429) but also the ability to rule wisely and maintain order within Saluces. She can function effectively both within the domestic and the public sphere when required.

From a male perspective Griselda exhibits also a pleasing disinterest in exploiting marriage as a means of feathering her own nest. Griselda brings to their union 'wrecched clothes, nothyng faire, / [...] But feith, and nakednesse, and maydenhede' (850, 866). Without the money even to pay for his daughter's merchet that would be due to Walter as her lord, her father, Janicula, neither expects nor exacts any pre-nuptial contract for his daughter but agrees,

> [...] 'Lord,' quod he, 'my willynge
> Is as ye wole, ne ayeynes youre likynge
> I wol no thyng, ye be my lord so deere;
> Right as yow lust, governeth this mateere.'
> (319–22)

He does this, even though, as the narrator admits later, Janicula was always suspicious of the marriage and worried that, perceiving it as degrading, Walter would discard Griselda having slept with her (904–10). Unlike the Wife of Bath and May who inhabit the bourgeois and aristocratic worlds in which the making of a marriage is as much a business transaction as it is a personal relationship, it never enters the head of the peasant Griselda that she might have value to a prospective husband that can be exploited to her advantage. Through marriage, the Wife of Bath acquires land and treasure as well as presents and movables, and May obtains not only the jointure agreed in the pre-nuptial contract but also all of Januarie's inheritance (2175). In contrast, Griselda walks away from a marriage that she believes is annulled, with nothing more than the dowry that was habitually returned to a wife whose marriage was declared invalid for reasons other than her adultery.[67] Griselda returns the wedding ring, clothes and jewels that Walter has given her and requests only a shift to cover her nakedness in replacement for her dowry: her virginity that Walter cannot return to her.

In the *Merchant's Tale* the ideal bride described in a lengthy encomium to marriage shares many of the qualities exhibited by Griselda,

---

67 Fleming, *Family and Household*, p.83.

> Thanne sholde he take a yong wyf and a feir,
> On which he myghte engendren hym an heir,
> And lede his lyf in joye and in solas [...]
> For who kan be so buxom as a wyf?
> Who is so trewe, and eek so ententyf
> To kepe hym, syk and hool, as is his make?
> For wele or wo she wole hym nat forsake;
> She nys nat wery hym to love and serve.
> (1271–73, 1287–91)

Again this recalls the *mulier fortis* of Proverbs who is youthful, fertile, beautiful and obedient. That said, Januarie's choice from all of the young girls who live locally is determined as much by a sexual fantasy. The ranking of attributes in his fantasy bride is telling. First and foremost, this lecherous old man wants a young nubile goddess of 'fresshe beautee,' with a 'myddel smal,' and 'armes longe and sklendre' (1601–02). With this satisfied only then does he require the 'wise governaunce,' 'gentillesse,' 'wommanly berynge' and 'sadnesse' (1603–04) of the *mulier fortis*. The marriage sermon in John Myrc's *Festial* makes no mention of physical features, rather advising that in choosing a wife a man should select one 'lyke of age, lyk of condicions, and lyk of burth; for þereos þese ben acordyng, it is lyk to fare wel, and ellys not' (*Sermo de Nupcijs*, folio 117a). Januarie, however, is obsessed by his bride's face and body. In exchange for marriage to a sexy, young thing, Januarie is willing to ignore the potential problems that might arise from the fact that May is radically younger than he and from a lower social class (1625). He even turns the age gap into a positive attribute: the pliable nature of youth permits a young wife to be moulded to her husband's taste (1429–30). Elaine Tuttle Hansen sees his definition of an ideal wife as 'the "heighe fantasie" of a male who is anxious about his waning manliness and wants to see his own lost youth and powers of discernment reflected in the image of a young wife'.[68] Januarie wants in a wife what he lacks in himself. His desire for a *mulier fortis* is combined with the sexual fantasy of a lecherous

---

[68] E. Tuttle Hansen, *Chaucer and the Fictions of Gender* (Oxford: University of Oxford Press, 1992), p.250.

old man. Both are fictions powerful enough to make Januarie deny the reality that he sees before his very eyes up the pear tree.

Marquesses and knights are not the only husbands to wish for wifely obedience of Griseldan proportions. Such a desire spreads across all classes. While recognising that the Clerk denounces Griselda's contemporary currency as a wifely role model, Lesley Johnson observes how for the Host and the Merchant she remains the ideal wife.[69] The Clerk may argue that no such women exist, that they are merely a textual construction, and encourage wives to expunge them from life and all future texts, but it is the married men who have the last word on Griselda's interpretation. The Host asserts that in preference to a barrel of ale (a not insignificant source of income for the publican of the Tabard Inn) he would rather that his wife heard the story of Griselda (*Clerk's Tale*, 1212b–d). Similarly the Merchant bemoans the

> [...] long and large difference
> Bitwix Grisildis grete pacience
> And of my wyf the passyng crueltee.
> (*Merchant's Prologue*, 1223–25)

Thus Griselda, regardless of the best efforts of the Clerk, in demanding that she not be read as the role model of what men desire in a spouse, is interpreted precisely as such by the married men in the company of pilgrims. The Sultan, Walter, Januarie, Harry Bailey and the Merchant all seek the *mulier fortis* of Proverbs. The scripture writer warns she is hard to find because in seeking the *mulier fortis* they seek a textual construction, a male fantasy not a real woman. Regardless, the attitude of Chaucer's married male pilgrims reveal how this textual construction retained a remarkable hold over men and cast a long shadow over the literary representation of wives and the lives of real women.

Those of Chaucer's tales that engage with becoming a bride intimate that appearing to have primarily the obedience, but preferably all of the attributes, of the *mulier fortis* is what gets a girl chosen as a bride. The Sultan, Walter, Januarie, and Alisoun of Bath's first three husbands sought this obedient, industrious paragon of virtue, adept in both

---

69   L. Johnson, 'Reincarnations of Griselda: contexts for the *Clerk's Tale?*', in Evans and Johnson, *Feminist Readings*, pp.195–220 (p.210).

bedroom activities and household economy. The Sultan has little opportunity to see Custance live up to the reputation of a *mulier fortis*: this is experienced by her second husband, Alla. Walter has found the Holy Grail since Griselda never wavers from the behaviour expected of the *mulier fortis*, in spite of her husband's maltreatment of her. The Wife of Bath's first three husbands may well have believed that they were getting a fertile young woman, well-tutored in running a house and the business of the cloth trade. May demonstrates most visibly that women understood the appeal to prospective husbands of the *mulier fortis* and that, with a little play-acting, this could be used to their advantage. This young woman valiantly out-Griseldas Griselda in the charade played out for Januarie, sitting at the wedding feast like Queen Esther famed for her meekness and beauty (1742–46).

Chaucer's representation of Custance, Griselda and May affirms that literature promoted the cliché that men desired wives who were chaste, silent and obedient. By the time of her fourth marriage, no longer young, probably barren, gap-toothed and vocal in opinions in which she is not malleable, Alisoun of Bath no longer holds the attraction of a Custance, Griselda or May. Yet she admits that she was 'nevere withouten purveiance / Of mariage' (*Wife of Bath's Prologue*, 570–71), and two further men choose to marry her. Put bluntly, her attraction lies in her money and her childlessness, attributes that Barbara Hanawalt suggests made widows a popular choice of bride especially at those times in the fourteenth century when land was in short supply.[70] Our selection from the *Canterbury Tales* reveals the persistent appeal of the *mulier fortis* and women's understanding of this. The Wife of Bath's *Prologue* persuades that once they have aged beyond beauty and fertility older women are judged by a new wifely paradigm. Wealth and childlessness was a desirable combination for prospective husbands interested in breeding not heirs but coin and the social advancement that cash brought with it.

Not only do these tales examine what it was that men wanted in a wife, but they reveal also that a bride might desire certain things in a husband, even if she came from those social classes for which arranged

---

70 B. Hanawalt, 'Marriage as an Option for Urban and Rural Widows in Late Medieval England', in Walker, *Wife and Widow*, pp.141–64 (p.149).

marriages were the norm and her wishes, at best, secondary. The Man of Law is uncritical of the politically arranged marriage that takes a young woman far away from her family and even her culture, for when negotiations are underway for Custance's union to the Sultan he concludes 'What nedeth gretter dilatacioun?' (*Man of Law's Tale*, 232). From a patriarchal perspective the answer to his rhetorical question must be 'none whatsoever', for the Emperor has disposed of his goods (his daughter) in a socially approved of and time-honoured way and the Sultan too is happy with his side of the bargain. But Chaucer's tales present not only the husbands' perspective but also those of wives on becoming a wife about which there is much more to say. One need only recall Alisoun's admission of not loving her first three husbands (*Wife of Bath's Prologue*, 208) to be reminded that women, as well as men, have an attitude towards the kind of husband who they wish to marry. The wives of the *Canterbury Tales* indicate that a number of attributes might feature on a woman's wish list.

Custance is distressed at leaving her family to go 'unto the Barbre naciuon' (*Man of Law's Tale*, 286), suggesting the importance of the cultural and geographical proximity of the groom to her family and to the life that she has known. This is not always possible, particularly if like Custance, the bride was making a royal match. In England, until the mid-sixteenth century, royal brides had been foreign, usually members of the French or Spanish Royal families. The exceptions were few; Isabella, daughter of the Earl of Gloucester and first wife of John (divorced 1199); Mary of Bohun (d. 1394), first wife of Henry IV; Elizabeth Woodville (d. 1492) wife of Edward IV; Anne Neville (d. 1485) wife of Richard III, and Elizabeth (d.1503) wife of Henry VII. Of the nineteen monarchs who ruled England between 1066 and 1547, two never married (William II and Edward V) and of the other seventeen, fourteen had one or more foreign brides. Homesickness, anxiety about sex and getting on with the relatives must have been stresses suffered by many brides, especially by women like Custance from royal and aristocratic families whose match involved considerations other than simply personal happiness. Custance's reception and treatment by both of her mothers-in-law illustrates, in exaggerated form, the very real fear from which many brides may have suffered of being accepted into their new husbands' families.

In her second marriage, in the absence of any male relative or political consideration to satisfy, Custance is able to exercise her own free choice of partner. Her union with King Alla of Northumberland is a much quicker affair, lacking the negotiations and monitory exchanges of her first. Custance is alone in Northumberland, is no longer a political pawn worth bartering for, and is without male relatives to initiate and gain from a pre-marital agreement. She marries Alla through choice, certainly a choice influenced by being an undefended stranger in a foreign land, but it is a choice nonetheless and the pity that Alla shows toward her, along with his willing conversion to Christianity, sways her decision.

Alisoun of Bath and May's marital experiences demonstrate that although financial security is important, money is not everything. Chaucer acknowledges that women experience sexual desire. Although she admits to having selected her first three husbands as much for their money as their sex appeal, 'Of whiche I have pyked out the beste, / Bothe of here nether purs and of here cheste' (44a–b), Alisoun reveals that her provision from chest and scrotum is progressive rather than simultaneous, and that husbands four and five are chosen to meet her sexual needs. Alisoun quotes men who complain that cattle, utensils, cutlery and furniture can all be tried out before purchase but not wives, and that this can lead to a bad investment on the part of the man (285–92). Her narrative demonstrates how the same holds as true for the bride as it does for the groom. May's adulterous desire for Damyan illustrates the adage that old age should not marry youth. Real women expressed their desire too. The feelings of Margery Brews for John Paston III, who she called 'right wurschypfull and welebelouyd Volentyne', and her admission that should he accept the marriage contract proposed by her parents that she would be 'þe meryest mayden on grounde'[71] reveals the importance of physical attraction and sexual desire for one's husband, even if one had been brought up to expect an arranged marriage.

Becoming a bride was the first step in the process of becoming a wife and it was subject to the influence of canon law that stipulated who could and could not marry, the age at which this could take place,

71   Davis, *Paston Letters*, II, letter 416.

and the importance of freely given consent. Chaucer demonstrates how becoming a bride was bound up with a woman's age, social status and the operation of canon law. Alisoun's choice of husbands four and five takes her out of her own social group in search of a mate and indicates how the canon law of eligibility might impact upon the selection of a life partner.

Chaucer's presentation of Custance's marriage negotiations illustrates the long-lived custom of arranged marriages for financial and blood benefit, in which the woman might have little or no say. Alisoun of Bath's fourth and fifth marriages and Custance's second union, suggest how things might be different when a mature woman married without the influence of relatives, and/or with material wealth to dispose of as she wished. The marriage negotiations of May and Januarie, along with those of the Wife of Bath, disclose how a wife might benefit from a pre-nuptial agreement or jointure settled on her later during her marriage should she pre-decease her spouse.

The qualities in a spouse as looked for by the Sultan, Walter, Januarie, Harry Bailey, the Merchant narrator and the first three husbands of Bath reveal the tenacious influence of the chaste, silent and obedient *mulier fortis* of biblical tradition. May's playing of this role illustrates women's understanding of its continued attraction and their ability to exploit it to their benefit. Alisoun of Bath reveals how disposable wealth might offer the older, previously married woman the opportunity of becoming a bride again. The portrayals of Alisoun, May, and to a lesser degree Custance, expose how women, even if unable to exercise the freedom to choose their own life partner, might have certain qualities in mind that they deemed necessary in an ideal spouse. The perfect husband is one who can offer financial security within a loving and considerate relationship that is sexually satisfying. Such is not always forthcoming. Chaucer's presentation of the experiences of Alisoun and May admits to the fact of female sexuality and that her spouse might fail to live up to a wife's (s)expectation. Chaucer is fair in his estimation of choosing a spouse: in as much as his husbands could be disappointed in their brides so a bride too could end up with a pig in a poke.

Before she discovered if marital bliss might exist, a girl experienced some form of ceremony that marked her transition from maiden to wife. How a woman got married was an event over which both the Church and secular custom exerted significant and often competing influence. It is to this moment that we now turn.

Chapter Two
Ceremonies and Feasts

Wedding Ceremonies:
Canon Law and Secular Custom

Having agreed to the union, the next stage in becoming a bride was the wedding. This was an experience that the discourses of canon and secular law, instruction manuals for priests, sermons and spiritual guides sought to influence and regulate, with varying degrees of success. The Church preferred that marriages be solemnised *in facie ecclesiae*, that is, in church, in the presence of a priest and witnesses. Its canon law stated that all that was necessary for the creation of a full and licit marriage was the freely given consent, expressed in the present tense, of two, currently unwed individuals, eligible to marry. The *Sententiae* of Peter Lombard explained how an indissoluble, licit marriage results there and then if consent is given in the present tense (*verba de presenti*) between two people for whom no impediment exists.[1] The definition of marriage as activated by words of present consent became the prevailing canonical marriage doctrine throughout Europe and many took the Church at its word: the words of present consent did not have to be exchanged *in facie ecclesiae*.[2] The indissolubility of a licit marriage between two people free to wed even if the marriage is contracted clandestinely is illustrated in the experience of Margery Paston. Margery's story reveals how, despite significant pressure from her wealthy family, the Church supported and affirmed the permanent nature of her marriage to someone whom her family

---

1   Brundage, *Law, Sex and Christian Society*, p.264.
2   In England a series of thirteenth century synods demanded that a wedding be publicly celebrated but James Brundage finds little evidence that this was ever systematically enforced, *Law, Sex and Christian Society*, p.436.

considered unsuitable because the marriage was made with present consent between two individuals free to marry. Margery accepted an offer of marriage from the family bailiff, Richard Calle, considered most unsuitable by the family due to their social disparity, as indicated in a letter dated May 1469, between her brothers in which the younger John states that he would never consent to let his sister sell candle and mustard in Framlingham. Richard and Margery married but did not do so *in facie ecclesiae*. After the event it is clear from his comments, that the Pastons plagued the Bishop of Norwich to intervene, with a view to annulling the marriage. Margery was brought before him. The Bishop reminded her of her duty to be guided by her family and friends, and enquired into the precise words that Margery and Richard exchanged. Clearly satisfied that the marriage had been contracted in the present tense, he found in their favour and there was nothing that her affronted family could do to void the union. They took their revenge for being related to a bailiff, by never acknowledging Calle as a member of the family (although they permitted him still to serve them) and Margaret Paston disinherited her daughter.

In an effort to avoid cases concerning the disputed existence of a marriage coming before its courts, the Fourth Lateran Council decreed that a pending marriage should be announced publicly (the reading of the banns), in church, with a suitable time being fixed beforehand in which any lawful impediment could be identified.[3] In the *Instructions for Parish Priests*[4] (*c*. 1400) John Myrc, an Augustinian canon of Lilleshall in Shropshire, advised that priests 'do ryȝt as seyn the lawes, / Aske the banns thre halydawes' (202–03). The banns were to be pronounced in the vernacular, on three holy days, with at least one weekday intervening between each holy day, and in a final asking at the wedding itself. Their wording survives in a fifteenth-century manuscript, 'I aske þe banes between I de B and A de C. ȝif any man or woman kan sey or put any lettenge of sybrede, wherefor they may not,

---

3 [...] *statuimus ut cum matrimonia fuerint contrahenda, in ecclesiis per presbyteros publice proponantur, competenti termino praefinito, ut infra illum qui voluerit et valuerit legitimum impedimentum opponat.* Tanner, *Decrees*, p.258.

4 *Instructions for Parish Priests by John Myrc*, ed. by E. Peacock, EETS OS 31 (London: Trübner, 1868).

ne owght not, to come togedere be lawe of holy chirche do vs to wete'.[5] Anyone who became engaged in a parish might be married in that parish (*Instructions for Parish Priests*, 876–77) but a couple might have to wait a while before the event could take place. The *Sarum Missal* prohibited marriages between Advent and Epiphany, Septuagesima (the third Sunday before Lent) up until Easter, the Monday of Rogation week (the week before Ascension Day) until the day after Trinity Sunday.[6] In effect, church weddings were restricted from taking place during December until after the 6 January, from February to April or thereabouts depending on the date of Easter and throughout most of May.

With the exception of the wealthy for whom a church wedding was crucial for any subsequent claim to dower to be considered in the secular courts, historical records show that many married when and where the mood took them. In 1381 Alice Baumburght witnessed the wedding of Robert and Agnes while the couple were in bed in 'a certain high room'.[7] At a later date, Robert contested its ever having taken place and so the matter came before the Dean and Chapter of York. Ecclesiastical court records between 1300 and 1500 suggest that the majority of matrimonial cases arose to enforce marriages that became litigious because they were clandestine, that is neither publicly announced nor witnessed.[8] Many weddings went unwitnessed because of the high incidence of marriages still taking place away from church in

---

5   *English Fragments from Latin Medieval Service-Books*, ed. by H. Littlehales, EETS ES 90 (London: Kegan Paul, Trench, Trübner, 1903), p.5.
6.   *The Sarum Missal in English, Part II*, trans. by F. Warren (London: Alexander Moring Ltd. The De La More Press, 1911), pp.143–44.
7   Goldberg, *Women in England*, pp.117–18.
8   Brooke, *Medieval Idea of Marriage*, p. 251. Brooke quotes from R. Helmholz, *Marriage Litigation in Medieval England* (Cambridge: Cambridge University Press, 1974), pp.27–30, whose findings are replicated in M. Sheehan's analysis of the Consistory Court register of Thomas Arundel's reign as Bishop of Ely between 1374 and 1382 in 'The Formation and Stability of Marriage in Fourteenth-Century England: Evidence from an Ely Register', *Medieval Studies*, 33 (1971), 228–63 and C. Donahue Jnr's examination of the York Consistory Court between 1301 and 1499 in 'Female Plaintiffs in Marriage Cases in the Court of York in the Later Middle Ages: What Can We Learn from the Number?', in Walker, *Wife and Widow*, pp.166–83.

a range of locations; under an ash tree, in a garden, in a storehouse, in a field, a blacksmith's shop, in a kitchen, by an oak tree, in the alehouse, on the King's Highway and, as in the case of Robert and Agnes, even in bed.[9] Indicative of the Church's concern at the persistence of clandestine weddings is Myrc's advice in the *Instructions for Parish Priests*, that a couple,

> come and wytnes brynge
> To stonde by at here weddynge;
> So openlyche at the chyrche dore
> Lete hem eyther wedde othere.
> (204–07)

John Myrc was not alone in encouraging that weddings be celebrated in church. Earlier Robert Mannying of Brunne had warned in *Handlyng Synne*, a manual of spiritual instruction for the laity written in 1303,[10] how women in particular are at risk of breach of promise if they marry clandestinely,

> 3yf þou haue trouþë pryuyly
> To bygyle a womman to lygge here by,
> Þogh no wedlok were yn þy þoght,
> But þat wuldest þy synne were wroght;
> 3yf she vndyrstode weddyng of þe.
> (1625–29)

Any marriage should be made before witnesses *in facie ecclesiae*, with a ring as a visible symbol of the union. Myrc's concern that women, in particular, are at risk should the existence of a clandestine wedding be denied later, is heard also in the narrator's advice in *How the Good Wijf Tauȝte hir Douȝtir* that 'If ony man biddiþ þe worschip, and

---

[9] Helmholz, *Marriage Litigation*, p. 29. For a further example of marriage contracted in bed see Goldberg, *Women in England*, pp.117–18.

[10] *Robert Mannying of Brunne's Handlyng Synne*, ed. by F. J. Furnivall, EETS OS 119 (Washington DC: Microcard Editions, 1964). The same fear about false marriage contracts is evident in a number of love lyrics in London, British Library MS Harley 2253, M. J. Franklin, '"Fyngres Heo Haþ Feir to Folde": Trothplight in some of the Love Lyrics of MS Harley 2253', *Medium Aevum*, 55.1 (1986), 176–87.

wolde / wedde þee [...] That man þat schal þe wedde bifor god wiþ a ryng' (32–33). In spite of the Church's encouragement that weddings be celebrated *in facie ecclesiae*, its own canon law insisted that this was not essential and, throughout the Middle Ages, many weddings remained do-it-yourself affairs.

The Church developed a liturgy (with regional variations) with which to celebrate marriage.[11] Though mostly in Latin, some of the later liturgies, such as the *Ordo ad faciendum Sponsalia* of the *Sarum Missal*,[12] had the vows of consent in English. From the twelfth century it was customary to begin the celebration of a marriage before the church door, where the contract (the *dos* or *dotalium* in which the dower and dowry were identified) was read aloud, and the couple expressed their consent to marry. After this they entered the church for the exchange of vows, ring-giving and participation in a nuptial mass in which they might take communion. In a symbolic gesture of dowry exchange and as a good luck token, Edward II contributed money to be thrown over the heads of aristocratic brides and grooms at the church door.[13] In many medieval parish churches a porch covered the public entrance to the nave. Christopher Brooke suggests a connection between the practice of solemnising marriages at the church door and the development of impressive porches in the later Middle Ages.[14] Alisoun of Bath marries five men at the church door (*General Prologue*, 460, *Wife of Bath's Prologue*, 6). That she mentions that part of the ceremony in

11 Marriage liturgies from England dating between the ninth and fifteenth centuries have survived in many documents, as discussed in *The Publications of the Surtees Society*, 63 (1874), Appendix 4. The Bury St Edmunds liturgy is described by J. K. Leonard, 'Rites of Marriage in the Western Middle Ages', in *Medieval Liturgy: A Book of Essays*, ed. by L. Larson-Miller (New York: Garland Publishing, 1997), pp.165–202 (pp.188–91).
12 *Missale ad Usum Insignis et Praeclarae Ecclesiae Sarum*, ed. by F. H. Dickinson (Oxford: J. Parker, 1861–83, republished 1969).
13 In 1318 Edward II paid £3 in money thrown over the heads of Sir Hugh Audley, junior at his wedding to the Countess of Cornwall and £2 10*s*. at the wedding of Oliver de Bourdeaux and the Lady Maud Trussel, with a further 19*d*. to be distributed at the nuptial mass. T. Stapleton, 'A brief Summary of the Wardrobe Accounts of the tenth, eleventh and fourteenth years of King Edward the Second', *Archaeologia*, 26 (1836), 318–45 (pp.337–39).
14 Brooke, *Medieval Idea of Marriage*, p.253.

which the *dos* is given is, for Priscilla Martin, indicative of Alisoun's financial interest in matrimony.[15] I suggest that it is symptomatic too of her character's pragmatism: her unions are openly witnessed and a binding contract from which her husband cannot easily withdraw at a later date. Fourteenth-century marriage liturgies indicate that, in some parts of the country, it was customary for all of the rituals to take place within the body of the church. With the church ceremony completed, the priest might then visit the couple's home and say prayers specifically to bless the couple's bedchamber.

Bridal feasts

A wedding was usually followed by some kind of celebration commensurate with the families' means to provide for the newly-weds. For brides and grooms from wealthy backgrounds a wedding feast might be held in the hall of the family home, accompanied by music, traditionally before, during and after the serving of dishes.[16] Love songs, obscene gestures, lewd jokes and dancing were also common features.[17] Etiquette manuals reveal that at the bridal feast special guests and the hosts sat at the centre of the high table with other tables perpendicular to them, so that the honoured could see all the guests who sat in descending order of social rank and be seen by them.[18] The seating arrangement might be circumscribed also by gender. In 1486 at her wedding to Charles, Duke of Burgundy, the Princess Margaret, sister of Edward IV was seated between her mother-in-law, the Dowager Duchess of Burgundy, on her right and her sister-in-law on her left,

---

15   Martin, *Chaucer's Women*, p.98.
16   M. P. Cosman, *Fabulous Feasts: Medieval Cookery and Ceremony* (New York: George Braziller, 1976), p.18.
17   Brundage, *Law, Sex and Christian Society*, p.191.
18   Cosman, *Fabulous Feasts*, p.16.

accompanied by fifty-two ladies on one side of the table.[19] Her husband sat on the other side with the Lords and Knights.

A Feste for a Bryde [20] that survives in a treatise dating from the close of the fifteenth or start of the sixteenth century, indicates that it was customary at the weddings of the wealthy to provide guests with a sumptuous meal comprising many meats, game, fish and symbolic, decorated food sculptures – subtleties – that carried messages conveying what culture hoped for its married couples. The text recommended the first course comprise brawn, frumenty (hulled wheat boiled with venison), swan and pig, pheasant, a great custard (a pie without a lid filled with eggs and milk) and a subtlety of a boar's head lying in a field and surrounded by the legend:

> Welcombe you bretheren godely in this hall!
> Joy be unto you all
> That en [*sic*] this day it is now fall;
> That worthy lorde that lay in an Oxe stalle
> mayntayne youre husbonde and you, with your gystys
> > alle!
>
> (*Feste for a Bryde*, p.375)

Recalling the magnificence of the decorated boar's head served at another important feast, that of Christmas,[21] the legend welcomes the guests and commends the bride and groom to Christ.

This was followed by venison in broth, roast venison, crane, rabbit, a meat pie and 'leche damaske' (a kind of jelly made from cream, almonds and clarified, set honey with damask roses). After this came a third course of cream of almonds, a diamond shaped cake or wafer in syrup, wildfowl, spiced veal, jellied veal with an egre-douce (seafood sauce), and a meat pie with a subtlety of an angel bearing the legend 'thanke all, god, of this feste' (*Feste for a Bryde*, p.376). The fourth course was dessert: a pie with a soft crust, cheese, cheesecake, hot

---

19　T. Phillipps, 'Account of the Ceremonial of the Marriage of the Princess Margaret, sister of King Edward the Fourth, to Charles, Duke of Burgundy, in 1468', *Archaeologia*, 31 (1846), 326–38 (p.334).
20　*Ffor to serve a Lord* in Furnivall, *Babees Book*, pp.367–77.
21　See 'The Boar's Head Carol' in *Medieval English Lyrics*, ed. by R. T. Davies (London: Faber & Faber, reprint 1981), p.278.

67

bread and the wedding cake on top of which is a wife lying in childbed and a legend that reads 'I am comyng toward your bryde, yf ye dirste onys loke to me ward, I wene ye nedys muste' (*Feste for a Bryde*, p.377). The wedding cake promoted fertility in its suggestion of the childbed that awaited the bride. The feast concluded with brawn with mustard, deer or sheep offal, swan, capon and lamb.

Chaucer is economical in his description of Alisoun of Bath and May's wedding ceremonies, presenting his audience with only those moments pertinent to the characterisation of each woman. Although the Wife of Bath marries five times at the church door, not one of these ceremonies is described in detail. The reading of the marriage contract is the key interest of this acquisitive serial spouse and, as we shall see, that which Alisoun would have vowed before God and her husband are promises that she chooses to ignore in the quotidian living of her marital life. In contrast, when describing Januarie and May's wedding ceremony, Chaucer includes only its concluding moment: the blessing of the wife that exhorts her to be like Old Testament virtuous wives, a blessing that rings out ironically throughout the rest of the tale. A work does survive in which the rituals of marriage *in facie ecclesiae* are described in detail. The wedding in question is for medieval Christians the most spiritually significant ever to have taken place: that of the Virgin Mary and Joseph. Most probably East Anglian in origin,[22] the *Mary Play* that survives in the N-Town Plays[23] alone among surviving medieval English plays dramatises the marriage of the Mother of God.

Medieval literature provides examples of wedding feasts of those who can afford to spend on such items. The wedding feast of Dame Ragnell and Sir Gawain is described in great detail in the anonymous *Wedding of Sir Gawain and Dame Ragnell* (hereafter *Dame Ragnell*), a parody of courtly romance dating from around 1450.[24] In this work Sir Gawain marries a loathly lady, in a tale analogous with that told by

---

22 *The Mary Play From the N.town Manuscript*, ed. by P. Meredith (London: Longman, 1987), pp.6–7. All quotations are taken from this edition.
23 *The N-Town Play: Cotton MS Vespasian D. 8.*, ed. by S. Spector, 2 vols, EETS SS 11 and 12 (Oxford: Oxford University Press, 1991).
24 *Middle English Verse Romances*, ed. by D. B. Sands (Exeter: University of Exeter Press, 1986), pp.323–47 (p.341).

the Wife of Bath. Chaucer describes Januarie and May's wedding reception. In both instances, the feast is the arena for the new wife's first appearance in public, and her behaviour at which marks her transition from being a representative of her father and his success in bringing her up, to that of her husband and his ability to select a *mulier fortis*. In both texts there is a gap between how these new wives behave and what these women are really like. Both authors exploit the husbands' misunderstanding to full comedic potential.

The Marriages of Mary and Joseph, Ragnell and May

People believed that Mary had been a wife. The many medieval reproductions of the apocryphal narratives of Mary's early life[25] and the seminal *Legenda Aurea*[26] tell how Mary and Joseph married in the Temple of Jerusalem when she was twelve (fourteen in the *Pseudo-Matthew*). In the *Mary Play* Mary and Joseph marry in a recognisably medieval church ceremony replete with exchanges of vows and ring-giving. The correspondences between the *Mary Play* and the *Ordo ad faciendum Sponsalia* of the *Sarum* (Salisbury) *Missal* marriage liturgy are many. Peter Meredith acknowledges that the play version is 'sufficiently similar to have the ring of truth and reality'.[27] The setting, words, action and music of the ceremony render it identifiably so and

---

[25] For the *Protevangelion* and the *Pseudo-Matthew* see *The Apocryphal New Testament: A Collection of Apocryphal Christian Literature in an English Translation*, trans. and ed. by J. K. Elliott (Oxford: Clarendon Press, 1993) and for the *Evangelium* see *Evangelia Apocrypha*, ed. by C. Tischendorf (Avenarius et Mendessolin, 1853), pp.92–105.

[26] *Jacobus de Voragine Legenda aurea vulgo historia lombardica dicta*, ed. by J. G. T. Graesse (Leipzig: Arnold, 1846), pp.585–95; *Jacobus de Voragine, The Golden Legend: Readings on the Saints*, trans. by W. G. Ryan, 2 vols (Princeton NJ: Princeton University Press, 1993), II, pp.149–57.

[27] Meredith, *Mary Play*, p.104, note 883.

in such a memorable way that, as Richard Rastall suggests, a deliberate reference to the marriage liturgy must be assumed.[28]

In contrast to those that took place in pubs, under trees or in bed, the *Mary Play* impresses upon its audience that Mary and Joseph's wedding occurred in a sacred location, was publicly witnessed and officially blessed. Although Mary goes 'Into þe tempyl a spowse to wedde' (612) a medieval audience was encouraged to transpose the wedding to their own contemporary setting. It is likely that the Temple of Jerusalem was represented on a single platform or structure.[29] This could be transformed, through the use of props, into a setting analogous to a medieval church interior replete with an altar. Guild records testify that in the pageant of the *Purification of Our Lady* (that also takes place in the Temple of Jerusalem) just such a transformation did indeed occur. The 1571/2 accounts of the Chester Smiths, Cutlers, and Plumbers evidence that the guild paid 'to the clarke for lone of a cope, an Altercloth & Tunecle xd' for their *Purification* play.[30] Between 1541 and 1558, tapers or candles and incense were all part of the Coventry Weavers' stage expenditure for their *Purification* play, to which was

28 R. Rastall, *The Heaven Singing: Music in Early English Religious Drama*, vol 1 (Cambridge: D. S. Brewer, 1996, reprint 1999), p.286. Martial Rose notes that the Marian material is full of ritualistic action and Richard Axton argues that the singing of liturgical texts in this material is crucial to its devotional effect. M. Rose 'The Staging of the Hegge Plays' in *Medieval Drama*, ed. by N. Denny, Stratford-Upon-Avon Studies, 16 (London: Edward Arnold, 1973), pp.197–222 (pp. 204–5); R. Axton, *European Drama of the Early Middle Ages* (London: Hutchinson University Library, 1974), p.172.
29 Critics of the *N-Town Plays* concur that the Marian section of the cycle required a fixed stage production involving multiple playing places. Alan Nelson conceives of one *loca* that he terms the 'heaven complex' that includes a temple with an altar and the fifteen steps of the 'Presentation of Mary,' in 'Some Configurations of Staging in Medieval English Drama', in *Medieval English Drama: Essays Critical and Contextual*, ed. by J. Taylor and A. H. Nelson (Chicago: The University of Chicago Press, 1972), pp.116–47 (p.135). Peter Meredith argues for a combination of five locations in total within the *Mary Play*: the Temple, Heaven, the houses of Joachim and Anne, Mary and Joseph and Elizabeth and Zacharias presented as five scaffolds bordering a playing place. Meredith, *Mary Play*, p.20.
30 *REED: Chester*, ed. by L. M. Clopper (Toronto, Buffalo: University of Toronto Press, 1979), p.91.

added, in the second half of the sixteenth century, a fee for James Hewett to play the regal or small, portable organ.[31] Collectively, candles, incense, ecclesiastical vestments and the use of music might recreate the sights, sounds and smells of a plausible, contemporary church interior. Given the lack of evidence about staging the *Mary Play*, Peter Meredith proposes that it 'is as likely to have been performed indoors as out, and the main central scaffold could easily be the rood screen and loft of a church, or the screen and gallery of a medieval hall'.[32] The verisimilitude of a church interior would enhance the solemnity of proceedings while a medieval hall was a location associated also with weddings as it was where newly weds from wealthy backgrounds dined on the dais, in front of all of their guests.

For the actual wedding celebration the dramatist borrowed heavily from the Sarum *Ordo ad faciendum Sponsalia*. The Sarum rite used the mass of the Holy Trinity (normally used on Whitsunday and Trinity Sunday) as its nuptial mass[33] and the *Mary Play* ceremony too contains sequences or hymns belonging to this mass. The wedding commences with *Benedicta sit beata Trinitas* [Blessed be the Holy Trinity], the sequence for the Commemoration of the Holy Trinity and concludes with the Pentecost hymn *Alma chorus domini nunc pangat nomina summi* [now the choir shall sing the gracious names of the highest Lord] (after 906).[34] The audience witnessed a wedding whose solemn ritual was as clearly introduced and concluded as if it were taking place in their local church. Having a man play the part of Mary may have been neither as distracting nor detrimental to verisimilitude as might first be thought. Mary's part would have been performed by a pre-pubertal male actor who, Richard Rastall suggests, could be as old as seventeen or eighteen and possess already the acting experience

---

31   *REED: Coventry*, ed. by R.W. Ingram (Toronto, Buffalo: University of Toronto Press, 1981), pp.156, 206, 208 and 210.
32   Meredith, *Mary Play*, p.20.
33   Meredith, *Mary Play*, p.103, note 874 and p.104, note 907. See also J. Vriend, *The Blessed Virgin Mary in the Medieval Drama of England* (Purmerend: J. Muusses, 1928), p.58, note 1.
34   Rastall, *Heaven Singing*, p.289.

that would enable him to convey with dignity and command 'her' shyness and reluctant obedience to marry.[35]

The Sarum rite began with the couple consenting to the union by saying 'I will':

> N. wilt though have this woman to thy wedded wife, wilt thou love her, and honour her, keep her and guard her, in health and in sickness, as a husband should a wife, and forsaking all others on account of her, keep thee only unto her, so long as you both shall live ?
> The man shall answer 'I will'.

> Then the priest shall say unto the woman, N. wilt thou take this man to thy wedded husband, wilt thou obey him, and serve him, love, honour, and keep him in health and in sickness, as a wife should a husband, and forsaking all others on account of him, keep thee only unto him, so long as you both shall live?
> The woman shall answer 'I will'.[36]

The *Mary Play* presents a close rendition of what it is to which a man consented when the bishop asks Joseph 'wole ȝe haue þis maydon to ȝour wyff / And here honour and kepe as ȝe howe to do?' (875–76). Joseph's first response is every bride's nightmare, 'Nay, sere, so mote I thryff!' (877) and one that might readily encourage the same nervous laughs and gasps from the watching congregation (comprising Mary's other suitors, her parents, Joachim and Anne, the officiating bishop and, of course, the playgoers) should such a reply be given at a genuine wedding. Reminded that it is God's will, Joseph acquiesces '[…] to

---

35 Rastall, *Heaven Singing*, pp.309–15.
36 The Latin reads: *N. vis habere hanc mulierem in sponsam et eam diligere et honorare, tenere et custodire, sanam et infirmam, sicut sponsus debet sponsam; et omnes alias propter eam dimittere; et illi soli adhaerere, quamdiu vita utriusque vestrum duraverit?*
Respondeat: Volo.
Item sacerdos ad mulierem.
N. vis habere hunc virum in sponsum, et illi obedire et servire, et eum diligere et honorare, ac custodire sanum et infirmum sicut sponsa debet sponsum; et omnes alios propter eum dimittere; et illi soli adhaerere, quamdiu vita utriusque vestrum duraverit?
Respondeat: Volo.
Dickinson, *Missale ad Usum Insignis, Ordo Sponsalium*, column 831.

performe his wyl I bow þereto,' (881). Although he does not state 'I will,' Joseph can be understood to promise to Mary precisely the loving, honouring, keeping, guarding and forsaking of all others that is encompassed in the man's consent. His words served as a timely reminder to the husbands in the audience of their vows to their own wives.

When Mary replies to the question of consent, 'wole ȝe haue þis man / And hym to kepyn as ȝour lyff?' (887–88), her response is not 'I will' but rather 'In þe tenderest wyse, fadyr, as I kan, / And with all my wyttys fyff' (889–90). Although in the affirmative, Mary's vow too is different from Sarum in that she promises to take Joseph as her husband, most tenderly and with all her five senses. This phrase is heard in an earlier episode of the *Mary Play*. As a young child in the Temple, Mary prays to God to be allowed, once in her lifetime, to see the lady who will bear God's son, in order that she 'may serve here with my wyttys fyve' (524). Peter Meredith explains that the phrase is a greatly contracted translation of the '*oculos, linguam, manus, pedes, genua*' [eyes, tongue, hands, feet, knees] with which Mary promises to serve the yet unknown Mother of God in the *Meditationes Vitae Christi*, another source of the *Mary Play*.[37] In the wedding ceremony, however,

---

[37] Meredith, *Mary Play*, p.98, note 524. The phrase appears in Chapter III of the *Meditationes Vitae Christi* in which Mary's life in the Temple and her seven prayers to God are described. Her fifth prayer is to be allowed to see the virgin who will bear God's son and the complete petition reads as follows; *Quinto petebam, ut faceret me videre tempus, in quo esset nata illa beatissima Virgo, quae debebat Filium Dei parere; et ut conservaret oculos meos, ut possem eam videre; linguam, ut possem eam laudare; manus, ut possem ei servire; pedes, ut possem ire ad servitium suum; genua ut possem adorare Dei Filium in gremio suo. S.R.E. Cardinalis Bonaventura Opera Omnia*, ed. by A. C. Peltier, XII (Paris, [n.p.], 1868), p.513. This text was translated into Middle English by Nicholas Love, Prior of Mount Grace Charterhouse, Yorkshire (1410–1421) and reads: [...] þe fift peticion I made to god þat he wolde lete me se þe tyme in þe whech þat blessed maiden schold be born, þat schuld conceyue & bere goddus son, & þat he wolde kepe myn eyene þat I miȝt se hire. Min eres.' þat I miȝt here hire speke. My tonge'. þat I miȝt praise hire. Myn handes.' þat I miȝt serue hire wiþ. Myn fete þat I miȝt go to hire seruice, & myn kneene.' with þe whech I miȝt honour and wirchip goddus son in hire barme. *Nicholas Love The*

the referent of Mary's promise to have, keep and serve with her five senses is her husband, Joseph. She does not promise to obey him. Her vow of service and fidelity recognises key facets of a woman's role in an earthly marital relationship while not compromising the status held by the Mother of God and Queen of Heaven.

The Betrothal window in St Mary's, Fairford in Gloucestershire (*c*. 1500–17)[38] depicts Joseph standing on the priest's right and Mary on his left at the moment in which Joseph takes hold of Mary's left hand. The Sarum Missal explains the woman's place on the left is the result of her formation out of a rib from Adam's left side.[39] This gesture, known as handfasting, occurred when the priest transferred the woman from her father's keeping into the legal power of the husband. During handfasting a second exchange of vows, in the vernacular, takes place:

> I N. take the N. to my weddyd wyfe, to have & to holde fro this day forward, for better for wurs, for rycher, for porer, in sykenesse & in helth, tyll deth vs depart, yf holy Church will it ordeyn: & therto I plyght the my trouth (*manum retrahendo* [withdrawing his hand]).
> I N. take the N. to my weddyd husbonde, to have & to holde fro this day forward, for better for wurs, for rycher, for porer, in sykenesse & in helth, to be bonoure & buxum, in bed & at borde, tyll deth vs depart, yf holy Church will it ordeyn: & therto I plyght the my trouth (*manum retrahendo*) [withdrawing her hand].[40]

In the *Mary Play* Joseph's vow is performed in some detail:

> *Episcopus (et idem Joseph)* [The Bishop (and likewise Joseph)]
> Sey þan after me: Here I take þe, Mary, to wyff ...
> To hauyn, to holdyn ... as God his wyll with us wyl make ...

Mirror of the Blessed Life of Jesus Christ: A Reading Text, ed. by M. G. Sargent (Exeter: Exeter University Press, 2004), pp.20–21.

38   H. Wayment, *The Stained Glass of the Church of St Mary, Fairford, Gloucestershire*, The Society of Antiquaries of London, n. s. Occasional Paper 5 (London, 1984), p.2; *Life, Death and Art: the medieval stained glass of Fairford Parish Church*, ed. by S. Brown and L. MacDonald (Stroud: Sutton, 1997), p.67, supports Wayment's proposal of a date of *c*. 1500–17 for the project.
39   Warren, *The Sarum Missal in English*, p.144.
40   Dickinson, *Missale ad Usum Insignis, Ordo Sponsalium*, columns 831–32.

>   And as longe as bethwen us ... lestyght oure lyff ...
>   To loue ȝow as myselff ... my trewth I ȝow take.
>   (*nunc ad Mariam, sic dicens*) [Now to Mary, saying as follows].
>   (883–87)

As indicated in the stage directions and the use of *punctus* in the manuscript, the performance replicates the repetition of the celebrant's words by the male voice and the alternation between male and female responses as found in the wedding service.[41] In performance nothing could be more appropriate than for Mary to stand on Joseph's left, for them to clasp hands and then withdraw their hands on completion of the vow, thus incorporating the gesture of handfasting.

A striking similarity exists between Joseph's second vow, made at the moment of handfasting, and the man's response as given in the Sarum liturgy. Joseph's 'I take þe Mary, for my wife' replicates the opening of the male vow as found in Sarum. In addition, his promise to 'have and hold' Mary, that is, to take over the authority and care of her from her parents, is a phrase found verbatim in the liturgy. In what appears to be an echo of 'yf holy Church will it ordeyn,' Mary and Joseph's wedding is sanctioned by the authority of God, 'as God his wyll with us wyl make'. The *Mary Play* includes the promise made by all husbands that Joseph would remain with his wife until separated by death 'And as longe as bethwen us ... lestyght oure lyff'. This promise confirms Joseph's role as Mary's protector and therefore presents little problem doctrinally. Joseph's handfasting vow concludes with 'my trewth I ȝow take,' a close version of '& therto I plyght the my trouth'.

In deference to Mary's chastity that remains unaltered even in marriage, the dramatist is required to be more creative in his use of the woman's vow in handfasting, and there is greater discrepancy between it and that given by Mary. In the Sarum liturgy much of the vow in which the woman promised to be gentle and obedient in bed and at board (at table) until death separated them is highly inappropriate for Mary and Joseph's chaste marriage. Thomas Aquinas explained in the *Summa Theologica* how their marriage was understood, 'Afterwards, when she had taken a husband, the acceptable thing to do in those

---

41   Meredith, *Mary Play*, p.104, note 883.

days, she with her husband took a vow of virginity.'[42] In order to circumvent the difficulty of tying Mary to any promise of obedience, sexual and otherwise, the *Mary Play* omits the content of this second vow. Instead, Mary's response, 'In þe tenderest wyse, fadyr, as I kan, / And with all my wyttys fyff' (889–90), serves both as her answer to the first vow of consent and to the vow that would normally accompany handfasting. In so doing Mary promises Joseph love, honour and service in all ways but sexual.

Following the handfasting, the marriage liturgy required the man to give to the woman a ring that is then blessed. A gold ring was given by those who could afford it as its incorruptible nature was considered symbolic of the permanent tie of marriage while for the less well off, wire and pewter ones were available.[43] Wedding rings could be a plain band or set with a gemstone, usually in a cabochon setting. In the fourteenth and fifteenth centuries it became fashionable to have a love message or 'poesie' engraved on the outside, as recorded in the bequest, in 1434, of Margaret Ashcombe to a friend's wife of 'a rynge of golde with a stone, & a reson [motto] "*sans departir*"'[44] and in the couplet, 'Most in mynd and yn myn herrt Lothest from thee ferto deparrt' found on a fifteenth century ring.[45] What a woman did not want to receive was a rush or sedge ring, used during the thirteenth century to trick girls into believing a marriage had been contracted. This practice was outlawed in 1217 by Richard, Bishop of Salisbury, who ruled that any man who placed such a ring on a woman's finger so that she would 'the more willingly become friendly with him' would be con-

---

42 *Summa Theologica*, 3a, Question 28, article 4. The Latin reads, '*Postmodum vero, accepto sponso, secundum quod mores illius temporis exigebant, simul cum eo votum virginitatis emisit.*' Thomas Aquinas, *Summa Theologiae: Latin Text with English Translation, Our Lady*, 51, trans. by T. R. Heath (London: Eyre and Spottiswoode, 1969), pp.54–55.
43 G. Egan and F. Pritchard, *Dress Accessories c. 1150–c. 1450: Finds from Excavations in London* (London: HMSO, 1991), pp.327, 331–32.
44 Furnivall, *Fifty Earliest English Wills*, p.96.
45 G. F. Kunz, *Rings for the Finger* (Philadelphia: J. B. Lippincott Company, 1917), p.211.

strained to marry her.⁴⁶ In other places, when an ecclesiastical court enforced matrimony a ring of rush or straw was used in the ceremony,⁴⁷ perhaps in recognition of its pretended beginning.

In the *Mary Play* Joseph gives Mary a ring in the following exchange:

> *Episcopus*
> Joseph, with þis ryng now wedde þi wyff,
> And be here hand now þu here take.
> *Joseph*
> Sere, with þis rynge I wedde here ryff,
> And take here now here for my make.
> (891–94)

Comparison with the Sarum marriage liturgy is fruitful once more. In Sarum the ring is blessed,

> [...] Do thou, O Lord, send thy blessing upon this ring, that she who shall wear it may be armed with the strength of heavenly defence, and that it may be profitable unto her eternal salvation.
> Bless, O Lord, this ring which we bless in thy holy name; that whosoever she be that shall wear it, may abide in thy peace, and continue in thy will, and live, and increase, and grow old in thy love; and let the length of her days be multiplied.⁴⁸

46 Kunz, *Rings for the Finger*, p.206. Contained within the statute I Salisbury 83, identified by Conor McCarthy as the first English statute requiring a priest to be present at a marriage, is the statement, '*Nec quisquam annulum de iunco vel alia vili materia vel pretiosa iocando manibus innectat muliercularum, ut liberis cum eis fornicetur* [...]'. McCarthy, *Marriage in Medieval England*, p.31. Although McCarthy translates *annulum* as 'noose' I suggest that the text refers to the prohibition against the use of rush rings and reads, 'Nor should anyone entwine girls' hands with a ring made of rush or any other material, cheap or expensive, in order to fornicate with them more freely [...]'.

47 Kunz, *Rings for the Finger*, p.206.

48 The Latin reads: *tu, Domine, mitte bene✠dictionem tuam super hunc anulum; ut quae illum gestaverit sit armata virtute caelestis defensionis, et proficat illi ad aeternam salutem* [...] *Benedic, Domine, hunc anulum quem nos in tuo sancto nomine benedicimus; ut quaecunque eum portaverit, in tua pace consistat, et in tua voluntate permaneat, et in amore tuo vivat et crescat et senescat, et multiplicetur in longitudinem dierum*. Dickinson, *Missale ad Usum Insignis, Ordo Sponsalium*, column 832.

The ring is then placed upon the woman's finger in a symbolic gesture:

> The man shall take it [the ring] in his right hand with his three principal ingers, holding the right hand of the bride with his left hand, and shall say, after the priest, 'With thys ryng I the wedde and thys gold and siluer I the geue; and wyth my body I te worscype, and wyth all my worldly catell [chattels] I the honore.'[49]

The ring blessing requests heavenly defence and spiritual profit for the wearer, peace, fertility and a long life lived in God's will and love. This is as appropriate to the Virgin Mary as to any woman. Joseph gives Mary a ring as a visible token of their marriage with the words 'with þis rynge,' a recognisable echo of the liturgy. The associations of this ritual are problematic, however, because the giving of a ring symbolised not only the giving of the man's goods but also his body to his wife. The former poses little problem for Mary and Joseph and, indeed, Joseph leaves Mary after their marriage to work to pay for the cost of their home. The giving of his body is out of place in their chaste union. The playwright circumvents this difficulty by ignoring the specific words of the liturgy that should accompany the ring giving, substituting them with an incontrovertible truism: the ring is a symbol of the fact of Mary and Joseph's marriage. Joseph is concerned that the ring-giving is 'ryff' or openly done, since a ring served as the only visible symbol of a woman's married status.

It is possible in a play so fond of liturgical gesture that as Joseph gives Mary the ring; he does so in the manner as described in the liturgy,

> Then shall the bridegroom place the ring upon the thumb of the bride, saying, 'In the name of the Father', then upon the second finger, saying, 'and of the

---

49 The Latin instruction that accompanies the vow reads, '*quem vir accipiat manu sua dextera cum tribus principalibus digitis, a manu sua sinistra tenens dexteram sponsae; docente sacerdote, dicat.*' Dickinson, *Missale ad Usum Insignis, Ordo Sponsalium*, column 833.

Son', then upon the third finger, saying 'and of the Holy Ghost'; then upon the fourth finger, saying 'Amen,' and there let him leave it.[50]

Should Joseph leave the ring on Mary's fourth finger this would bear the significance, as explained in the *Sermo de Nupcijs* in John Myrc's *Festial*, of lying upon the vein that was believed to run from the finger to the heart with the band itself signifying the affection that the wife should have for God in the first instance, and her husband in the next (folio 117a). Audiences might even have expected a real ring to be used, since medieval Europe boasted more than one believed to be the actual ring with which Mary and Joseph had married. Mary's wedding ring of onyx or amethyst, bearing a representation of the flowers that budded miraculously from Joseph's staff when selected as her husband, held pride of place in the Cathedral of Perugia, built especially to house it.[51] Another was kept at Chiusi in Tuscany.[52] Closer to home Mary is shown wearing a ring embroidered with a magnificent sapphire on the orphrey (the decorative bands to adorn a priest's stole) made between 1415 and 1435 for Whalley Abbey in Lancashire.

After the ring giving the couple was brought before the altar steps where they prostrated themselves in prayer. In the *Mary Play* at this point the congregation sings *Alma chorus domini nunc pangat nomina summi* [Now the gracious choir shall sing the highest names of the Lord] (after line 906), the sequence of the nuptial mass.[53] Mary alone falls to her knees to be blessed, 'To haue зour blyssyng, fadyr, I falle зow before' (914). This may be in recognition of Joseph's advanced years that he moans have made him '[...] so agyd and so olde / Þat

---

50   The Latin instruction that accompanies the vow reads: *Et tunc proferat sponsus anulum pollici sponsae dicens, In nomine Patris; ad secundum digitum, et Filii; ad tertium digitum, et Spiritus Sancti, ad quartum digitum, Amen.* Dickinson, *Missale ad Usum Insignis, Ordo Sponsalium*, column 833.
51   R. W. Starr, *The Wedding Ring: Its History and Mystery* (London: S. W. Partridge, 1896), pp.27–28. The *Evangelium* states that Joseph's staff flowered as a sign that he had been selected as Mary's husband in a manner indebted to Numbers 16. 4–9.
52   M. Warner, *Alone of All Her Sex: The Myth and Cult of the Virgin Mary* (London: Picador, 1976, reprint 1988), p.294.
53   Meredith, *Mary Play*, p.104, note 907 and Vriend, *Blessed Virgin Mary*, p.58, note 1.

both myn leggys gyn to folde' and have left him 'ny almost lame' (799–801). It is also further indication of Mary's obedience to God's will as it recalls her previous gesture of kneeling, '*et genuflectet ad Deum*' [and she shall kneel to God] (294) when Mary is offered as a child into the service of the Temple, a role that she accepted willingly. If neither of the couple had been previously married, as they were blessed a pall or canopy was held above them by four clerks in surplices. As early as 1287 the synodal statutes of Bishop Quinel of Exeter stipulated that every parish church should contain a nuptial veil.[54] The *Mary Play* dramatist makes clear that Joseph 'haue be maydon evyr' (752) and was not previously married, as was stated in some apocryphal narratives.[55] It is not inconceivable that such a veil was used in their blessing since canopies were used in the Corpus Christi procession, as indicated by the payment recorded in the Coventry Smiths' Accounts of 1502 for 'a canopy of Sylke brodoryd with gold with ij Sydes of the same for the precession'.[56]

Old Testament wives, who were paragons of wifely virtue, were traditionally mentioned in the blessing included in the sixth century *Gregorian Sacramentary* and given for first marriages only:

> O God, by whom woman is joined to man, and the union, instituted in the beginning, is gifted with that blessing ✟, which alone has not been taken away either through the punishment of original sin, or through the sentence of the deluge, look graciously we beseech thee, on this thy handmaiden, who now to be joined in wedlock, seeketh to be guarded by thy protection. May the yoke of love and peace be upon her; may she be a faithful and chaste wife in Christ, and abide a follower of holy matrons. May she be as amiable to her husband as Rachel, wise as Rebecca, long-lived and faithful as Sara [...].[57]

54   C. Platt, *The Parish Churches of Medieval England* (London: Chancellor Press, 1995), pp.27–28.
55   Joseph's previous marriage by which he has sons is mentioned in both the *Protevangelion* and the *Pseudo-Matthew* but was excised from the *Evangelium* when the West stopped teaching about his former marriage.
56   Ingram, *REED: Coventry*, p.98.
57   The Latin text reads: *Deus, per quem mulier jungitur viro, et societas principaliter ordinata; ea bene✟dictione donatur; quae nec sola per originalis peccati poenam, nec per diluvii est ablata sententiam; respice, quaesumus, propitius super hanc famulam tuam, quae maritali jungenda consortio, tua se expetit protectione muniri; sit in ea jugum dilectionis et pacis; fidelis et casta nubat in*

The wife, in particular, was blessed so that she might have the good nature of Rachel (a wife of Jacob), the wisdom of Rebecca, wife of Isaac, and the longevity and faithfulness of Sara, wife of Abraham. On kneeling, Mary is blessed not with reference to Sara, Rachel or Rebecca whose goodness and salvific importance she far outweighs, but in the name of the Trinity, '*In nomine Patris et Filij et Spiritus Sancti* [in the name of the Father and Son and Holy Ghost]' (916) with whom she is soon to be so closely linked.

'in the open halle I will dine'
The Weddings of Dame Ragnell and May

The *Mary Play* does not contain a bridal feast, but elsewhere this event is considered worthy of comment in texts designed for those classes with an interest in the cost and consummation of luxuries. Although her physical appearance has been bewitched, Dame Ragnell's wits are not and it is at her insistence that her wedding and bridal feast is as public and conventional as possible. Banns are proclaimed 'in all the shire, / Bothe in town and in borrowe' (558–59) and although Dame Gaynor (Guinevere) suggests a clandestine wedding 'in the morning erly [...] "As privaly as we may"' (570–71), Ragnell insists on a church wedding and a public wedding feast,

> I woll be weddid alle openly, [...]
> I wolle not to churche tille highe masse time
> And in the open halle I will dine,
> In middis of alle the route.
> (*Dame Ragnell*, 575–80)

Christo, imitatrixque sanctarum permaneat feminarum. Sit amabilis ut Rachel viro, sapiens ut Rebecca, longaeva et fidelis ut Sara. Dickinson, *Missale ad Usum Insignis, Ordo Sponsalium,* column 840. It is based on a blessing-prayer that appears in the sixth century *Gregorian Sacramentary.* See Stevenson, *Nuptial Blessing,* p.246.

This unattractive woman is very aware that, if clandestine, the existence of her wedding might be challenged at a later date, so for her own protection the astute Ragnell makes her wedding ostentatiously public. Her wedding dress too is impressively grandiose:

> She was arrayd in the richest maner,
> More fresher than Dame Gaynour;
> Her arrayment was worthe three thousand mark
>
> Of good red nobles stiff and stark,
> So richely she was begon.
> (590–94)

Dressed more attractively than Queen Guinevere, Dame Ragnell's dress is expensive having a value of almost £2000.[58] This suggests fabric like that worn by Isabella Despenser, Countess of Warwick who, in 1439, bequeathed her 'weddynggown And all my clothis of gold, and clothis of silk, with-oute ffurreur' to the House of Tewkesbury.[59] It is likely that these dresses were intended, ultimately, for altar cloths and vestments for use in the Abbey and its convent. Royal brides were married in expensive dresses. A Wardrobe Account describes the wedding gown worn by Princess Philippa, daughter of Henry IV, on her marriage to Eric King of Denmark, in the cathedral at Lund in 1406. She wore a tunic with sleeves furred with ermine and a mantle with a long train of white satin worked with velvet, lined with pured miniver (the white winter coat of the ermine) and edged with a border of ermine.[60] When she married Charles, Duke of Burgundy, Princess Margaret (sister of Edward IV) wore 'clothe of golde cremysine, hir

---

58 *The Wedding of Sir Gawain and Dame Ragnell*, ed. by J. Withrington, Lancaster Modern Spelling Texts, 2 (Lancaster: The University of Lancaster, 1991), p.60, note 592.
59 Furnivall, *Fifty Earliest English Wills*, p.118.
60 W. P. Baildon, 'The Trousseau of Princess Philippa, wife of Eric, King of Denmark, Norway, and Sweden', *Archaeologia*, 67 (1915–16), 163–88 (pp.164, 174). The abbreviated Latin reads: *ad unam tunicam, unum mantellum cum trayn 'long' de satyn albo operato cum velvett fac' et furrur' cum minever pur' et purfil' cum ermyn, et manicas dicte tunice fur' cum ermyn, pro die solempnizacionis matrimonii* [...].

surcote and hir mantell whit clothe of golde, furred w[ith] ermyne, and she hirself richlye corroned'.[61] Dame Ragnell's wedding garments are meant to be noticed and that the cost is mentioned suggests that the author has done his level best to make this romance appeal to the financial interests and pretensions of a bourgeois audience.

Dame Ragnell places herself, centre stage, at the memorably flamboyant wedding feast held in the hall of King Arthur's court. The wedding celebrations of the wealthy might be grandiose affairs. When Thomas Mowbray, earl of Nottingham, married Elizabeth Montague (née Arundel) in 1384, the celebrations at Arundel Castle lasted over a week.[62] Dame Ragnell and Sir Gawain sit on a raised dais separately from the rest of the guests, probably either side of King Arthur and Queen Guinevere or to the Queen's right.[63] The capons, curlews and baked meat pies that provide the basis of the feast suggest the menu and structure of proceedings as set out in the *Feste for a Bryde*. Dining in the open hall does nothing, however, to disguise that Dame Ragnell's appetite and table manners are as monstrous as her appearance. She devours 'three capons and also curlues three, / And great bake metes she ete up, perdé' (*Dame Ragnell*, 610–11). Although medieval banquets contained many courses each comprising a multitude of dishes, the compiler of the *Boke of Nurture*, John Russell, indicates that small portions delicately carved were considered correct for the most noble, discriminating palates.[64] The narrator is shocked at Ragnell's unlady-like table manners, as with her three-inch nails she 'breke her mete ungoodly' (*Dame Ragnell*, 608) in a fashion far from the gracious dexterity of Chaucer's Prioress who

> At mete wel ytaught was she with alle;
> She leet no morsel from her lippes falle,
> Ne wette hir fyngres in hir sauce depe;
> Wel koude she carie a morsel and wel kepe
> That no drope ne fille upon hire brest.
> (*General Prologue*, 127–31)

61 Phillipps, 'Account of the Ceremonial', p.331.
62 Jewell, *Women in Medieval England*, p.141.
63 Withrington, *Wedding of Sir Gawain*, p.60, note 601.
64 *The Boke of Nurture Folowing Englondis Gise by John Russell* in Furnivall, *Babees Book*, pp.117–99 (p.145).

The narrator is shocked also by Dame Ragnell's gargantuan appetite: she can eat whatever is put in front of her from the start of the feast until the hand washing that concludes it, 'So she ete tille mete was done, / Tille they drewe clothes and had washen / As is the gise and manner' (*Dame Ragnell,* 619–21). Although a feast might be enormous, appetites should not be so. Dan Michel's *Ayenbite of Inwyte* (1340)[65] warns against the lecherous effect of the kind of great meats that Ragnell devours so voraciously, 'Ac þe greate metes and þet stronge wyn aliȝteþ and nourisseþ lecherie ase oyle oþer grese aliȝteþ and strengþeþ þet uer [fire]'.[66] Her consumption of food suggests that her sexual appetite too may be gluttonous, and befitting of her monstrous and unladylike appearance. Although this public spectacle demonstrates how far from an ideal bride Dame Ragnell is, her insistence on a public display provides irrefutable evidence of the fact of her marriage to Sir Gawain and makes any attempt by Gawain to rescind it at later date much more difficult.

This same attention to public witness of the wedding ceremony and the feast occurs in the *Merchant's Tale*. Januarie and May marry *in facie ecclesiae* and 'receyve the hooly sacrement' (1702).[67] This provides incontrovertible evidence of the union's existence to the benefit of May, whose position might become unsure should Januarie have doubts later about marriage to someone his social inferior, and whom he (quite rightly) suspects of adultery. As in the Wife of Bath's *Prologue* so here too, the moment of the ceremony described in detail is deliberately chosen. The tale's focus on the final blessing emphasises how Januarie's sexual desire has joined him, until death, to a young woman who could not be further from the Old Testament wifely exemplar who the Raguel blessing exhorts her to replicate and 'be lyk Sarra and Rebekke, / In wysdom and in trouthe of mariage' (1704–05). In this instance May's blessing is ironic, even more so when the complete version of this prayer is understood:

---

[65] *Dan Michel's Ayenbite of Inwyt or Remorse of Conscience*, ed. by P. Gradon, EETS OS 23 (London: Oxford University Press, 1866, reissue 1965), pp.52–53.
[66] Ibid., p.205.
[67] J. S. P. Tatlock, 'The Marriage Service in Chaucer's *Merchant's Tale*', *Modern Language Notes*, 32 (1917), 373–74, (p.374).

Look in your mercy on this your handmaid who is to be joined in wedlock and implores protection and strength from you. Make the yoke of love and of peace be upon her. Faithful and chaste may she wed in Christ; and may she ever follow the pattern of holy women; may she be dear to her husband like Rachel, wise like Rebecca, long-lived and faithful like Sara. May the author of deceit work none of his evil deeds within her, may she ever be firm in faith and in keeping the commandments. May she be true to one husband, and fly from unlawful companionship. May she fortify her weakness by firm discipline. May she be graceful in demeanour and honoured for her modesty. May she be well taught in heavenly lore. May she be fruitful in offspring. May her life be good and sinless. May she attain in the end to the peace of the blessed and the kingdom of heaven. May they both see their children's children to the third and fourth generation, and reach that old age which they desire.[68]

The disparity between the Church's hopes for a young bride and May's subsequent behaviour is glaring. Januarie discovers, to his cost, that May will be neither faithful nor chaste, and will embrace rather than fly from unlawful companionship with Damyan.

The Merchant-narrator provides expansive detail of Januarie and May's wedding feast with a professional eye for the expensive and exotic imports featuring in the marriage of a wealthy knight. The feast too is very publicly and memorably celebrated. The couple are described as taking pride of place 'With othere worthy folk upon the deys' (*Merchant's Tale*, 1711). There is much food and music accompanies each course. This heady combination coupled with May's beauty inflames the lust of her husband. After dancing and drinking January and May's reception concludes with 'spices al about the house they caste' (1770), also indicative of the wealth into which May has married. Here is yet another example of a public and witnessed wedding and feast used to sure up an uneven marriage, the existence of which might be contested at a later date should Januarie become wise to May's antics. Having been endowed with so much wealth in jointure, a public wedding secures May's right to sue for dower in the secular courts should she need to. Additionally, the public show of Januarie's desperation to get his bride into bed at the conclusion of the feast serves May well. It suggests to those present that May and Januarie will consummate their marriage and the probability that any child that May

---

68   Stevenson, *Nuptial Blessing*, p.246.

might be carrying at the close of the tale could well be her husband's heir, regardless of her adultery.

Participating in some form of wedding transformed the single woman into a wife. The Church attempted to regulate where a woman married by imposing rules about banns and encouraging a church ceremony for which it created a liturgy with accompanying ritual. Marrying *in facie ecclesiae* was recommended in sermons and conduct books and in the *Mary Play* the Church's most powerful and influential female icon was presented as marrying in this way. The 'solempn dede' of the wedding in the *Mary Play*, so heavily influenced by the Sarum *Ordo ad faciendum Sponsalia*, reinforced upon an audience already accustomed to look to Mary for guidance that the kind of wedding advocated by the Church was worthy of the Mother of God and so was to be recommended to all. In her *Book*, Margery Kempe recollects that whenever she saw church weddings it made her meditate on how Mary was joined to Joseph (Chapter 82). As an East Anglian resident, it is possible that Margery saw either the *Mary Play* or the N-Town cycle, or indeed both. That other women made a connection between their own married status and that of Mary is suggested by the number of wedding rings that wives bequeathed to statues of Our Lady, intended to adorn her fingers or to have enhanced the store of wealth that the image attracted. In 1499, Agnes Petygrewe of Publowe in the diocese of Bath and Wells left to 'the B[lessed] M[ary] "de le Peler" [Pillar] of the said Church of Publow my weding ryng'.[69] In 1504, Anne Barett of Bury St Edmunds, bequeathed to Our Lady of Walsingham '[...] My corrall bedys of thrys fyfty, and my maryeng ryng, wt all thyngys hangyng theron'.[70] In 1527, Joane Serne, widow of the parish of Shepton Mallet in Somerset, bequeathed her gold wedding ring to

---

69 *Somerset Medieval Wills (Second Series) 1501–1530 with some Somerset Wills preserved at Lambeth*, ed. by F. W. Weaver, Somerset Record Society, 19 (London: Printed for the Subscribers only, 1903), p.2.
70 S. Tymms, *Wills and Inventories from the Registers of the Commissary of Bury St Edmunds and the Archdeacon of Sudbury*, Camden Society Series 1, 49 (London: J. B. Nicholls and Son, 1850), p.95. J. C. Dickinson, *The Shrine of Our Lady of Walsingham* (Cambridge: Cambridge University Press, 1956), pp.46–47, notes that Anne Baret's [sic] gift was among the other humbler gifts at this time.

Our Lady of the brotherhood of the parish church of Shepton Mallet.[71] In that same year another Somerset widow, Alice Hensley of Porlock, left her wedding ring to the store of the Blessed Virgin Mary of Pilton.[72] Leaving one's wedding ring to Marian churches was also a feature of female piety in pre-Reformation Sussex. In 1520–21, Alice Ball of Midhurst, left her wedding ring to the cross of the Church of St Mary, Harting, in 1524 Margaret Hartill left her wedding ring to the gold cross at Our Lady of Climping and on August 21 1539, Joan Gawwyn bequeathed her wedding ring to the high altar of the Church of Our Lady at Felpham.[73]

The *Mary Play* portrays the Mother of God participating in a recognisably medieval marriage *in facie ecclesiae*. Mary makes the same kind of commitment and a version of the promises before God, as those women in the audience who had married in church. Although Mary does not promise to be obedient, the Bishop does assure Joseph that she is indeed 'buxum' (848). The manner in which Mary marries endorses the advice of John Myrc, that a wedding should be performed in church before witnesses. As observed by Meg Twycross, one feature of medieval plays is that they work particularly effectively as a mnemonic device and leave the viewer with a 'vividly memorable image for future use'.[74] Through its performance techniques, the *Mary Play* recalls marriage *in facie ecclesiae* to an audience whose own marriage celebrations were often other than the Church desired. Its formality and witnessing curtailed a disaffected spouse's ability to walk away from an unhappy union with an abusive or now unattractive partner for cohabitation elsewhere, with someone who suited better. Although undoubtedly some did self-divorce and move on to a new life elsewhere, the danger existed that should one do so and get caught, one faced punishment and public humiliation. The *Letter-Book* of William of Hoo, Sacrist of Bury St Edmunds, 1280–94, demonstrates how the Church

---

71   Weaver, *Somerset Medieval Wills*, p.261.
72   Ibid., p.268.
73   W. H. Godfrey, *Transcripts of Sussex Wills, Volume II*, Sussex Record Society, 42 (1937), pp.269, 27 and 144.
74   M. Twycross 'Beyond the picture theory: image and activity in medieval drama', *Word and Image*, 4.3/4 (July–December 1988), 589–617 (p.591).

treated those around Bury St Edmunds, should they walk out on licit marriages.[75] Adulterers were caught up with and might be excommunicated, as indeed happened to John of Mote, painter, and Beatrice of Ely At Lane's End, wife of Peter of Soham, who in 1289 were both in hiding in Bury.[76]

Marriage *in facie ecclesiae* did have its advantages in the protection that it offered a woman. Because publicly witnessed the union's existence and validity could not be easily challenged (a danger illustrated in the example of Robert and Agnes cited above). William Hoo's *Letter-Book* demonstrates that for those couples who followed the Church's advice concerning the publication of Banns and celebrated marriage *in facie ecclesiae*, they were protected against contracting illicit marriages and future trouble. William responded to the enquiry by the Bishop of London that he found no obstacle on the side of Beatrice of C. to her marriage to W. of M., and that the Banns had been called in Bury St Edmunds.[77] A church ceremony's provision for reading aloud the marriage contract permitted a widow to sue for her dower rights in the secular court should this become necessary at a future date. The Virgin Mary, Dame Ragnell, May and the Wife of Bath all marry *in facie ecclesiae*, replicating the manner in which the aristocracy and bourgeoisie, most particularly, embraced the incontrovertible evidence of a marriage provided by a church ceremony.

Although the woman alone promised to be 'buxom', the benefits of marriage *in facie ecclesiae* were not one-sided. In as much as a wife promised obedience, love and sexual exclusivity to her husband, he, in turn, made as binding and public a promise to her of his love, sexual exclusivity and maintenance of her for life with all his worldly wealth. There was, of course, no guarantee that a husband would meet his financial commitment to his wife (after all, it was a vow made 'For better or for worse'). This Alisoun discovers in her fourth marriage and, as we shall see, Mrs Noah also learns to her cost. The *Mary Play* shows such spousal protection at work. After their marriage Joseph is con-

---

75 *The Letter-Book of William of Hoo Sacrist of Bury St Edmunds 1280–1294*, ed. by A. Gransden, Suffolk Records Society, 5 (1963).
76 Ibid., p.52.
77 Ibid., p.65.

cerned to provide a home for Mary and rents '[…] a lytyl praty hous / […] and laboryn in fer countré / With trewth to maynteyn oure householde so' (1032, 1040–41). May and the Wife of Bath, in relation to her first three unions, also benefit materially from their marriages.

Literature engages also with what went on in the bedroom: the Wife of Bath and the Merchant leave the door ajar on this very personal and private moment. The author of Dame Ragnell and Margery Kempe both have something to say on the subject. In the following chapter we examine the discourses that sought to regulate what went on in the bedroom and what it is that late medieval literature reveals about the sexual relationships experienced by literary wives.

Chapter Three
'Bonoure & buxum in bed & at borde'

The unknown author of *Dame Ragnell* leaves the bedroom door ajar on Ragnell's wedding night. Chaucer provides details of Januarie and May's first night as husband and wife and Alisoun of Bath relishes recounting her bedroom exploits. Before she even got as far as the bridal suite patriarchal discourses predetermined a woman's sexuality about which much anxiety was expressed throughout the Middle Ages. Canon law sought to regulate a woman's sex life. Cultural productions warned about women's sexual voracity. L. R. Poos provides evidence from Church courts that women, rather than men, were most often the target of sexual defamation[1] because the culture was predisposed to believe that women will behave in this way. In its endeavour to maintain a woman's sexual health and enjoyment of sex, medical and scientific discourse, however, were fundamentally at odds with theology.[2] A bride was caught in a web of conflicting and competing discourses with regard to her body, her performance of conjugal rights and duties and her own sexual desire.

'Fleshly ded': Canon Law and Marital Sex

If married *in facie ecclesiae*, a woman vowed during handfasting to be 'bonoure & buxum, in bed & at borde, tyll deth vs depart'.[3] No such promise to be meek and obedient in the marital bed was required of

[1] L. R. Poos, 'Sex, Lies and the Church Courts of Pre-Reformation England', *Journal of Interdisciplinary History*, 25.4 (Spring 1995), 585–607 (p.586).
[2] M. Green, 'Female Sexuality in the Medieval West', *Trends in History*, 4.4 (1990), 127–58 (p.141).
[3] Dickinson, *Missale ad Usum Insignis*, columns 831–32.

the husband. Obligatory of both spouses, however, was that each paid the marital debt, an obligation that the Church took seriously and offered annulment (with the opportunity for remarriage) to those men and women whose partners were discovered to be impotent.

Canon lawyers devised legislation that defined spiritually-safe sex. Sex was not simply a matter of anywhere, anytime. There were times when couples were required to abstain; in time of prayer (vigils of the saints, Sundays and all other feasts), before taking the Eucharist, on Christmas and fast days (Lent, Ember days, Fridays), processional days (rogation days on the feast of St Mark (25 April) and the days before Ascension) and while performing any penance that one had been allotted.[4] Debra Hassig has calculated that if all regulations were obeyed, medieval married couples (taking advantage of all available opportunities) could have sex on about forty-four occasions only every year.[5]

If when one had sex was important, why one had sex was crucial, and for pleasure was not the best motivation in a culture in which the pursuit of *eros* or passionate, sensual love was disapproved of by the Church. James Brundage credits the canonist Raymon de Penyafort (1175/80–1275) with writing the definitive medieval pronouncement on marital coitus.[6] To have intercourse to procreate and/or pay the marital debt was sinless; to have coitus to avoid sexual incontinence was a venial sin while it was a mortal sin to have sex for pleasure.[7] The *Book of the Vices and Virtues* explained how marriage redeemed coitus so that sex became spiritually efficacious:

---

[4] P. J. Payer, *The Bridling of Desire: Views of Sex in the Later Middle Ages* (Toronto, Buffalo: University of Toronto Press, 1993), pp.98–99.

[5] D. Hassig, 'Sex in the Bestiaries', in *The Mark of the Beast: The Medieval Bestiary in Art, Life, and Literature*, ed. by D. Hassig (New York: Garland, 1999), pp.71–98 (p.75).

[6] In 1230 Raymon began a collection of extant decretals about marriage at the direction of Pope Gregory IX, Brundage, *Medieval Canon Law*, p.222.

[7] In his *Summa* 4. 2. 8 (479), Raymon refines Lawrence of Spain's (d. 1248) four sinless acts of marital coitus by synthesising them with Huguccio of Pisa's (d. 1210) view of coitus as inherently sinful. Raymon concludes that '*In primo et secundo casu nullum est peccatum, in tertio veniale, in quarto mortale*'. Kelly, *Love and Marriage*, p.257, note 39.

> þe staat of marriage is so holi and so honest þat the dede þat was erste dedly synne wiþ-out marriage is wiþ-oute synne in mariage, and not onliche wiþ-out synne, but in many caas grete þanke-worþi of God to wynne bi þe lif wiþ-outen ende [...].
> (fol. 95b, p.246)

This was only if sex was had for three, specific purposes; in the hope of offspring, in payment of the marital debt and in prevention of adultery.

Canon lawyers defined the natural and moral fashion in which intercourse should take place. Canon law prohibited intercourse that impeded conception. The vagina was considered the only appropriate orifice as its use alone rendered any act of coitus potentially fertile.[8] Experimentation with erotic sexual positions was discouraged.

The Church sought to stamp its authority on the marital bed and sanctify the activity therein on a couple's wedding day. The Sarum marriage liturgy made provision for blessing the marriage chamber and its occupants,

> Ble✝ss, O Lord, this chamber and all that dwell therein, that they may be established in thy peace and abide in thy will and grow in thy love, and that the length of their days may be multiplied.[9]

It made specific reference to conception, 'God ble✝ss your bodies and souls; and bestow his bless✝ing upon you, as he blessed Abraham, Isaac and Jacob.'[10] Having requested God's protection for the couple,

---

8   J. Brundage, 'Sex and Canon Law' in *Handbook of Medieval Sexuality*, ed. by V. Bullough and J. Brundage (New York: Garland, 1996), pp.33–50 (pp.40–41). In the Canon *Adulterii Malum* Gratian identifies the evil of using a sterile orifice and that '[...] the worst of all these things [the evils of adultery] is what is done contrary to nature, as when a man wishes to use a member of his wife not conceded for this', as quoted in Danielle Jacquart and Claude Thomasset, *Sexuality and Medicine in the Middle Ages* (Princeton: Princeton University Press, 1988), p.89.

9   The Latin reads *Bene✝dic, Domine, thalamum istum et omnes habitantes in eo; ut in tua pace consistant, et in tua voluntate permaneant, et in tuo amore vivant et crescant et multiplicentur in longitudinem dierum.* Dickinson, Missale ad Usum Insignis, Ordo Sponsalium, column 845.

10 The Latin reads '*Bene✝dicat Deus corpora vestra et animas vestras; et det super vos bene✝dictionem, sicut benedixit Abraham, Isaac, et Jacob.*' Dickinson, *Missale ad Usum Insignis, Ordo Sponsalium*, column 845.

and sanctified the bedchamber, the priest sprinkled holy water on the couple and departed.

The canon law that it devised demonstrated the Church's concern that when a couple had sex it was for the appropriate reason, at an approved time and in the correct position. To do otherwise was to imperil one's soul.

Sex education in Sermons and Manuals for Spiritual Guidance

Guidance about spiritually safe sex was disseminated from pulpit and text. Underpinning much of the advice offered was the belief, as stated by Thomas Aquinas (d. 1274) in the *Summa theologica*, that sexual activity should be moderated in frequency by the requirements of conservation of the species, and governed in its nature by reason through the operation of the virtue of temperance.[11] The prose sermon collection, *Jacob's Well*, surviving in a unique manuscript dating from around 1440,[12] makes very clear that sex should occur with moderate frequency and be inspired by an appropriate motive. It warns that marital coitus must be regulated,

> Þerfore, folow þe ordre of matrimonye, & fare þou noȝt as a beste vnresonable. For wedlok trewly knytt, trewlly kept, & vsed in ordre, is of suche vertu, þat it kepyth here fleschly ded fro dedly synne. Also, ȝyf þou vse þi wyif or þin husbonde as þi lemman in entente hollyche for lust, takyng non hede ne reward to þe mede, ne to þe loue, ne to þe fruyte of wedlok, ne to þe honeste, but as an vnresonable beeste takyng hede to þi luste, be ware of þe feend Asmodeus þat slowe þe vij husbondys of Sare [...].
> (*Jacob's Well*, Chapter XXIV, folio 53 a., pp.161–62)

---

11 See Aquinas, *Summa theologica* 2–2.141.6 as explained in Payer, *Bridling of Desire*, pp.151–53.

12 *Jacob's Well: An Englisht treatise on the Cleansing on Man's Conscience*, ed. by A. Brandeis, EETS OS 115 (London: Kegan Paul, Trench, Trübner, 1900).

Sex constituted lechery if indulged in purely for pleasure. The writer advocated couples recall the fate of the six husbands of Raguel's daughter, Sara (*Book of Tobit*, Chapters 5–8), each of whom were slain by the devil, Asmodeus, on their wedding night because they approached her with lecherous intent. Only her seventh, Tobias, survived the wedding night because he was not driven by lust when he lay with her. Sex should be approached with the appropriate intention, otherwise lust reduces men to beasts, and the act is detrimental to one's spiritual well being. The work warned also that kissing and touching permitted the slime of evil to enter one's body,

> Whanne þou felyst or towchyst with mowth in kyssyng, wyth hand in gropyng, & with ony membre of þi body in towchyng þat steryn þe to synne & luste, þanne entreth be þe gate of þi felyng in-to þi pytt þe watyr & wose of wykkydnesse.
> (Chapter XXXIV, folio 70a, p.219)

This sentiment was echoed in a requirement in Myrc's *Instructions* that a priest ask any man during confession if he had committed lechery by 'Clyppynge, or kyssynge, or towchynge of lyth [body] that thy flesch was styred with?' (1365).

The *Book of the Vices and Virtues* advised that sex be avoided during a woman's period because of the threat of conceiving 'maymed folk, þat is þe blynde, þe halte and lame, an þe messeles [measles or leprosy]' (folio 96b, 14–15, p. 248). Menstrual blood was believed poisonous and that children who were conceived during a woman's period would be born afflicted with either measles or leprosy.[13]

The *Book of the Vices and Virtues* identified as one of the more serious facets of lechery doing anything with one's wife 'aȝens kynde and aȝens þe ordre of wedloke' (folio 17a, 7–8, p.45). Canon lawyers

---

13 The medieval belief in the toxicity of menstrual blood was in accordance with a tradition recorded in Pliny who recounts its ability to sour of new wine, dull the surfaces of mirrors, kill bees, rust iron and bronze (see *Pliny: Natural History with an English Translation* trans. by H. Rackham, 10 vols (London: William Heinemann, 1961), ii, Book VI, xv.64–xvi.67, pp.548–49. Children were believed afflicted with measles or leprosy as a result of their bodies' attempts to purge the menstrual blood taken in during gestation. For a description of the physiology of menstruation see Jacquart and Thomasset, *Sexuality and Medicine*, pp.71–78.

defined the natural and moral fashion in which intercourse should take place as the missionary position since, as Albertus Magnus (1200–80) explained, 'Nature teaches that the proper manner is that the woman be on her back with the man lying on her stomach.'[14] Deviation from this was sanctioned only when physical obesity necessitated or there was danger of smothering the foetus in the advanced stages of pregnancy.[15] To act contrary to nature was to use a bodily member or vessel not granted by nature for such use – that is, oral and anal sex while coitus with the woman on top was also prohibited because the position was believed to impede conception.[16]

The dangers of adultery were made very clear in *Jacob's Well*. Its results were many, visible and destructive; 'false eyrys, false maryagys, manslaughter and many oþere' and, according to Pope Boniface,

> ȝif englyschmen brekyn þe knott of matrimonye, & folowyn avowtrye & spousebreche, of hem schal springe in tyme comynge a wycked seed. þat seed schal ben here chylderyn, falsely begetyn in avowterye as bastardes & false eyres: þe which schul multyplie so fer-forth in Inglond, þat þe peple schal be graceles, vnmyȝty in batayle & vnstedfast in þe feyth of holy cherch. and so þei schul haue no worschip of oþere landys, as to þe word: god schal hatyn hem [...].
> (Chapter XXIV, fol. 52b, p.161)

Adultery held dire consequences, not only for the individuals concerned but also for the nation, as the bastards sired would be so great in number as to make the country weak in battle, and wavering in its faith. The worst consequence predicted was that England would not be respected by other countries and would be hated by God. Sex was not something to be taken lightly.

---

14 Albertus Magnus, *Commentarii in IV Sententiarum (Dist. XXIII–L)* in *Opera Omnia*, ed. by S. C. A. Borgnet, 27 (Paris, 1894), 30.263 and translated in Payer, *Bridling of Desire*, p.219, note 66.
15 Payer, *Bridling of Desire*, p.78.
16 Ibid., pp.77, 79.

Cultural construction of Woman's 'croked instrument'

A variety of texts warned against the dangers of female sexuality. In the *Etymologiae*, Isidore of Seville declared that women were more lustful than men[17] and it was believed that due to the weakness of their nature, women would hardly ever remain chaste unless closely watched and guarded.[18] This belief was so commonplace that even the Virgin Mary was not exempt from the accusation of adultery. In the N-Town *Trial of Mary and Joseph* the Primus Detractor or Reysesclaundyr [Raises slander] quotes the perceived wisdom that Mary (and, by extension, any woman) who is

> Such a ȝonge damesel of bewte bryght,
> And of schap so comely Also
> Of hire tayle ofte tyme be lyght
> And rygh tekyl vndyr þe too.
> (61–64)

Mistrust of women's sexuality is revealed also in the paternal advice given to his son and heir, Thomas, at some point between 1445 and 1450 by Peter Idley, a twice married father of six. In his *Instructions to his Son* Idley assimilated the prose Latin writings of Albertanus of Brescia and Robert Mannying's vernacular prose treatise, *Handlyng Synne*, to couple their sentiments with his own experience.[19] In a section of Book II original to Idley,[20] and in a departure from his hitherto measured and good-humoured attitude, Idley betrays anxiety about woman's sexuality and warns his son against the power of

---

17 Blamires, *Woman Defamed and Woman Defended*, p.43.
18 Huguccio in his *Summa* and John of Salisbury, *Policraticus* as quoted in Brundage, *Law, Sex and Christian Society*, p.301, note 194.
19 *Peter Idley's Instructions to his Son*, ed. by C. D'Evelyn, The Modern Language Association of America, Monograph Series 6 (Boston: D.C. Heath and Company, 1935).
20 For Idley's immediate sources for this section of the *Instructions* see D'Evelyn, *Instructions*, pp.45–57.

woman's 'croked instrument' (II, 1790 *et passim*). In the Middle Ages 'croked' had the meaning of bent and also that of a bodily deformity, distortion of an organ, and figuratively, wickedness, moral or spiritual perversity.[21] Idley explained to his son that the primary use of woman's 'croked instrument' was the pursuit of sexual pleasure because she had most delight in 'suche foule lust' (II, 1791).

Some believed that a woman's body could physically endanger the penis. The author of *De secretis mulierum* [On the Secrets of Women], a late thirteenth-century text attributed falsely to Albertus Magnus,[22] warned about women with whom intercourse could wound the penis because of iron strategically placed in the vagina.[23] Even if unwounded, the penis might become painfully and embarrassingly trapped. Probably a form of vaginismus, the fear of *penis captivus* captured the medieval imagination, as tales warning of its dire consequences appear in literary compositions. In his *Book of the Knight of La Tour-Landry*, written in around 1372 for the instruction of his three daughters who had been left motherless,[24] Geoffrey de La Tour-Landry tells of an extreme case with mortifying social consequences. In chapter thirty-five he relates the story of Pers Lenard who had sex on an altar with an unnamed woman. The result of such blasphemy was that he and his lover became joined 'fast like a dogge and a biche togedre' all night and throughout the following day, were marvelled at by the townsfolk and separated

---

21 *Middle English Dictionary*, editor S. M. Kuhn, associate editor J. Reidy (Ann Arbor: The University of Michigan Press, 1963), volume C, 1a, 2a and 4, p.755.

22 M. Green, 'From "Diseases of Women" to "Secrets of Women": The Transformation of Gynecological Literature in the Later Middle Ages', *Journal of Medieval and Early Modern Studies*, 30.1 (Winter 2000), 5–39 (pp.14–15). For a translation of the work see H. Rodnite Lemay, *Women's Secrets: A Translation of Pseudo-Albertus Magnus's 'De Secretis Mulierum' with 'Commentaries'* (Albany, NY: SUNY Press, 1992).

23 H. Rodnite Lemay, 'Some Thirteenth and Fourteenth Century Lectures on Female Sexuality', *International Journal of Women's Studies*, 1.4 (1978), 391–400 (p.395).

24 As quoted in J. Rolleston, 'Penis Captivus: A Historical Note', in *Sex in the Middle Ages: A Book of Essays*, ed. by J. Salisbury (New York: Garland, 1991), pp.232–36 (pp.233–44). For an edition of the text see *The Book of the Knight of La Tour-Landry*, ed. by T. Wright, EETS OS 33 (London: Kegan Paul, Trench, Trübner, 1868, revised edition, 1906).

only after the people had held a procession around them (*Book of the Knight*, pp.51–52). For their penance, the couple had to go naked before the congregation on three Sundays, beating themselves and admitting their sin.[25] Clearly the Knight believed that his young daughters required warning against the power of their own bodies. He replicates the folk fear that reinforced the belief that woman's sexuality emanated from a secret and dark orifice that promised pleasure but also threatened its converse: pain and danger.

Medicine and Female Sexuality

Thomas Laqueur demonstrates how from Aristotle (384–322 BC) and Galen (129–c.216? AD) the Middle Ages inherited a one-sex model of humanity that understood women's anatomy as an inverted and inferior form of men's.[26] This belief is heard in Lanfrank's statement in his *Science of Cirurgie* (1296) that 'þe maris [womb] in a womman is maad neruous & is schape as it were a ȝerde [penis] þat were turned aȝenheer'.[27] It is repeated in the description of the womb found in the *Cyrurgie*, a Middle English translation of Guy de Chauliac's *Inventarium seu collectorium in parte cyrurgicali medicine*, written in Avignon in 1363.[28] To the body of classical knowledge the Middle Ages contributed interest in and discussion of sexual pleasure[29] that con-

---

25 Wright, *Book of the Knight*, p.52.
26 T. Laqueur, *Making Sex: Body and Gender from the Greeks to Freud* (Cambridge, Mass: Harvard University Press, 1990), p.33.
27 For the Middle English translation of Lanfranco of Milan's work see *Lanfrank's Science of Cirurgie*, ed. by R. Fleischhacker, Part One, EETS OS 102 (London: Kegan Paul, Trench, Trübner, 1894), Section II. ix, p.175.
28 *The Cyrurgie of Guy de Chauliac*, ed. by M. S. Ogden, EETS 265 (London: Oxford University Press, 1971), p.67.
29 J. Cadden, *Meanings of Sex Difference in the Middle Ages: Medicine, Science, and Culture* (Cambridge: Cambridge University Press, 1993), p.135.

cluded that women experience more pleasure in coitus than did men.[30] This too was based on the belief in women being an inverted form of men. It was understood that, during intercourse, both men and women emitted seed that united to form the embryo but that if the woman did not emit her sperm, conception could not take place, as was explained in the *Canon* or medical compendium of Avicenna (d. 1037),

> There is no shame in the doctor speaking about the increase in the size of the penis, or the narrowing of the receptive organs, or of the woman's pleasure, since these are factors that play a part in reproduction. For the small size of the penis is often a hindrance to climax and emission in the woman. Now, when the woman does not emit any sperm, conception cannot take place.[31]

Joan Cadden observes that the formula for sexual pleasure that was perpetuated recognised that 'man's pleasure came from the emission of his own semen, whereas woman's pleasure derived only partially from her own emission and depended for the rest upon the man.'[32] How the man might help is suggested in cures for female sterility that recommended erotic touching as foreplay. To encourage simultaneous female emission one fourteenth-century medical author recommended that the husband 'smoothly stroke his lady, breasts and belly, and excite [her] for having intercourse'.[33] The *Rosa Anglica* of John Gaddesden, the fourteenth-century Oxford doctor of physic appointed to Edward II, was much more detailed in his advice, and took into consideration a woman's erogenous zones:

> To excite and arouse a woman to intercourse, a man ought to speak, kiss and embrace [her], to touch her breasts, to caress her breasts and to touch the whole [area] between her perineum and her vulva and to strike her buttocks with the

---

30 J. Salisbury, 'Gendered Sexuality', in Bullough and Brundage, *Handbook of Medieval Sexuality*, pp.81–102 (p.93); Cadden, *Meanings of Sex Difference*, pp.97–98.
31 Avicenna, *Canon*, Book III, fen 20, tr.1, ch. 8, as quoted and translated in Jacquart and Thomasset, *Sexuality and Medicine*, p.130.
32 Cadden, *Meanings of Sex Difference*, p.161.
33 The Latin reads: '*Maritus [...] debet dominam suaviter palpare mamillas et ventrem et excitare ad coytum.*' *De impedimentis conceptionis* as quoted in Cadden, *Meanings of Sex Difference*, p.252, note 86.

purpose that the woman desires sex [...] and when the woman begins to speak with a stammer, then they ought to copulate.[34]

In respect of its understanding of women's seed and the mechanics of its emission, medical opinion supported generally the theological belief that women were sexually voracious, although the visionary abbess Hildegard of Bingen (d. 1179) defended her sex, and argued that men were more prone to lechery than women.[35] Unlike Canon law that saw spiritual danger lurking in sexual intercourse medicine, however, recognised coitus in moderation as healthy for the individual.[36]

Medical advice focused specifically on women is located in vernacular versions of material ultimately derived from the Latin *Trotula* ensemble; the *Liber de Sinthomatibus Mulierum* [Book on the Conditions of Women], *De Curis Mulierum* [On Treatments for Women] and *De Ornatu Mulierum* [On Women's Cosmetics].[37] Women's access to, and the level of literacy required for understanding such works, has engaged scholars in lengthy debate. Monica Green's research suggests compellingly that the majority of high and later medieval gynaeco-

---

[34] The Latin reads: *Mas excitare foeminam debet ac sollicitare ad coitum, loquendo, osculando, amplectendo, mamillas contractando, tangendo pectinem et perinaeum totamque vulvam accipiendo in manus et nates percutiendo hoc fine atque proposito ut mulier appetat venerem [...] et cum mulier incipit loqui balbutiendo, tunc debent se commiscere.* John of Gaddesden, *Rosa Anglica* (Augsburg, 1595), p.555 as quoted in Jacquart and Thomasset, *Sexuality and Medicine*, p.222, note 99, translation my own.

[35] In her *Book of Compound Medicine* Hildegard states that since a woman's desire is less violent she is more able to contain herself because of the moistness 'where the pleasure burns' and because of either fear or shame, as quoted in J. Cadden, 'It Takes all Kinds: Sexuality and Gender Differences in Hildegard of Bingen's "Book of Compound Medicine"', *Traditio*, 40 (1984) 149–74 (p.159). Jacquart and Thomasset, *Sexuality and Medicine*, p.213, note 105, identify Hildegard's belief as unique in the medieval period.

[36] N. Siraisi, *Medieval & Early Renaissance Medicine: An Introduction to Knowledge and Practice* (Chicago: The University of Chicago Press, 1990), p. 111. See also *The Trotula: A Medieval Compendium of Women's Medicine*, trans. and ed. by M. Green (Penn, Philadelphia: University of Pennsylvania Press, 2001), p.26.

[37] The standardized ensemble comprises these three texts. For their contents see M. Green, *The Trotula*.

logical texts (Latin and vernacular) were written for men, that when laywomen owned medical texts they were generally of the most basic nature (including recipe collections) and for information about obstetrics (that remained a largely feminised area of medical practice) women relied on oral tradition as the normative means of dissemination.[38] Medical opinion, whether acquired from a university trained physician by those few women could afford it, or from recipe books, or by the majority from other women with obstetrical knowledge, sought to maintain a woman's reproductive health and promote pleasurable intercourse.

The Knowing of Woman's Kind in Childing, a late medieval gynaecological treatise written for a female audience,[39] offers a very different attitude to women's sexuality from that encouraged by canon law. While canon lawyers decreed that a woman could become a bride and sexually active at twelve, the narrator of *The Knowing of Woman's Kind* advises that,

> Euery mayde schulde kepe here from þe dedyut [intercourse] at þe leste telle here flovrys be fall & comyn, þat ys till sche be xv yere olde, þat nature & þe ma't'rys [womb] myth fulfyll & bere þat þat longith to hem of kynde [...]. (250–53)

The concern here is at what age a girl became physically ready for intercourse. The text recommended that a woman's first sexual encounter be delayed for a further three years than that permitted under canon law, that is, until she reached fifteen, and was physically more

---

38 M. Green, *Women's Healthcare in the Medieval West: Texts and Contexts* (Aldershot: Ashgate Variorum, 2000), Chapter VII, 'The Possibilities of Literacy and the Limits of Reading: Women and the Gendering of Medical Literacy', pp.2–76 (pp.45–47).

39 The *Liber de Sinthomatibus Mulierum* is one of its sources. See *The Knowing of Woman's Kind in Childing: A Middle English Version of Material Derived from the Trotula and Other Sources*, ed. by A. Barratt (Turnhout: Brepols, 2001), p.1. I have used the version throughout that appears in Oxford MS Douce 37 (SC 21611), written in the first half of the fifteenth century, whose compact size Barratt suggests, indicates that it was made for practical use and carrying to the bedsides of women in labour, Barratt, *The Knowing of Woman's Kind in Childing*, p.12.

mature. The text warned of three possible results should intercourse be experienced too early: the girl will be barren, have halitosis or 'sche schall be to lauy [unruly] of here body to oþer þan to here hosbande' (256–57). Marital litigation found in ecclesiastical court records supports the danger of sex at too early an age as warned of in *Knowing of Woman's Kind*. In a testimony before the ecclesiastical court at York, Alice de Rouclif,'s former companion, Joan de Rollaston, reported to William Marrays, the abbot of St Mary's, York, that she overheard Alice complain about how the force of her husband's 'labouring' hurt her.[40] Alice was twelve years old. Unlike the many clerics who regarded women as inherently lustful, medical opinion in this instance argued that a woman became sexually voracious only if she began her sex life too early. *The Knowing of Woman's Kind* suggests that men are implicated in creating their own worst nightmare.

Medicine sought to facilitate a woman's enjoyment of sex and offered help should this become impaired by the frequent childbirth that was the usual outcome of spiritually-safe sex. *The Knowing of Woman's Kind in Childing* pointed out that a woman might develop 'slaknesse of þe wyket,' heavy menstruation, and hate 'þe deduit of drewry' (974–76). The *De Curis Mulierum* offered a recipe to promote a woman's sexual pleasure by artificially constricting the vagina.[41] The author of the *Liber Trotuli*, a highly condensed translation of the *Trotula* ensemble that survives in London, British Library, MS Additional 34111, acknowledged that personal hygiene might aversely affect a woman's sex life and advised women use a deodorising vaginal douche made from a variety of herbs and gums.[42]

In contradiction to canon and secular law, medicine offered contraceptive and abortion advice. Contraceptives were recommended ranging from talismans to various plant extracts. The *Liber de Sinthomatibus Mulierum* recommended any woman not wishing to con-

---

40 Goldberg, *Women in England,* p.62.
41 Green, *The Trotula*, p.42.
42 The manuscript was copied between 1420 and 1450, M. Green, 'Obstetrical and Gynecological Texts in Middle English', *Studies in the Age of Chaucer*, 14 (1992), 53–88 (p.68). Excerpts from the *Liber Trotuli* are from the text found in *Women's Writing in Middle English*, ed. by A. Barratt (London: Longman, 1992), pp.35–38 (p.36).

ceive to carry against her body either the womb of a goat that has never had kids or the testicles of a castrated weasel wrapped in goose skin or that she taste or carry 'gagates' [jet] in her hand.[43] In addition to apotropaic remedies, barrier contraceptive methods existed as did recipes for compounds that functioned as spermicides.[44] Bizarre and outlandish as many of these recipes seem, Jacquart and Thomasset suggest that some of them may have worked quite efficiently by modifying the vaginal pH.[45] Some understanding of *coitus interruptus* should not be discounted, even if, as is argued by John Riddle, the degree of co-operation required of the man meant that it was not universally practised.[46]

Should a woman become pregnant, a termination might be achieved by taking a menstrual regulator such as that given in *The Knowing of Woman's Kind in Childing*:

> Now will I tell yow medycyns for þe retencion or faylynge of flowrys [*menses*], as whanne a woman hath nonne or ryȝht few. [B]vt yf ye woll vndyrtak for-to mak þe flowrys of eny woman to comme, ye muste fyrst vse þys medycyn viij dayes be-fore þe day & þe tyme þat sche was wonte to have hare flowrys, of þe wyche ye must be certayne of here-selfe.
> (664–69)

The concoction is drunk once on the eighth day before her period is due, twice on the seventh and so on, increasing up until the day of menstruation. In addition the woman should be bathed daily in a mixture of ground ivy, catmint, wild thyme, and savin (675) and her vagina and womb fumigated with the steam (as hot as she can bear it) from bay leaves, savin, catmint and dittany (677–80). These remedies may have been intended for non-pregnancy induced dysmenorrhoea and amenorrhea and as such can be disassociated from abortion *per se*,

---

43 Green, *The Trotula*, pp.97–99.
44 J. Riddle, *Contraception and Abortion from the Ancient World to the Renaissance* (Cambridge, Mass. and London: Harvard University Press, 1992), pp.128–29.
45 Jacquart and Thomasset, *Sexuality and Medicine*, p.91.
46 Brundage, *Law, Sex and Christian Society*, p.358; Riddle, *Contraception and Abortion*, p.143.

but Riddle asserts that the women who took them probably knew what they would do to a pregnancy.[47]

As controversially medicine also offered remedies for those sexually active women who wished to appear virgin on their wedding night. Recipes for vaginal constrictives claimed to replicate the tautness of an unpenetrated vagina.[48] Others offered 'sophistication,' the means by which to construct a false hymen (the *sine qua non* of virginity). For this recipes recommended dried egg white mixed with other herbs or rainwater combined with well-ground fresh oak bark.[49]

Medieval medicine recognised that sex was more than simply the impregnation of a wife, achieved preferably without the pleasure that so imperilled the soul. Medical texts sought to keep wives sexually active and healthy, and to provide the means, even if of dubious efficacy, to avoid repeated pregnancy. While secular law criminalised actions and potions that brought about abortion, and some medical writers expressed doubt about the probity of using vaginal constrictives, contraceptives and abortifacients, such recipes existed.[50]

Literature is not written in a vacuum. Literary wives are shown caught within the same web of conflicting and competing discourses of canon law and medical doctrine regarding the body, the performance of conjugal rights and duties, and individual sexual desire as were real women. Literature offers a female perspective of a wife's conjugal

47 J. Riddle, 'Contraception and Early Abortion in the Middle Ages', in Bullough and Brundage, *Handbook of Medieval Sexuality*, pp.261–77 (p.269).
48 The recipe 'to mak streyt the prive member' offered in the *Liber Trotuli* that survives in London, British Library, MS Additional 34111, suggests the powder's efficacy 'for woman hathe han part of man and wolde be holde for a mayden', Barratt, *Women's Writing*, p.37. Another recommended method is for a girl to insert a fresh leech on her labia the day before her wedding, permitting blood to trickle out and form a crust over her vaginal orifice: the flow of blood tightens the passage, as quoted from the *Collectio Salernitana* recipes by J. Wogan-Browne, 'The Virgin's Tale', in Evans and Johnson, *Feminist Readings*, pp.165–94 (p.168).
49 Wogan-Browne, 'The Virgin's Tale', p.168. The use of dove's intestine filled with blood to simulate rupture of the hymen is another recommendation, E. Lastique and H. Rodnite Lemay, 'A Medieval Physician's Guide to Virginity', in Salisbury, *Sex in the Middle Ages*, pp.56–79 (p.65).
50 Lastique and Rodnite Lemay, 'A Medieval Physician's Guide', p.65.

rights and duties and opportunity to talk back to the cultural influences on female sexuality.

'Broght abedde as stille as stoon': May's Transition from Maiden to Wife

Chaucer examines women's view of sex in his engagement with the fabliau tradition, a genre whose purpose Charles Muscatine sees specifically as interrogating the obstacles in the ways of sexual satisfaction.[51] The *Merchant's Tale* goes some way in describing the sex-life of May and the elderly knight, Januarie, an experience that cannot have been unfamiliar to the many young women married off to much older, wealthy men. Both the Merchant-narrator and Januarie misinterpret May's attitude to sex while the Merchant, in particular, attempts to silence May's opinion. Her actions, however, speak volumes. We begin with the couple's wedding night.

The *Merchant's Tale* relates how, surrounded by the groom's friends, Januarie and May are escorted to their bedchamber. May is brought to the bed, presumably by her female servant, and before the whole company a priest blesses the bed (1818). The chamber and bed blessings of the Sarum rite commend the couple to God's protection and sanctify the bed as a place of tranquil sleep and a site for producing offspring. What follows emphasises the gap between what the Church required from the marriage bed and Januarie and May's own sexual desires.

Fortified by aphrodisiacs (1807–08) as recommended by Constantine the African in his *De Coitu* [On Intercourse],[52] Januarie satisfies his sexual appetite repeatedly as 'Thus laboureth he til that the day gan dawe' (1842). This is contrary to canon law that warned that sex for

---

51   C. Muscatine, *The Old French Fabliaux* (New Haven: Yale University Press, 1986), p.109.
52   P. Delaney, 'Constantinus Africanus' *De Coitu*: A Translation', *Chaucer Review*, 4.1 (1969), 55–65 (pp.62–65).

pleasure was a mortal sin and advocated moderation of its frequency. Januarie maintains this level of sexual activity on other occasions, from the moment 'that the coughe hath hym awaked [...] Til evensong rong and that they moste aryse' (1957, 1966).

Throughout the summer in his secret walled garden Januarie repeatedly demands and is paid the marital debt. His garden is deliberately evocative of those in which illicit lovers meet in romance tradition and a parody of the enclosed garden metaphor for the Virgin Mary's sealed womb in the Song of Solomon (4.12). It has one notable and distinct difference. Perhaps out of pride, or more in hope, Januarie's garden silences Priapus, the classical Roman god who was the proector of gardens, garden produce and a fertility deity, usually portrayed with an oversized, erect member. Regardless of his garden's splendour, and despite Januarie's confidence in his ability 'To do al that a man bilongeth to' (1459), old age was understood to dampen potency.[53] Januarie is the literary stereotype of the *senex amans* or lecherous old man, whose thought is preoccupied with sex when it should be on the preparation of his soul for the afterlife that beckons shortly. His over-indulgence in sexual activity would have been understood as undermining his physical health,[54] and indeed he wakes up in the night with a cough. Over a century after Chaucer's work, the danger to men of too much sex was still matter for concern. In his sermon on Psalm 38, John Fisher, Bishop of Rochester (1459–1535) warned,

> Physycyens saye that a man taketh more hurte by the effusyon of a lytell sede than by shedynge of ten tymes so moche blode [...] Euery synne that a man dooth is outwarde from his body, but he that dooth fornycacion or lechery offendeth god & also hurteth his body.[55]

In the garden Januarie performs acts on May's body 'that were nat doon abedde' (2051), possibly sex not according to nature, either not in the appropriate vessel or not in the approved position. He is confident

---

53 Hallissy, *Clean Maids*, p.157.
54 S. Shahar, *Growing Old in the Middle Ages: Winter Clothes Us in Shadow and Pain* (London: Routledge, 1997), p.78.
55 *The English Works of John Fisher, Bishop of Rochester (1459–1535), Part I*, ed. by J. E. B. Mayor, EETS ES 27 (London: N. Trübner, 1876), p.64.

that matrimony legitimates his actions, 'For in oure actes we mowe do no synne. / [...] For we han leve to pleye us by the lawe' (1838, 1841). But he is wrong. As Helen Phillips comments, Januarie's desire for May exhibits all the features of the inordinate desire of lechery,[56] the effects of which become manifest upon his body. Taking May as his 'lemman in entente hollyche for lust,' he does indeed devolve into the 'vnresonable beeste takyng hede to þi luste' warned of in *Jacob's Well*, becoming 'al coltissh, ful of ragerye, / And ful of jargon as a flekked pye' (*Merchant's Tale*, 1847–48). The *Aberdeen Bestiary* (University Library MS 24), written and illuminated in England around 1200, reveals the following characteristics about the *pica* or magpie,

> Magpies are like poets, because they utter words, with a distinct sound, like men; hanging in the branches of trees, they chatter rudely, and even if they cannot get their tongues round words, they nevertheless imitate human speech.[57]

Januarie's post-coital behaviour is akin to a frisky young horse, his crowing recalls that of a cockerel and his language descends to the chatter of the magpie that replicates that of man but is, in fact, meaningless. He becomes, ultimately, the horned cuckold, a monstrous fusion of human and beast. Januarie exhibits other physical conditions associated with lechery. His boast that, before married, he always 'folwed ay his bodily delyt / On wommen' (1249–50), is borne out by his leanness (1849). Leanness was considered symptomatic of too frequent intercourse, as exemplified in the lyric, 'Too Much Sex', of around 1500, in which the narrative voice warns about the man who,

> [...] Haste so blowen atte the cole,
> That alle thy rode is from thine face agoon, [...]

---

56 H. Phillips, *An Introduction to The Canterbury Tales: reading, fiction, context* (Basingstoke: Macmillan Press, 2000), p.125.

57 *De pica / Pice quasi poetice, quod verba in discrimi / ne vocis exprimant ut homo, per ramos enim / arborum pendule importuna garruli / tate sonantes, et si nequeunt linguas in / sermone explicare, sonum tamen humane / vocis imitantur, de qua congrue quidam ait: Pica loquax / certa dominum te voce salutat. Si me non videas esse ne / gabis avem. Picus a Pico Saturni filio nomen sumpsit, eo quod / in auspiciis utebatur. Nam ferunt hanc avem quiddam habere.* See http://www.abdn.ac.uk/bestiary/ folio 36v.

That fleesh upon thy carkeis is there noon:
There is nought lefte but empty skinne and bone.[58]

Januarie loses his eyesight, an affliction also believed indicative of over indulgence in coitus.[59] Some two and a quarter centuries after Hildegard of Bingen's observation, Chaucer's portrayal of Januarie demonstrates that, contrary to cultural opinion, a voracious sexual appetite is not the sole preserve of women.

May is 'broght abedde as stille as stoon' (1818) and maintains her silence: throughout the Merchant's description of the wedding night, during the encounter in which Januarie strips her and makes love to her until evensong, and throughout the antics in the garden. The sex scenes between husband and wife are presented either by the narrator or Januarie, and thus from a male perspective. From the outset Januarie boasts that he doubts May will be able to endure his 'corage' that is 'so sharp and keene' (1759). Clearly a phallic pun is intended. His ego encourages Januarie to interpret May's silence as maidenly modesty and fear of his male power that will rupture her hymen. Januarie assumes also that May will perceive sex as a 'trespace' or sin that will 'greetly offende' (1828–29). In his turn, the Merchant too assumes much about May's attitude to sex with her husband. He concludes that May values the *senex amans*' sexual performance 'nat worth a bene' (1854) and that she keeps to her room until the fourth day (1860) after their marriage because she is tired out from her sexual initiation (1862–63). His comment that May keeps to her room is the Merchant's ironic reference to the tradition of the 'Nights of Tobias', in which newly-weds were counselled, out of respect for the nuptial blessing, to defer the consummation for three nights and devote themselves instead to prayer.[60] As John Myrc explained in his sermon for

---

58   *Medieval English Lyrics: A Critical Anthology*, ed. by R. T. Davies (London: Faber & Faber, 1963), p.260.
59   Jacquart and Thomasset, *Sexuality and Medicine*, p.56.
60   In his interpretation of the Arnolfi *Betrothal* Edwin Hall informs that medieval Italian couples were reminded of the 'Nights of Tobias', a custom that was introduced in Carolingian times in the actual wedding ceremony, *The Arnolfi Betrothal: Medieval Marriage and the Enigma of Van Eyck's Double Portrait* (Berkeley: University of California Press, 1994), p.53.

the feast of St Anne, Tobias restrains himself for three nights and on the fourth 'ʒode to her bed and hade childyrne'.[61] Januarie is no Tobias and May is no Sara. Having said this much, the Merchant refuses to engage with May's feelings about sex with Januarie, 'But God woot what that May thoughte in hir herte' (1851), 'be hire lief or looth. / [...] Or wheither hire thoughte it paradys or helle' (1961, 1964).

From her arrival in the marriage bed and throughout the sexual encounters with her husband in the garden, all that we see and hear of May is Januarie's fantasy of silent obedience from a sexy, compliant body to which the Merchant is reluctant to grant a voice. When the Merchant suggests that May sets no store by her husband's lovemaking that she evaluates at 'nat worth a bene,' one feels that his real interest lies not in laying bare May's feelings, but in scoring sexual points against his older, social superior. Although in his prologue he bemoans his wife's 'cursednesse' (1238), the Merchant is keen to intimate that, unlike May, his wife had no complaints in bed.

Sex with May is refracted through a male prism and, as Helen Phillips comments, from her 'we never hear of any response'.[62] Although she says nothing, Phillips and Anne Laskaya concur that the 'nat worth a bene' evaluation of Januarie's wedding night performance is, indeed, the experience from May's perspective.[63] That May takes a lover suggests strongly that, emotionally and physically, Januarie's bedroom antics are indeed worth very little to her. Taking a lover permits her to discover if sex with someone else might be 'worth a few beans at least'.[64] If, like the Merchant, we too assume that Januarie's lovemaking cannot be worth a bean to his young wife, I think that we fail to see the whole picture. May is no fool, as her quick-thinking destruction of Damyan's love-letter attests. While it is most probable that the prospect of sex with her husband is met with silence through repulsion, less probably through maidenly modesty, and least likely through fear of his sexual prowess (although, of course, Januarie chooses to interpret it in this way), I suggest that May's silence indicates also that she has work-

---

61 Erbe, *Mirk's Festial*, p.214.
62 Phillips, *Introduction to the Canterbury Tales*, p.129.
63 Ibid., p.129; Laskaya, *Chaucer's Approach to Gender*, p.94.
64 Tuttle Hansen, *Chaucer*, p.260.

ed out the value of her vow to be 'bonoure and buxom' in bed. She is obedient not because she has vowed before God to be so nor because she is naturally compliant and dutiful, but because it is to her own financial benefit. Should Januarie predecease her, and medical texts and sermons suggest that he will should he maintain his current immoderate level of sexual activity, in exchange for her sexual obedience and fidelity May will obtain not just the part of his wealth stipulated in the prenuptial contract, but all of his 'heritage, toun and tour' that he has promised will be made over to her in legally binding 'chartres' (2172–73). By taking a young and attractive lover May confirms that in terms of physical satisfaction Januarie's lovemaking is, indeed, worthless but the Merchant fails to consider that financially, sex with Januarie is worth a whole heap of beans to this prospective widow. May is an image of the youthful Wife of Bath, thinking ahead to that time when she will be a player once more in the marriage market. Jill Mann's advice is timely, that we not waste our sympathy on attributing to May repugnance about her husband that she does not possess since she has willingly married the old fool for his money.[65] May is prepared to act the part of a Griselda to secure Januarie's money and the prospect of future, more appealing suitors, who this would attract.

May's adultery is consistent with the representation of women in the anti-feminist tradition, warned about from the pulpit, and a stock character in the fabliaux genre to which the *Merchant's Tale* belongs.[66] At the same time, it reveals that, contrary to medical scientific discourse, woman is not simply an inverted man but that her private parts signal, to quote Elaine Tuttle Hansen, 'true difference' that has its own sexual desire and needs.[67] Her encouragement of Damyan indicates that May has 'han no plesaunce' (1434) with Januarie, and that what she desires from Damyan is sexual pleasure, pure and simple. Unlike Januarie, May makes no mention of a desire for children. Elaine Tuttle Hansen's view is compelling that May's behaviour with her squire is illustrative of her awakening as she comes into a subjectivity and

---

[65] Mann, *Geoffrey Chaucer*, p.68.
[66] Laskaya, *Chaucer's Approach to Gender*, pp.96–97.
[67] Tuttle Hansen, *Chaucer*, p.260.

sexuality of her own.[68] We see her take charge of her sexuality by the most memorable metaphor. May fashions a wax impression from which Damyan can create his own key to the 'smale wyket' (2045) of the walled garden. Januarie has exclusive ownership of the key and unlocks the gate or 'wyket,' a term that was employed in medical texts to describe a woman's genitalia,[69] when he desires entry of both the garden and May. Januarie's exclusive access to his wife's body is sanctioned and affirmed in canon law and has been promised by May in her wedding vows. In fashioning a duplicate key, May effectively removes her vagina/sexuality from the sole possession of her husband and gifts it to the young squire.

To fulfil her desire, May climbs into the pear-tree, a site associated, in at least one medieval lyric, with illicit love affairs. In 'Love in the Garden',[70] the grafting of a pear tree's shoot is metonymic for the impregnation of a beautiful maiden, who the narrator boasts that he 'gryffid [...] / ryȝt vp in her home' (18–19). May elicits her husband's help in climbing into the pear tree, by suggesting that her sudden longing for its fruit arises from pregnancy. While May's craving (2335) may indeed be indicative of this condition, it is as likely that it is feigned,[71] for there are a number of contra indicators of pregnancy in the passage. May's assignation in a pear-tree may signal her use of contraception. If carried in contact with a woman's body, the pear tree and its roots were believed to have contraceptive virtues.[72] Her upright position in

---

68   Ibid., *Chaucer*, p.258.
69   The Middle English derives from the Old French '*guichet*' and Anglo-Norman '*wiket*'. Terminology used to describe body parts is explored in J. Norri, *Names of Body Parts in English, 1400–1550* (Helsinki: Finnish Academy of Science and Letters, 1998). Norri cites the use of the Anglo-Norman term '*wiket*' used in this way in a late fifteenth-century translation of the works of John of Arderne (writing in the 1370s) in a cure for the retention of afterbirth, 'þe roote of lylye soden vppon colys with oyle & after stamped & putte vppon þe wykett bryngeþ out the secundine [afterbirth]', Norri, p.216. It appears too in *The Knowing of Woman's Kind in Childing*, as quoted above.
70   Robbins, *Secular Lyrics*, number 21, pp.15–16.
71   Benson, *Riverside Chaucer*, p. 889, note 2335–37; Laskaya, *Chaucer's Approach to Gender*, p.95; Hallissy, *Clean Maids*, pp.157–59.
72   Jacquart and Thomasset, *Sexuality and Medicine*, p.91. Albert the Great indicates of the pear tree that, *Qui autem magicis insudant, dicunt quod radix pyri,*

the tree and leaping down from it immediately after coitus were recognised contraceptive practises since horizontal sex was considered best for conception because if 'the woman gets up at once, and moves, or jumps [...] the seed being slippery [...] passes out'.[73] Unreliable as these contraceptive methods were, their presence suggests that May tried to have her cake and eat it. Through the use of contraceptive practices, should they succeed, May will appear faithful and obtain her husband's money while being able to take a lover and avoid discovery through pregnancy. She will also avoid conceiving children, either legitimate or illegitimate who, as Hallissy points out, would at best dilute her share of Januarie's money and, at worst, wreck her marriage.[74] One wonders how many young women married off to older, wealthy men and surrounded by attractive squires of their own age, secretly applauded May's break for sexual freedom. If using contraception, May is playing a dangerous game. In 1530 Joan Willys, along with her husband, John Hunt, were sentenced by the church court at Harpenden, in the diocese of Lincoln, to do public penance because Joan had drunk a potion to kill the child that she carried.[75] Discovery might be the least of a woman's worries. On 12 December 1503, Joan Wynspere of Basford, died from the poisonous effects of the draughts that she had imbibed to kill the child in her womb.[76]

The actual sex scene, however, is an anticlimax. It is *coitus interruptus* and not just from Damyan's point of view. May's actions in taking a lover and giving him access to her 'wyket,' reveals that women

> *et praecipue stiptica et tarde maturi portata et ligata super mulierem, impedit conceptum: et similiter si mulier se vel iuxta habuerit pyra, difficulter pariet.* [Moreover those who toil with magic, say that the root of the pear, specially an astringent variety [small, hard stewing pears] and slowly ripened carried [by] and bandaged on a woman, prevents conception: and in the same way if a woman will hold a [piece] of pear-tree close to her, she will give birth with difficulty.] From *De Vegetalibus et Plantis* VI, I, quoted in Jacquart and Thomasset, p.215, note 11. Translation my own.

73 Albertus Magnus as quoted in Hallissy, *Clean Maids*, p.160. Sneezing and jumping around had been considered a means of avoiding pregnancy since the time of Hippocrates, Jacquart and Thomasset, *Sex and Medicine*, p.93.
74 Hallissy, *Clean Maids*, p.157.
75 Goldberg, *Women in England*, p.122.
76 From a Coroner's Inquest quoted in Hanawalt, *The Ties that Bound*, p.101.

have sexual desires of their own. At the very moment in which we might anticipate May to voice this, we are disappointed. Missing is any statement of her joy in sex, such as that experienced by Alison in another fabliau, the *Miller's Tale*, about whose night of passion with the 'hende Nicholas' we learn that the couple both 'lith [...] / In bisynesse of myrthe and of solas, / Til that the belle of laudes gan to rynge' (3654–55). Had this tale been told by the Wife of Bath, we would have heard how Damyan's efforts compared with Januarie's and how May felt about the experience since Alisoun of Bath readily compares the sexual performances of her five husbands and admits that Jankyn in bed was 'so fressh and gay' (*Wife of Bath's Prologue*, 508).

It should not surprise that in the *Merchant's Tale*, not only the wedding night but also the adulterous sex scene is related from the male point of view. In silencing May a patriarchal conspiracy is at work. We are given a very blunt description from the Merchant's perspective of how Damyan 'Gan pullen up the smok, and in he throng' (2353) and then Januarie's outcry 'Ye, algate in it wente! [...] / He swyved thee' (2376, 2378). May says nothing (even though Proserpina has granted her and all women the ability to talk themselves out of tricky situations) at the very moment in which she might be expected to voice her opinion about men's sexual performance, for having had two lovers she is now in a position to judge. In silencing May, the *Merchant's Tale* demonstrates men's fear that women have sexual needs of their own and that they hold an opinion regarding how well these are met by the men in their lives. The Merchant-narrator refuses his female lead space to advocate this and so create a sexual-textual discourse of her own. The Merchant's description of May's coupling with Damyan disappoints because of May's emotional absence from the moment: she is the smock to be lifted and the hole to be filled, reduced to the stereotypically voracious vagina that characterises many a wicked wife. There is no thought to how May might feel about this young man's sexual ability, if she has enjoyed the experience, or if she might want more sensitivity and satisfaction than that provided by Damyan's 'thronging' or 'thrusting in'. The focus of the encounter is the Merchant and Januarie's reaction to Damyan's actions. It is the bare-faced cheek of this that they criticise, not the sexual performance that most tellingly neither perceives as lacking in any way nor as anything other than is expected.

In solidarity with a patriarchy that has much to lose should men acknowledge that women assess men's sexual performance as much as men do women's, and that men too can be found wanting, the Merchant balks at giving May opportunity to admit this. It is one thing for the Merchant to assume, on May's behalf, that a man apparently much older than the Merchant cannot pleasure a woman but another matter entirely to permit her to admit that women prefer young, virile men or, even worse, that men, old and wealthy, young and attractive alike, simply do not know how to sexually satisfy their women. He does allow May speech with which to condemn herself and all other women as adulterous whores, and demonstrate their sex's ability, so praised by the Wife of Bath (*Wife of Bath's Prologue*, 227–28), to lie their way out of trouble.

The Merchant moves swiftly from the sex scene and we leave the tale as Januarie 'on hire wombe [...] stroketh hire ful softe' (2414), an image that critics interpret as fondling either May's womb or her genitalia.[77] Whichever is intended, it is a gesture of ownership: Januarie believes his wife's 'wyket' is back in her husband's rightful control and we never discover what May thought of sex with a younger man or if she would like, or indeed can have, further sexual encounters with her squire. May escapes punishment because sexual voracity and adultery engineered through deceit is precisely what fabliaux literature, and culture in general, readily expects of its wives. Access to May's thoughts and actions are limited within the *Merchant's Tale* but Chaucer does have a narrator who gives voice, at great length, to her perspective on sex and who is unwilling to be silenced by patriarchal discourse: Alisoun of Bath.

---

77   Benson, *The Riverside Chaucer*, p.889, note 2414.

'In wyfhod I wol use myn instrument':
The Wife of Bath's Vagina Monologue

The Wife of Bath is no silent, obedient and malleable body. Alisoun repeatedly questions man's authority over and knowledge of woman's sexuality. E. Jane Burns' interpretative strategy of listening to the speech, what she terms 'bodytalk', of heroines is illuminating when applied to the Wife of Bath, as she has much to say, both within and against the dominant discourses that construct her. Unlike the stony silence to which the Merchant condemns May Alisoun is loquacious about her lovers, having the longest dramatic monologue of any pilgrim.

In Alisoun's speech one can hear both the dominant discourses that construct women's sexuality, and her talking back to those traditions that criticise how she has conducted her marital career and her sex life therein. So frequent is her quotation of texts about remarriage, marital sex, and medical and cultural attitudes to the female body, that Jill Mann argues that what comes out of her mouth is an extensive corpus of anti-feminist commonplaces.[78] Anne Laskaya too notes how Alisoun

> damns herself before her clerical listeners when she claims for herself all the attributes of women the antifeminist tradition identifies: she relishes her sexuality; she enjoys acquiring wealth and power; she boasts that no man can 'swere and lyen' half so well 'as a womman kan'; and she absolutely tingles at the prospect of deceiving men.[79]

Stewart Justman concludes that 'the Wife boasts of her *pudenda* (literally 'things to be ashamed of'), vaunting the shamelessness and the perverted reason that were long said to be women's by nature'.[80]

When she admits that she cannot deny any good man her 'chambre of Venus' (618), Alisoun sounds like the stereotypically libidinous,

---

[78] Mann, *Chaucer*, p.70.
[79] Laskaya, *Chaucer's Approach to Gender*, p.176.
[80] S. Justman, 'Trade as Pudendum: Chaucer's Wife of Bath', *Chaucer Review*, 28.4 (1994), 434–52 (pp.348–49).

shameless woman. This is not the measured and thoughtful response to sex required by canon law. She quotes her husband's patriarchal assumption about woman's sexual desire, 'Thou liknest it also to wilde fyr; / The moore it brenneth, the moore it hath desir / To consume every thyng that brent wole be' (373–75), a belief that her behaviour would seem to bear out. Alisoun kindles her lechery still further, by doing precisely what the *Book of Vices and Virtues* warned against, in its advice that women be 'sobre in etyng & drynkyng, for of to moche etyng and drynkynge comeþ moche quekenyng of þe fier of lecherie' (fol. 95b., p. 245). When Alisoun 'had dronke a draughte of sweete wyn' (459) the effects are dramatic: she sings and dances 'And after wyn on Venus moste I thynke, / [...] A likerous mouth moste han a likerous tayl' (464, 466). As is her right, Alisoun demands the conjugal debt from each husband who will 'have his tribulacion withal / Upon his flessh, whil that I am his wyf' (156–57) but does so with such immoderation that her three older husbands 'pitously a-nyght [...] swynke!' (202) and 'many a nyght they songen "Weilawey!"' (217). Like Januarie, the Wife of Bath exhibits an inordinate interest in sex, problematic in itself according to theologians at a time in life when the Church advocated that one's thoughts be on matters more heavenly.

The correspondences between Januarie and Alisoun suggest that, in sexual terms, as she ages she becomes, increasingly, a female counterpart of the knight. Each has had sexual encounters in their youth that contravene canon law. Like Januarie's pre-marital affairs, Alisoun's juvenile sexual experiences are sinful and constitute fornication (*General Prologue*, 461). Both use their wealth as a means of attracting a younger spouse. Both are aroused by the effect of alcohol. Alisoun's confession that she is both 'ful of ragerye' and 'joly as a pye,' echoes the Merchant's description of the post-coital Januarie, 'al coltissh, ful of ragerye, / And ful of jargon as a flekked pye' (*Merchant's Tale*, 1847–48). Both admit to remaining wanton in their maturity and are compared with magpies.

As a much younger wife, however, Alisoun has much in common with May. Like May, Alisoun discovers, from an early age, that sex is a powerful bargaining tool and that it can be as much a commodity with a price as any cloth that she might sell. She knows how supply and demand can influence a market,

> Greet prees at market maketh deere ware,
> And to greet cheep is holde at litel prys:
> This knoweth every womman that is wys.
> (522–24)

Contrary to her boast and the teaching of St Paul, throughout her first three marriages sex is either deliberately withheld or overwhelmingly proffered. Alison deliberately does not use her instrument freely. On some occasions, she refuses to pay the marital debt and withholds sex from each of her first three husbands, until they literally pay up,

> I wolde no lenger in the bed abyde
> If that I felte his arm over my syde,
> Til he had maad his raunson unto me;
> Thanne wolde I suffre hym do his nycetee.
> (409–12)

Here 'ransom' or penalty suggests that the price her husband pays for his legitimate enjoyment of his wife's body is some form of jointure and/or other property and gifts. Because she rations her supply of sex this puts a higher premium on those occasions when she does acquiesce. In a perversion of St Paul's dictate that sex within marriage is a mutual debt between partners, and in blatant disregard for canon law, Alison sees the debt entirely as belonging to her husbands who she makes 'bothe my dettour and my thral' (155). When she does give them what they want, her husbands are so grateful that they bring her 'gaye thynges fro the fayre' (221). When she pays the marital debt, Alisoun does so solely for financial gain, behaviour that some see as only saved from being prostitution in that it occurs within matrimony and between spouses.[81] Alisoun is, without doubt, the self-confessed queen of (s)exploitation for economic gain and enjoys the pleasure of outwitting her three old husbands in the best fabliau tradition. In the case of four and five, she is driven by lust and pleasure to seek their payment

---

[81] R. Mazo Karras, *Common Women: Prostitution and Sexuality in Medieval England* (Oxford: Oxford University Press, 1996), p.88. Justman sees Alisoun as a comical grotesque functioning somewhere between widow, wife and whore, 'Trade as Pudendum', p.346.

of the marital debt. At no stage does she mention the only sinless reason for sex: the procreation of children.

But at the same time that her bodytalk confirms male fear of uncontrolled and uncontrollable female sexuality, it resists this formulation by presenting knowledge different from the dominant tradition, exposing 'the fraud of male knowledge'.[82] The Wife of Bath talks back to those discourses whose purpose it is to define and control her sexuality. Alisoun's attitude toward her sexuality is formulated not from the written 'auctoritee' (1) of clerics who fear and distrust women 'down there', but is the result of accumulative experience of five marriages since the age of twelve and 'diverse practyk' (44d) with five husbands. A striking feature of her prologue is the number and tone of the references to the uniquely female orifice that punctuate her speech. In her anecdotal focus on her vagina, the Wife of Bath anticipates by nearly six centuries Eve Ensler's *Vagina Monologues*,[83] a collection of autobiographical stories that permit the vagina to talk back and address 'the popular belief that men, whether as lovers or physicians, knew more about women's bodies than women did'.[84]

Alisoun's experience tells her that, whatever clerks may say, her genitals are made for more than simply 'purgacioun / Of uryne, and, [...] to knowe a femele from a male' (120–22), and 'ese of engendrure' (127–28). Experience has also taught Alisoun that her vagina is an organ of pleasure, that pleasure is something to be sought within marriage and against which, the canonical prohibition of sex purely for enjoyment is powerless within the privacy of a woman's own bedroom. She rejects expressions that signify her genitals as a bodily part of which to be ashamed: *pudendum* is Justman's term not hers. Alisoun employs morally neutral language to describe this area; 'membres maad of generacion' (116), 'thynges smale' (121) and 'instrument' (132). In stark contrast to Peter Idley, who sees the vagina as 'croked,' Alisoun perceives hers as neither bodily deformity, distortion nor a symbol of

---

[82] Burns, *Bodytalk*, p.39.
[83] The monologues were produced first by HOME for Contemporary Theatre and Art at the HERE Theatre, New York. They are published as E. Ensler, *The Vagina Monologues* (London: Virago Press, 2001).
[84] Gloria Steinem in her foreward to Ensler, *Vagina Monologues*, p.xi.

moral and spiritual perversity. God has given all women a vagina to use lawfully in marriage (149–50), and her celebration of her sexuality is detectable in her repeated references to her 'bele chose' (447, 510) and 'chambre of Venus' (618). In contradiction to Januarie's assumption that sex is a trespass against woman, Alisoun's bodytalk indicates that, if performed with a woman's satisfaction in mind, sex for its own sake is a pleasure to be welcomed.

In the comparison of her first three marriages with her fourth and fifth, Alisoun openly admits what the Merchant feared May might voice: that women have an attitude towards sex and that a man's sexual prowess does not always satisfy his wife's expectations. In her first three marriages Alisoun describes how she remained unsatisfied sexually and emotionally,

> For wynnyng wolde I al his lust endure,
> And make me a feyned appetit;
> And yet in bacon hadde I nevere delit.
> (416–18)

Alisoun's confession of enduring sex and faking her desire indicates that she did not enjoy an affectionate and intimate relationship with any of her first three husbands. Her reference to bacon is to the competition held annually in Dunmow in Essex for the Flitch or side of bacon. If a married couple could live a year and a day without arguing and regretting having married, they could win the Flitch.[85] In none of her first three marriages to much older men, has Alisoun enjoyed bacon – metonymic both of her husband's sexual member and a strife-free marital relationship.

Alisoun's complaint about her older husbands' lack of sexual ability serves as a rebuttal of Januarie's confidence in the power and appeal of his masculinity having remained unaltered as he has aged. It

---

85   The couple was required to swear their oaths on the 'Kneeling Stones' which may still be seen in Little Dunmow Priory today. It is likely that the bacon was given by the ecclesiastical authorities of the Augustinian Priory of St Mary the Virgin at Little Dunmow, as a kind of edible bonus if people took marriage vows with the Church's blessing, details from the anonymous, *Little Dunmow Priory. A Brief History and Guide to the Parish Church Today* ([n.p.]: [n.d.]).

recalls too, the lyric in which ten wives gather in a tavern, to discuss the relative size and utility of their husbands' penises or 'ware'.[86] According to their gossip, the measurements vary from 'The lengthe of a snayle' (15), 'The lengthe of thre bene' (24), to a 'warbrede' (36). The husbands are said to suffer from 'the fydefalle' (47), that is the drooping ailment, and from impotence (71). In another lyric, 'Old Hogyn's Adventure',[87] the narrator finds that her lover, Hogyn, is useless since 'The old chorle he cowld do nowght' (15). She punishes him with a misdirected kiss of her backside, as suffered similarly by Absolon in *The Miller's Tale*. The women in these lyrics make clear that size really does matter. In so much as she benefits from her first three marriages in terms of finance and power, Alison loses out in relation to her husbands' 'ware'. Like the wives in the lyric, Alisoun acknowledges that, contrary to the cultural assumption that women are sexually insatiable, if a husband does not appeal to his spouse and the sex is not good, the marital debt is something that women 'tolde of it no stoor' (203). Wealth is not everything in a lifetime partner: sexual desire and sexual satisfaction have their place too.

In her hunt for a fourth and fifth husband, Alisoun prioritises sex appeal, even though this means that her spouse brings rather less financially to the union than that to which she has become accustomed. Number four promises much in terms of sexual satisfaction but fails to come up with the goods. Alisoun discovers that to which Januarie remains blind: money can buy a spouse but not affection nor fidelity. As a mature woman, Alisoun's sexual favours do not hold the same value to a 'revelour' (453) as they did to her first three, older husbands. She falls foul of sexist, age discrimination, as expressed by Januarie, 'I wol no womman thritty yeer of age; / It is but bene-straw and greet forage' (*Merchant's Tale*, 1421–22). Although Alisoun considers herself still 'yong and ful of ragerye, / Stibourne and strong, and joly as a pye' (455–56), this is not her husband's perception. She is denied her sexual right by a man who is not overwhelmed by desire for her, most probably, because he can get the same or better *gratis*, from a mistress who may not be so demanding in terms of presents from the fair. Through

---

86 Salisbury, *The Trials and Joys of Marriage*, pp.95–102.
87 Robbins, *Secular Lyrics*, number 37, pp.33–34.

husband number four's treatment of her, Alisoun discovers that, like any commodity, a woman's sex appeal – and any power that this might give her – is subject to depreciation with age, losing its attraction and value as a bargaining tool. This can occur, even if the woman considers herself still to be the vibrant and sexy creature that she was in her youth.

In a form of wish-fulfilment, in her tale Alisoun reverses the physical effects of old age, and transforms the unattractive hag into a young beauty whom the knight desires. In the fictional Bath established in her monologue, bodies do not magically transform and Alisoun understands the vital importance of re-packaging her wares. Parading herself to her best advantage in eye-catching, scarlet robes (559), Alisoun secures the attention of Jankyn and marries him. Alisoun readily admits what the Merchant fears May might reveal, that sex with a much younger lover is a pleasurable, tactile, satisfying but all too infrequent experience,

> But in oure bed he was so fressh and gay,
> And therwithal so wel koude he me glose,
> Whan that he wolde han my *bele chose*; [...]
> I trowe I loved hym best, for that he
> Was of his love daungerous to me.
> (508–10, 513–14)

She recalls fondly Jankyn's performance in bed. This she describes in a very different fashion from the ability of her first three husbands whose efforts are akin to the 'swyving' experienced by May up the pear tree. Alisoun reminisces that Jankyn was 'fesshe and gay' in bed, a portrayal that conveys a variety of meanings; fresh, new, vigorous, lusty, joyous, wanton, amorous, any number of which indicate that he brought virility, pleasure and invention to his lovemaking. Alisoun reveals that Jankyn 'gloses' her body. 'Glose' could mean to cajole and flatter, suggesting that Jankyn began his lovemaking with erotic speech, seducing his wife mentally before attempting anything physical.[88] The verb also means to gloss a body of writing, that is, the insertion of an explanatory or interpretative comment between the lines or margins of a text after its care-

---

88 See 'glosen', 3b in *Middle English Dictionary*, vol 4 (G–H), p.173.

ful scrutiny. The Wife of Bath is familiar with this second meaning, and also that some 'glose' or interpret more accurately than others, for she uses the term to dismiss both the interpretation of the Gospels' stance on digamy, 'Men may devyne and glosen, up and doun' (Prologue, 26) and, as we have already seen, clerical interpretation of the purpose of the genitalia. Glossing implies the slow and careful study of a text, fingering the lines of a manuscript as it read, taking the time to explore and understand its minutiae. In this context, the Wife leads us to understand that during their lovemaking Jankyn took the time to appreciate the minutiae of his wife's body, applying the same close reading techniques of his studying one membrane to another skin that bore similar lines, hairs, scar marks and discolourations. Jankyn 'gloses' his wife's body, suggesting the slow, careful touching of its lines, lacunae or orifices, scars and birthmarks, such as the one of Mars that she bears upon her 'privee place' (620). Alisoun recalls that he did this so 'wel', intimating that Jankyn learned to understand her body and that she finally achieved sexual arousal, the memory of which still retains its power to move her. Chaucer's audience might have expected Jankyn to succeed where her other husbands had failed. Andreas Capellanus' *De Amore* (1184–86) placed clerics at the summit of the hierarchy of lovers because of their attention to detail that extended to lovemaking:

> The cleric is seen to be more careful and wise in all things than the layman. He orders himself and his affairs with greater control, and is accustomed to governing everything with more fitting measure; because he is a cleric he has knowledge of all things, since scripture gives him this expertise. So his love is to be accounted better than the layman's, because nothing on earth is established to be so vital as that the lover should have experience in diligent application of all things.[89]

---

89   The Latin reads: *Clericus enim in cunctis cautior et prudentior quam laicus invenitur, et maiori moderamine se suaque disponit et competentiori mensura solitus est omnia moderari, et quia clericus omnium rerum scientiam habet scriptura referente peritiam. Unde potior ipsius quam laici amor est iudicandus, quia nil in mundo tam necessarium invenitur quam omnium industria rerum amorosum esse peritum.* Sections 487–8 of Andreas Capellanus, *De Amore, VI, Loquitur nobilior nobiliori* at http://www.thelatinlibrary.com/-capellanus1.html

Capellanus praises a cleric as a better lover than a layman because of the former's ability to apply to his lovemaking the knowledge and control gained from study. Danielle Jacquart and Claude Thomasset have gone so far as to claim that what Capellanus has encoded here is clerical ability to practise *coitus interruptus*.[90] Alisoun intimates that Jankyn was a different kind of lover from her previous husbands. He practised measured and inventive lovemaking, in which she delighted and about which she expresses sentiments similar to the unnamed female narrator of the lyric, 'Our Sir John', who admits that when,

> Ser Iohn ys taken In my mouse-trappe:
> ffayne wold I haue hem [Sir John/his penis] bothe nyght and day.
> he gropith so nyslye a-bought my lape,
> I haue no pore to sa[y hym nay].[91]

Alisoun is 'glosed' and the lyric narrator experiences being 'nyslye gropith'. Both women respond positively to partners who explore their bodies, and their sexual pleasure is very different in quality from the 'swyving' up a pear tree experienced by May. Alisoun has argued throughout her prologue that conduct books and other male produced texts were written to assist a woman in perfecting being a wife. Her discussion of sex reveals that men also required tutoring in the role of a husband. Her praise of Jankyn's sexual technique reveals that a man can perfect the art of sex, if, with her tutoring, he frequently and diligently studies his wife's body.

Unlike the description of Januarie's 'ragerye' that encourages revulsion, the Wife of Bath's confession that in older age 'ragerye' does not diminish, and her description of sex with the much younger Jankyn, engenders a sympathetic response. This is elicited, in part, by the emotional turmoil of sexual frustration, brought about through unrequited passion, to which Alisoun admits in the description of her treatment by the 'revelour'. In addition, I suggest that Alisoun's description of her and Jankyn's lovemaking encourages the audience to be comforted, rather than disgusted, that this vibrant woman has found, at last, the sexual satisfaction so conspicuously absent from her previous

---

90 Jacquart and Thomasset, *Sexuality and Medicine*, p.104.
91 Robbins, *Secular Lyrics*, number 26, p.20.

marriages. Although Jankyn may well have married her for her money, there is no indication that their sex life is anything other than mutually pleasurable: unlike May, he does not seek sexual satisfaction outside of marriage. Their bedroom activities demonstrate how canon law's warning about the perils of touch and its prohibition of sex motivated purely by pleasure is sinful, holds no sway in the privacy of the bedroom.

Yet Alisoun remains discontented. Jankyn strives to assert the authority over his wife that the patriarchal institutions of Church and state condoned and facilitated him to wield. Alisoun's bodytalk concedes that, even if the sex is good, women bridle under male authority, a point repeated in her tale. Having complained about the canon law governing sex and cultural preconceptions about woman's sexuality, her relationship with Jankyn causes Alisoun to re-address a topic that she had already raised with regard to her first three spouses: the secular law that grants the husband power over his wife in all matters legal and financial. Alisoun has already protested that her first three husbands hid the keys of their money chests (308–09), when natural justice would have that the marital property 'is my good as wel as thyn, pardee!' (310). With them, in the private arena of the bedroom, Alisoun institutes a new kind of law, in which her husbands had to choose to exert either their rights in secular law over her goods, or their rights enshrined in canon law over her body, but could not exert not both:

> Thou shalt nat bothe, thogh that thou were wood,
> Be maister of my body and of my good;
> That oon thou shalt forgo, maugree thyne yen.
> (313–15)

Alisoun refuses to adhere to her wedding vow of absolute obedience in bed and at board, choosing to pay the marital debt only on those occasions when it benefits her financially. She re-interprets the vow in which the man to promises to honour his wife with 'all my worldly catell [chattels]'[92] to mean 'what's mine is mine and what's his is

---

92 The Latin instruction that accompanies the vow reads: *quem vir accipiat manu sua dextera cum tribus principalibus digitis, a manu sua sinistra tenens dexteram sponsae; docente sacerdote, dicat.* Dickinson, *Missale ad Usum Insignis, Ordo Sponsalium*, column 833.

mine'. Overwhelmed by those occasions on which Alisoun does pay up, she obtains from her first three husbands not only financial reward, but also treasure of another kind: their submission and obedience to her since she 'governed hem so wel, after my lawe' (219). She has them eating out of her hand and drains them, as Priscilla Martin observes, of their forms of power: their money, property, vitality and articulacy.[93]

Her fourth husband never participates in her scheme since he goes elsewhere for sex and they spend much time apart: she on pilgrimage and he on business in London. Jankyn too refuses, initially, to be ruled by Alisoun's law. He asserts his authority, by quoting from the significant body of literature that supports the exertion of male power over recalcitrant wives. Since 'He nolde suffre nothyng of my list' (633), Jankyn comes into conflict with Alisoun's *modus operandi*. Experience of husband number four has taught the ageing Alisoun that she can no longer rely absolutely on her sexual allure to persuade Jankyn to her way of thinking. Frustration erupts into violence and Alisoun, ironically, turns to the secular law whose property edicts she has just criticised, frightening Jankyn with the weight of criminal law. She accuses him of attempting to murder her for her land. Homicide was a felony whose judgement was reserved to the royal courts and the penalty for which was death.[94] Scared that he has killed her with his blow, Jankyn duly agrees to be governed by Alisoun's legal code and the threat of the hangman's rope recedes. He accepts a reversal of roles. Taking on the status of a wife, he becomes financially dependent on his spouse and agrees to let her be his master, granting her,

> [...] Al the bridel in myn hond,
> To han the governance of hous and lond,
> And of his tonge, and of his hond also.
> (813–15)

By burning his book, Jankyn symbolically destroys the patriarchal textual authority with which he has tried to constrain his wife. Her vow to be 'bonoure and buxum' made before God, is conveniently

---

93   Martin, *Chaucer's Women*, p.91.
94   Goldberg, *Women in England*, p.36.

overlooked within the privacy of their own home. If this way of living extended to when they appeared as a couple outside of the home, we never find out. Jankyn has neither the nerve nor the confidence in his social status of Arveragus who, in the *Franklin's Tale*, offers to obey his wife, Dorigen, yet demands that 'Save that the name of soveraynetee, / That wolde he have for shame of his degree' (751–52).

In Alisoun's bodytalk we hear her voice bullying her husbands and living up to every man's worst nightmare of women's sexuality, but also, more subversively, revealing that women have an attitude to sex and their sexuality other than that which men are willing to admit. In Alisoun's vagina monologue we hear her disagree with and reject the male-authored teaching about marriage and marital sex that disagrees with matrimony as she has experienced it. Her prologue reveals the influence wielded over men's and women's lives, of patriarchal discourses purporting to know women's sexuality. Alisoun knows only too well, that whoever paints the lion governs the perspective given. If women had written the stories of their sexuality, the tales would be very different from those told by clerks. She offers a glimpse of the possibilities, if those discourses that predetermine and constrain a wife's authority are discarded; by destroying the books in which the proper action of male sovereignty over recalcitrant wives is enshrined and devolving power to the wife. Defining a matrimonial relationship, for which neither texts nor authorities currently exist, proves difficult but not impossible, 'But atte laste, with muchel care and wo, / We fille acorded by us selven two' (811–12). This step into the unknown and unorthodox permits the wife's textual/sexual oppression to be broken and a different way of living to commence.

What results is disappointing, however, in that in constructing a new text by which to conduct a marital relationship, Chaucer permits Alisoun no more creativity than to institute a reversal of traditional roles. In turn, this suggests that women could not conceive of wifehood, in terms other than the absolute legal and corporeal sovereignty over an obedient spouse currently permitted to men in secular law, and vowed before God in the marriage service. In spite of Alisoun's criticism of the inadequate bedroom activities of her first four husbands, her praise of Jankyn's 'glosing' of her body reinforces, as do so many lyrics, that what women really desire is to be the recipient of a rigid, male member. Her prologue and tale close down any opportunity for consideration of female sexuality other than normative, penetrative sex. For a more creative revision of those discourses that define marriage and women's sexuality, one must turn to Margery Kempe, who forged her own, alternative sexuality and way of living as a wife.

'Grawnteth me that ye schal not komyn in my bed': The Sex(less) Life of Margery Kempe

We are fortunate that Margery Kempe (*c.* 1373–*c.* 1440) has left testimony of her marital experiences in her *Book*. Belonging to the prosperous middle-class and the daughter of a burgess, Margery was married at around the age of twenty to John Kempe, a successful Bishop's (now King's) Lynn merchant. Margery spent at least the next decade and a half occupied with fourteen pregnancies (Chapter 48). The references to her married life are scattered throughout her *Book* and their chronology has been usefully summarised by Kim Phillips,

> Margery's early twenties were a time of considerable change and crisis: marriage, pregnancy, childbirth, madness, and her first visionary experiences. The years between her recovery at twenty-one or twenty-two and her mid-thirties were strongly marked by worldly concerns. [...] It was probably at around thirty-five that Margery heard the heavenly melody which made her leap out of bed, and instigated her fervent wish for celibacy (3:11). The next few years were marked by sexual struggle as she tried to persuade her husband to become chaste and took to wearing a hair shirt, but after two years found herself once more prey to lust, and was subject to temptations for three years. She was at most thirty-eight when she was approached and rebuffed by, a man in church (4:14). [...] Certainly by the age of forty Margery's sexual and reproductive life was ended (11:23; 15:33).[95]

Margery begins her account of herself with marriage and sexual experience because, as Barry Windeatt suggests, 'to her mind every-

---

95 Phillips, 'Margery Kempe and the Ages of Woman', p.19.

thing follows from that'.[96] Margery's experience demonstrates how a real wife's sexuality was subject to precisely the patriarchal construction and control of which the fictitious Wife of Bath complains. In contrast to the view expressed by the Wife of Bath that a woman's sexuality does not diminish, Margery's text illustrates how female sexuality is something that can alter over time and that some women, who at one time thoroughly enjoyed active heterosexuality, desired its exchange for chastity as they matured and became enthused by a spiritual life. Margery yearned for, and eventually acquired, another way of living as a married woman: what Dyan Elliott calls spiritual marriage in which the sexual aspect of a married relationship was rejected.[97] Margery never denounced marriage and was not averse to calling to attention the fact of her wife– and motherhood when necessary, as a defence strategy against those who failed to understand her behaviour and manner of dressing.[98] She remained John's wife, in all ways except sexual, until his death in *c.* 1431.

Margery's *Book* contains references to the early years of her marriage. These references reveal a sex life led, initially, according to the text scripted by clerics and evinces the power of the Church's precepts in shaping a woman's self-image.[99] The effect of the Church's construction of female sexuality upon Margery's self-perception was not positive. Looking back in her mature years, Margery admits to having felt for John in their youth 'ful many delectabyl thowtys, fleschly lustys, and inordinat lovys to hys persone' (Chapter 76, 6076–77). The feeling was mutual for Margery states that in the payment of the marital debt they both shared 'inordynat lofe and the gret

---

96 Windeatt, *Book of Margery Kempe*, p.30.
97 D. Elliott, *Spiritual Marriage: Sexual Abstinence in Medieval Wedlock* (Princeton: Princeton University Press, 1993) and M. McGlynne and R. J. Moll, 'Chaste Marriage in the Middle Ages: "It were to hire a greet Merite"', in Bullough and Brundage, *Handbook of Medieval Sexuality*, pp.103–22.
98 L. Herbert McAvoy examines how Margery uses the labels and skills of being a wife and mother in her defence against accusations of heresy in *Authority and the Female Body in the Writings of Julian of Norwich and Margery Kempe* (Cambridge: D. S. Brewer, 2004), pp.58–63.
99 A. Goodman, *Margery Kempe and Her World* (London: Pearson Education Limited, 2002), p.63.

delectacyon that thei haddyn eythyr of hem in usyng of other' (Chapter 3, 357–59). Even as she enjoyed her sex life, unlike Alisoun, Margery was troubled by it because male authority encouraged her to feel this way. This is illuminated in a scene early on in her *Book* when Margery, fearing that she might die after the birth of her first child during which she endured a labour 'wyth grett accessys', summoned a priest to hear her confession of some 'thing' that she had long concealed (Chapter 1, 194). Although the precise nature of this 'thing' is never spelled out, Barrie Ruth Straus is convincing in suggesting that 'all indications point to some aspect of Margery's sexuality for which she feels Church-induced guilt'.[100] This opinion is supported by Liz Herbert McAvoy who concurs that Margery's guilt is of a sexual nature and considers it to be a composite of Margery's desire not to endure John's sexual advances (Chapters 11–12) and a potentially adulterous relationship with an unnamed man (Chapters 13–16).[101] It is indeed possible that the sin to which she wished to confess is especially complex due to Margery's retrospective view of her early life. Coming immediately after a traumatic labour, it is plausible that Margery repented her hitherto enthusiastic enjoyment of sex that resulted in the pain that she has just endured. Her description of the desire that she and John felt for each other suggests that both were in spiritual danger of having too much sex and of using each other as a 'lemman,' as warned of in *Jacob's Well*. After the birth of her first child, Margery possessed the experience to truly understand and wish to expiate the curse of Eve: 'In pain you shall bring forth children' (Genesis 3. 16).[102] But this is not the only sexual

---

100 B. R. Straus, 'Freedom through Renunciation? Women's Voices, Women's Bodies, and the Phallic Order', in *Desire and Discipline: Sex and Sexuality in the Premodern West*, ed. by J. Murray and K. Eisenbichler (Toronto: University of Toronto Press, 1996), pp.245–64 (p.256).

101 McAvoy, *Authority and the Female Body*, p. 34 and note 22. McAvoy acknowledges that there is some circumstantial and textual evidence that Margery's unspeakable 'sin' might have been an early flirtation with heresy, p.35.

102 Genesis 3.16 reads, '*mulieri quoque dixit multiplicabo aerumnas tuas et conceptus tuos in dolore paries filios et sub viri potestate eris et ipse dominabitur tui*' [He said also to the woman I shall multiply your pain in childbearing and you shall bring forth children in pain you shall be under the man's power, and he shall have dominion over you].

sin of which Margery may have believed herself guilty. Since St Paul had instructed her, and all wives, that they were obligated to pay the marital debt on demand her desire, developed later, of seeking to avoid paying the marital debt to John was sinful too. Finally, Margery's later behaviour would have emphasised too that she was not exempt from the temptation to the adultery to which many clerks believed every woman was prone. Although she knew that sex only with her husband was 'leful onto hir in leful tyme' (Chapter 4, 457) she was willing to jeopardise her soul by accepting an unnamed neighbour's sexual invitation. The time and the place in which the extra-marital affair was solicited can only have heightened her awareness of this sexual sin and how far she was from spiritual perfection for, as Samuel Fanous observes, Margery was propositioned on the eve of Lynn's patronal festival of the church dedicated to the virgin martyr Margaret of Antioch and all other virgins.[103] I suggest that Margery's unspecified guilt with which she commences her narrative is sexually induced and tripartite in composition. That she feels such guilt reveals the extent to which Margery had internalised the sexual behaviour that patriarchy demanded of its wives. To begin her *Book* in this fashion serves to emphasise the trauma that internalising these attitudes caused her, encouraging her to perceive herself 'as polluted, sexual being',[104] but also to signal the success with which Margery travelled the arduous road from being the sexually active *sponsa Johanni* to that of chaste and spiritual *sponsa Christi*.

Margery's vision of Heaven hardened her attitude toward sex into such aversion 'that sche had levar, hir thowt, etyn or drynkyn the wose, the mukke in the chanel, than to consentyn to any fleschly comownyng, saf only for obedyens' (Chapter 3, 347–50) and it was endured only for the sake of the obedience promised in her marriage vow. Again, this suggests the power that the social expectation of being a wife continued to wield over Margery. This suggests that Margery

---

103 S. Fanous, 'Measuring the Pilgrim's Progress: Emphases in *The Book of Margery Kempe*', in *Writing Religious Women: Female Spiritual and Textual Practices in Late Medieval England*, ed. by D. Reveney and C. Whitehead (Cardiff: University of Wales Press, 2000), pp.157–76 (p.162).
104 McAvoy, *Authority and the Female Body*, p.37.

took seriously her marital vows and the social role of being a wife. At some point in her mid-thirties, Margery developed a yearning for a sex-less marriage that permitted her to lead a spiritual life. In this desire too, Margery found herself caught between wanting to lead her own life and the one scripted for her by clerics. Margery wanted a chaste marriage that she believed would bring her closer to Christ. John did not and because married, she remained subject both to marital canon law and to her husband's authority that this upheld. Her problem was that John knew the canon law only too well and would have his conjugal rights, much to Margery's distress. When he 'usyd her as he had do befor, he wold not spar' (Chapter 3, 363–64), sex became, at best an act of canonical duty, 'I may not deny yow my body (Chapter 3, 351) and, at worst, marital rape. Margery's predicament reveals how canon law rated a wife's spiritual desires as secondary to her sexual duties.

Although clerics sought to encourage spiritually safe sex, they neither expected marriages to be sexless nor, judging from cultural attitudes to the vagina and medical works on women's health, for wives to be celibate therein. But, as Dyan Elliott demonstrates, during the Middle Ages spiritual marriage was recognised in which sexual intercourse and the marital debt is renounced, often late in life, where a full, licit marriage already existed and remained.[105] Lady Margaret Beaufort (1443–1509), countess of Richmond and Derby and mother of Henry VII, took a vow of chastity in 1499, after which she welcomed her husband, Thomas, Lord Stanley to his suite of rooms in her manor house at Collyweston, Northamptonshire 'as a friend not a husband'.[106] Although now living chastely, their continued friendship is suggested in a prayer book (c. 1500) commissioned, either by Margaret for her husband or by him for her, in which both the Beaufort portcullis and Stanley's eagle-leg badge appear throughout.[107]

In a spiritual marriage renunciation of intercourse should be made by either a solemn vow or a simple vow.[108] The former was made pub-

---

[105] Elliott, *Spiritual Marriage*, Chapter Five.
[106] Stafford, *Letters of the Queens*, p.146.
[107] *Gothic: Art for England 1400–1547*, ed. by R. Marks and P. Williamson (London: V&A Publications, 2003), p.252.
[108] Elliott, *Spiritual Marriage*, p.159.

licly into the hands of a church official and then became enforceable by the Church.[109] The latter was made without formalities and the couple remained living together.[110] If the woman alone stated her intention to live in a chaste marriage, this could be done only with her husband's permission that, even if given, according to Pope Innocent IV (d. 1254), could be retracted, as long as he did not vow himself. Although a wife's vow of chastity demonstrated her intention of never seeking the conjugal debt, the debt still existed and her husband might legitimately demand it of her unless he too forgoes this, grants her permission and, to all intents and purposes, made a simple vow of chastity himself. As Chaucer's Parson makes clear, a wife can live chastely within marriage 'by licence of hir housbonde' (*Parson's Tale*, 945). John Myrc's *Instructions for Parish Priests* advised priests to inform their congregation that wives were not to make vows unknown to their husbands,

> That heo a-vow no maner þynge
> But hyt be at hys wytynge;
> For þaȝ heo do, hyt may not stande
> But heo haue grawnte of hyre husbonde;
> And ȝef þe husbonde assente þer to,
> Þenne nedely hyt mote be do.
> (396–401)

In this ruling we can see how medieval patriarchy interfered with female spiritual practice; as stated earlier a wife's spiritual desires were secondary to her sexual duties and a wife's spirituality was subordinate to the will of her husband, as Margery finds out to her cost.

Christ promised to end Margery's sexual relations with John (Chapter 9) and matters came to a head one Friday, probably 23 June 1413, as Margery and John returned from York. They had been chaste for the past eight weeks, possibly more so from John's temporary impotence (that Margery interpreted as an act of God) rather than any acquiescence on his part and we are to understand that, at this point, John has not agreed to live in a chaste marriage. John asked Margery,

---

109   Ibid., p.159.
110   Ibid., p.164.

in what sounds like an expression of sexual frustration, if she would prefer him dead to having intercourse with him. Her response was unequivocal, 'I had levar se yow be slayn than we schuld turne ayen to owyr unclennesse'. So was his reply, 'Ye arn no good wyfe' (Chapter 11, 720–21, 722) and from a male perspective, this insult would ring true: Margery had reneged on payment of the marital debt, was sexually incompliant and had refused to follow the Pauline instruction that '*mulieres subditae estote viris sicut oportet in Domino*' [Wives, be subject to your husbands, as it behoveth in the Lord] (Colossians 3.18). Ignoring John's frustration and what her husband and society expected from her as a wife, Margery asked John's permission to grant her wish for chastity 'in what bysshopys hand that God wele' (Chapter 11, 734). Margery was outwitted by John's understanding of the text of canon law. He refused her request 'that wyl I not grawnt yow, for now may I usyn yow wythowtyn dedly synne and than mygth I not so' (Chapter 11, 735–36). Doctrinally, he was quite correct and clearly reluctant to make a simple vow of chastity himself, and forgo the pleasures of the flesh. His agreement was given only when Margery bartered payment of John's financial debt for her release from the marital one. Although not described in her *Book*, it is probable that Margery and John professed their mutual vow of marital chastity later in the summer of 1413, before Philip Repingdon, Bishop of Lincoln (Chapter 15), once John's agreement to this had been formally given.[111]

Familiar with what Sheila Delany calls the 'cash-nexus that pervades the bourgeois world',[112] Margery was able to buy back her chastity and her way out of a sexual marriage. Once this was done, Margery was able to forge her own, new way of married life. Margery rejected the provision made for those interested in preparing for Heaven yet who were unable to enter a monastery or nunnery, available in texts such as

---

[111] That John was not finally chaste until they professed their vow before Repingdon is suggested by Laura L. Howes who believes that Margery may have been between three and five months' pregnant when she left England on her pilgrimage to Jerusalem in the autumn of 1413 and gave birth to the child while abroad, 'On the Birth of Margery Kempe's Last Child', *Modern Philology*, 90 (1992), 220–25 (pp.220–21).

[112] Delany, 'Sexual Economics, Chaucer's Wife of Bath', p.108.

late fourteenth-century *The Abbey of the Holy Ghost*.[113] This work was written, as Christiania Whitehead points out, for a literate, urban lay audience who, like Margery, had become more individualistic in their quest for religious experience.[114] Designed for those unable to join religious houses 'for band [bond] of marriage', the *Abbey* suggested how lay folk could build an abbey of virtues within their conscience, so that those 'þat ne may noghte be bodyly in religyon, þat þay may be gostely' (7–8). For Margery being 'bodyly in religyon' was always the goal and so in this respect, and also in its failure to offer practical instruction in dealing with a spouse who wished still to exercise his or her conjugal rights, works like the *Abbey* would not suffice. Instead, Margery looked to the lives of saintly women who were once sexually active in marriage and bore children but who became chaste and went on to achieve Paradise. These were not the inviolate virgins and virgin martyrs of whom so many Church Fathers approved. A saint's life, such as that of Christina of Markyate, was neither any good as an exemplar to Margery nor any help to her self-perception and self-esteem, since Christina never lost her virginity. The difference between herself and a virginal saint was unequivocal and glaringly obvious to the Mayor of Leicester. He berated Margery that she was nothing like St Catherine of Alexandria but was rather 'a fals strumpet' (Chapter 46, 3690). At various times in her *Book*, Margery mentions both Bridget of Sweden (1303–73) who was married at thirteen, bore eight children and persuaded her husband to live chaste for two years, and Elizabeth of Hungary, another saintly married woman. Margery travels to the homeland of Angela of Foligno (*c.*1248–1309), who lived a worldly life as a wife and mother until the age of thirty-seven, and Dorothea of Montau (1347–94), who was married at sixteen to a much older man by whom

---

113   A late fourteenth-century translation of the French prose treatise *Li Livre du cloister de l'áme* (*c.* 1300), *The Abbey of the Holy Ghost* may be found in *Religious Pieces in Prose and Verse*, ed. by G. G. Perry, EETS OS 26 (London: N. Trübner, 1917), pp.49–59 and N. F. Blake, *Middle English Prose* (London: Edward Arnold, 1972), pp.88–102. All references are taken from Perry's edition.
114   C. Whitehead, *Castles of the Mind: A Study of Medieval Architectural Allegory* (Cardiff: University of Wales Press, 2003), p.77.

she bore nine children.[115] Collectively, the lives of these women provided authority for those aspects of Margery's life and spirituality upon which the male text traditionally frowned. They authorised that period of her life lived as a sexually active wife and mother, and affirmed that this was no bar to Paradise. Margery's weeping and affective outbursts, that so trouble many of the priests and ecclesiastical authorities whom Margery encountered, finds precedent and confirmation in the bouts of weeping and visions experienced by Elizabeth, Angela and Dorothea. Elizabeth and Angela participated too in a mystical marriage to Christ.

Even as she struggled to create a discourse of her own through living it, apparent is the tenacity of male texts that constructed woman as voraciously sexual. This construction resurfaces while Margery was living chastely but experienced twelve days of lustful thoughts and visions of men's (including priests and monks) naked genitalia (Chapter 59). It is perhaps of little surprise that Margery believed herself sexually tempted, taunted and tested, precisely by those who would expect such lascivious misbehaviour from a woman; especially one whom many, including her own husband, believed recalcitrant, unwifely and unwomanly. Margery remained haunted by the clerical assessment of virginity as much worthier than wifehood. She expresses frequently the belief, reiterated by much clerical instruction, that her sexual activity has rendered her permanently less than those who had never lost their virginity. Christ himself had to reassure her, while she was pregnant, that he,

> [...] Lofe wyves also, and specyal tho wyfys whech woldyn levyn chast, yyf thei mygtyn have her wyl, and don her besynes to plesyn me as thow dost [...] yet, dowtyr, I lofe the as well as any mayden in the world.
> (Chapter 21, 1568–70, 1573–74)

Christ recognises the difficulties experienced by wives who wishes to 'have her wyl' to live chastely but are bound by canon law and social

---

115 Margery's access to the lives of these saints and their influence upon her *Book* is set out in J. Dillon,' Holy Women and their Confessors or Confessors and their Holy Women? Margery Kempe and Continental Tradition' in R. Voaden, ed., *Prophets Abroad: The Reception of Continental Holy Women in Late-Medieval England* (Cambridge: D. S. Brewer, 1996), pp.115–40 (pp.116–18).

expectation to be 'bonoure and buxum' to their husbands. Even in his reassurance, however, can be heard the traditional hierarchy of virginity and widowhood over marriage, 'thow the state of maydenhode be mor parfyte and mor holy than the state of wedewhode, and the state of wedewhode more parfyte than the state [of] wedlake' (Chapter 21, 1571–73). In her mystical union with Christ Margery struggled to see beyond the text of the marriage liturgy, that threatens to overwhelm her description of the event,

> Therfore most I [Christ] nedys be homly wyth the and lyn in thi bed wyth the. Dowtyr, [...] thu may mayst boldly, whan thu art in thi bed, take me to the as for thi weddyd husbond, as thy derworthy derlyng, [...] and wil that thow love me, dowtyr, as a good <wife> owyth to love hir husbonde. And therfor thu mayst boldly take me in the armys of thi sowle and kyssen my mowth, myn hed and my fete as swetly as thow wylt.
> (Chapter 36, 2949–50, 2951–57)

Bubbling beneath the surface of her mystical union is Margery's perception of it in terms characteristic of an earthly marriage, an aspect of what Sarah Beckwith sees as her 'preference for embodied relationships rather than heavenly transcendence'.[116] As in the Sarum wedding ceremony, Christ instructs Margery to take him as her wedded husband. He speaks to her like a husband and instructs her to engage in physically intimate behaviour; kissing his mouth and his body from head to toe. Margery's ring, inscribed with '*Jhesus est amor meus*' [Jesus is my Love], that she begins to wear after she professed her vow of chastity, functions as a wedding ring (Chapter 31) whose value is immense to her. Later on in her *Book*, in words that again echo the marriage liturgy, Christ requests that Margery be 'buxom and bonowr' to his will (Chapter 66, 5418). Although Margery is unable to suppress completely the text of the marriage service, with its presumption of sexual relations between husband and wife, her marriage to Christ lacks the penetration that she fought so long to excise from her earthly union to John.

---

116 S. Beckwith, *Christ's Body: Identity, Culture and Society in Late Medieval Writings* (London: Routledge, 1993), p.78.

Wendy Harding sees in Margery's wailing, sobbing and oral communication, the antithesis of 'the hierarchical, ordered, masculine spirituality of the pulpit'.[117] I suggest that a similar antithesis to the hierarchical, ordered, masculine attitude towards sex expounded from the pulpit can be detected in Margery's fluid and changing sexuality. In her early married life, Margery behaved according to male assumption regarding female sexuality: she enjoyed frequent sex with John immensely and was tempted to adultery. Consequently, her subsequent desire for a chaste marriage shakes to its foundations male certainty that women's sexuality remained constant throughout life, and arose from the unwavering desire for penetrative sex from an erect male member. It disrupts too the canonists' expectations of a wife's sexuality. Her description of how Christ wished her to behave in their spiritual marital bed suggests that as she matured, Margery began to yearn for physical intimacy of a non-penetrative kind.[118] Margery makes clear that some women desired chaste marriages and to forgo sexual activity. It is little wonder that the Mayor of Leicester was afraid that Margery had come to his city, like some female Pied Piper, to entice away other men's wives (Chapter 48), that the Suffragen of the Archbishop of York berated her for advising Elizabeth, Lady Greystoke, to leave her husband (Chapter 53) or that various preachers, her own husband, and the many married women satisfied with their lot, failed to comprehend what it was that Margery wanted.

Margery lived her life in the face of great opposition and in so doing, created, then recorded, the text that supported and validated her renunciation of marital sex. Her book, written down by the very male establishment that caused her so much grief during her lifetime, was an alternative text for those other women to whom, like her, the patriarchal discourses regarding women's sexuality simply did not speak. Karma Lochrie reads her story as a successful quest for literary author-

117 W. Harding, 'Body into Text: *The Book of Margery Kempe*', in *Feminist Approaches to the Body in Medieval Literature*, ed. by L. Lomperis and S. Stanbury (Philadelphia: University of Pennsylvania Press, 1993), pp.168–87 (p.174).
118 K. Lavezzo sees expression of same-sex desire in many of Margery's relationships with other women in 'Sobs and Sighs Between Women: The Homoerotics of Compassion in *The Book of Margery Kempe*,' in *Premodern Sexualities*, ed. by L. Fradenburg and C. Freccero (London: Routledge, 1996), pp.175–98.

ity[119] and in it we hear the perspective of one of the lions of whom the Wife of Bath spoke.

Many late medieval texts expose wives as insatiable sexual beings. The Church endeavoured to legislate against the sins to which coitus invariably lead. Woman's sexuality emanated from her vagina, considered by churchmen an ever open and ever-ready orifice that was further confirmation of woman's unbridled sexuality and, subsequently, her inferior spirituality. As such, it was at best to be distrusted and its lusts satisfied, not only at the woman's spiritual peril, but also that of the man. May and Alisoun of Bath act out the stereotype of woman whose voracious and insatiable sexual appetite is so feared and distrusted. Their behaviour appears to justify and endorse the attempt by male texts; canon law, the patriarchal (mis)understandings about female physiology and the writings of such as Jerome and Theofrastus, to define and constrain women's sexuality. At one and the same time, literary wives are subversive. May's actions and Alisoun of Bath's speech reveal that women have their own sexual desires, an attitude to their sexuality, and to the way in which society's texts construct that sexuality. Margery's sexual history attests to the possibility of fluidity of female sexuality over a wife's lifetime which the canon law governing conjugal rights struggled to accommodate. The behaviour of literary wives suggests ways out of the sexual/textual trap in which a wife found herself caught. May appears to have acquired knowledge of contraception and, fallible as it may be, attempts to cheat her biology. When Jankyn's book is torn up, Alisoun destroys literally a text that paints the lion in a manner not to her liking. She offers her own, alternative text that redefines wifely behaviour, and suggests a recipe for a successful marital relationship from the woman's perspective: female power and satisfactory male penetration. Admittedly, Alisoun is permitted nothing more imaginative than a marriage in which unequal power relations still exist, but this time tilted in the wife's favour. In contrast, by living it in the face of vocal and often physically violent male opposition, Margery creates the text that validates her re-

---

119 K. Lochrie, '*The Book of Margery Kempe*: The Marginal Woman's Quest for Literary Authority', *Journal of Medieval and Renaissance Studies*, 16 (Spring 1986), 35–55 (p.55).

nunciation of marital sex, for its replacement by a non-penetrative variety that leaves her chaste by her own standards and able to become a *sponsa Christi*. This she has written down for the benefit of other women to whom, like her, the patriarchal discourses regarding women's sexuality simply do not speak.

Chapter Four
The Drama of Childbirth and Motherhood

> A, blyssyd babb, welcome thowe be.
> (York *Purification*, 316)

As the experience of Margery Kempe attests, medieval wives expected, and were expected, to become mothers. Late medieval hagiography reflects an appreciation of motherhood as an occupation, for example, in the popularity of the maternal Elizabeth of Hungary, Bridget of Sweden and in the Church's emphasis on the motherhood of the Virgin Mary and that of her own mother, St Anne. In her portrayal as *Mater Dolorosa* and the *Pietà*, Mary as mother broods over the arts. St Anne was associated with marriage and childbearing that comes of it. Her forthcoming motherhood was anticipated on a bride's wedding day. One need only recall the image of a woman lying in child-bed and its accompanying legend 'I am comyng toward your bryde' that decorated the wedding cake described in *A Feste for a Bryde*. The rigours of childbirth and repeated pregnancies brought with them somatic change and equal share of trauma and joy. For women, becoming a mother was accompanied by the joy and achievement of bringing a healthy baby into the world. Throughout the Middle Ages, for many, pregnancy and childbirth proved fatal to both mother and child.

Motherhood is yet another aspect of being a wife that men sought to regulate textually and, as with so many aspects of wifedom, discussion of mothering is based upon a long tradition of male-authored texts. St Paul makes clear that the primary function of married women is motherhood, so that the world may be populated with Christians. This act can be a woman's salvation, so long as she lives '*in fide, et dilectione, et sanctificatione cum sobrietate*' [in faith and charity and holiness with sobriety] (I Timothy 2.14). St Augustine considered that women were created by God to be man's helper 'for the sake of bearing children'.[1] While the locus and performance of the actual birth may have remained a closed book, even to the father, men wrote didactically and authoritatively regarding pregnancy, the childbirth to which they were rarely witness and the postnatal care of both mother and child. As Clarissa Atkinson observes, 'mothers did not write about motherhood, but their lives and experiences were profoundly affected by the work of those who did'.[2]

This chapter examines childbirth and mothering in religious drama that, as Kathleen Ashley recognises, has the ability 'to mirror proper social behaviours for women in its audience'.[3] In plays' representation of pre- and post-partum wives is detectable the influence of those texts that defined late medieval understanding of and attitude toward childbirth and motherhood.

'poure women that lye in Iseyne': Medical Advice on Childbirth

In the *Book of the Knight of La Tour-Landry*, Geoffrey de La Tour-Landry gives cold comfort to his girls about the childbearing that lay ahead of them. The best that he can offer is Christ's promise in the Gospel that, on the Day of Judgement, he will have mercy on 'poure women that lye in Iseyne' (Chapter LXXXVIII, 32–33, p.113). Medieval medicine offered rather more to those women who could afford good food, rest and the help of a skilful midwife.

Medical knowledge regarding the process of conception and pregnancy was based largely on classical texts. The *Cyrurgie of Guy de*

---

1   St Augustine, *De Genesi Ad Litteram*, IX.5 as translated in Blamires, *Woman Defamed and Woman Defended*, p.79.
2   Atkinson, *Oldest Vocation*, p.26.
3   K. M. Ashley, 'Medieval Courtesy literature and dramatic mirrors of female conduct', in *The Ideology of Conduct: Essays in Literature and the History of Sexuality*, ed. by N. Armstrong and L. Tennenhouse (London: Methuen, 1987), pp.25–38 (p.26).

Chauliac discussed childbirth in the assumption that it was midwives who directed proceedings. Monica Green challenges the widely held belief that medieval women's health was exclusively women's business, and indeed the patient list and cures prescribed in the commonplace book of fifteenth-century medical practitioner, Thomas Fayreford, support her belief.[4] Green acknowledges that social taboo would have insured women a place as assistant to the male physician and that the role of midwife can have been 'rarely challenged'.[5]

The Knowing of Woman's Kind in Childing takes a holistic approach to childbirth. It begins with pregnancy during which a mother-to-be needed to take care of herself. Plenty of rest was recommended and over-exertion (riding, walking) and stressful emotion, such as anger, avoided (*Knowing of Woman's Kind in Childing*, 267–71). From her seventh month, the mother-to-be should remain rested and calm because of the danger of miscarriage or malformation of the child, and should avoid binding herself too tightly beneath her bosom, to allow her breasts to fill with milk (271–81). In the eighth month, the woman should rest, eat moderately and rub her stomach with henna shrub, olive or mirton oil (presumably to help with stretch marks). In the ninth, she should be tightly bound beneath her breasts, to encourage the baby to take up the right position for delivery, and avoid sex, in case the 'secundine' (the amniotic sac) should burst and the child be aborted or destroyed (281–94). While much of the advice is sound, it is clearly aimed at those wealthy enough to go horse-riding, purchase the oil and who could afford to rest while others bore the burden of running the household.

---

[4] Monica Green urges caution in identifying women's health exclusively as women's business in 'Women's Medical Practice and Health Care in Medieval Europe', *Signs: Journal of Women in Culture and Society*, 14.2 (1989), 434–73 (p.468). Of Thomas Fayreford's list of 103 patients he states that he successfully treats 10 women for suffocation of the womb (corrupt fumes ascending from the womb to the brain and leading to all manner of ailments) providing evidence that gynaecological medicine was not regarded exclusively as women's work, P. Murray Jones, 'Thomas Fayreford: An English Fifteenth-Century Medical Practitioner', in *Medicine from the Black Death to the French Disease*, ed. by R. French et al (Aldershot: Ashgate, 1998), pp.156–83, (pp.159–61).

[5] Green, 'Women's Medical Practice', p.468.

The emotional aspect and the fear factor of labour are addressed by a combination of orthodox prayers and sympathetic magic performed by the midwife:

> Tak a lytyll scrowe & wryt þys with-in: + In nomine Patris et Filij & Spiritus Sancti Amen + Sancta Maria + Sancta Margareta + ogor + sugor + nogo + and kyt þat scrov in-to small pecys & ȝiffe here to drynk. Or wrytt in a longe scrow all þe psalme of Magnificat anima mea & gyrde hit a-boute here.
> (*The Knowing of Woman's Kind in Childing*, 369–74)

Strips of parchment, onto which were written the names of the Holy Trinity, the Virgin Mary, St Margaret (the patron saint of childbirth) or the Magnificat, in which Mary humbly accepts her forthcoming pregnancy, were recommended as talismans. Sometimes to this list were added the names of Anne and Elizabeth, mother of John the Baptist, whose successful motherhood was venerated.[6] Ogor–sugor–nogo is possibly a corruption of palindromic words held to have magical properties.[7] The parchment was either cut up and ingested, as suggested in the *Knowing of Woman's Kind in Childing*, or bound to the woman's thigh. In some instances to aid labour, the wearing of a belt was recommended, upon which was written the Magnificat.[8] Belts sanctified by contact with the Girdle of Our Lady or containing a thread from this relic were especially sought after, by women who could afford them.[9] The use of sympathetic magic and charms was limited to the preliminary stages of labour. Once the delivery was underway, a woman should 'let þe mydwyffe helpe' (*Knowing of Woman's Kind in Childing*, 376).

For those with neither the money nor the status to acquire such help, prayer remained freely available. The opening of the Athanasian Creed (the *quicumque vult*) or the popular 'O infant, whether living or

---

[6] For the charm in British Library MS Sloane 3160 (fifteenth century) see T. Hunt, *Popular Medicine in Thirteenth Century England: Introduction and Texts* (Woodbridge: D. S. Brewer, 1990), number 89, p.98.

[7] Barratt, *The Knowing of Woman's Kind in Childing*, p.123, note 369.

[8] E. Waterton, *Pietas Mariana Britannica: A History of English Devotion to the Most Blessed Virgin Marye Mother of God* (London: St Joseph's Catholic Library, 1879), pp.91, 207.

[9] Ibid., pp.90–91. The belt was brought from Jerusalem to Constantinople by the Byzantine Empress, Aelia Pulcheria Augusta (399–453).

dead, come forth because Christ calls you to the light',[10] was customarily recited, three times, at the bed of the woman in labour. A Middle English prayer to ease childbirth is recorded in a handbook for parish priests. In it, the author compares Christ's trauma on the cross with that suffered by his mother and the woman in labour, who prays, '[...] Merci iesu crist, fader / ant sone ant holi gost. Deleuere me of mine / childe aze wez aze yi moder milde was deleuered / of ye'.[11] The prayer should be followed by three paternosters and three ave marias. A similar prayer may have been the writing, believed efficacious for pregnant women, sent by Ellen de Rouclif to her neighbour, Annabilla Rawcliffe.[12]

The *Sekenesse of Wymmen*, the gynaecological text most widely disseminated in late medieval England, contained advice for the repair of damage sustained in childbirth.[13] Should a prolapse of the womb occur, the midwife was advised to reinsert it manually, having oiled her hand beforehand, after which the woman should be fumigated from beneath, with the vapour of camomile or dry ox dung, thrown onto hot coals.[14] If her perineum tore, the work recommended the use of stitches, bed rest and the insertion of 'a lynnen cloute into þe member after þe

---

10   S. Shahar, *Childhood in the Middle Ages* (London: Routledge, 1990), p.36.
11   M. P. Richards, 'A Middle English Prayer to Ease Childbirth', *Notes and Queries*, n.s. 27.3 (1980), 292 (p.292).
12   Goldberg, *Women in England*, p.74.
13   The material contained within the two basic versions is a translation of the gynaecological and obstetrical chapters of Gilbertus Anglicus' *Compendium medicinae* (c. 1240) whose source is the *Practica medicinae* of Roger Baron (Roger de Barone). For a comparison of the two versions see M. Green, 'Obstetrical and Gynecological Texts in Middle English', *Studies in the Age of Chaucer*, 14 (1992), 53–88, pp.72–82. One manuscript of Version 1 and one of Version 2 has been edited. British Library MS Sloane 2463, the manuscript of Version 2 is edited and translated by B. Rowland, *Medieval Women's Guide to Health: The First English Gynecological Handbook* (Kent: The Kent State University Press, 1981). Monica Green identifies and corrects a number of Rowland's assumptions regarding the authorship and presumed audience for this work in Green, 'Women's Medical Practice and Health Care', pp.463–73. Rowland's edition has been used because of the additional recipes that this text supplies related to post-partum conditions.
14   Rowland, *Medieval Woman's Guide to Health*, p.101.

quantite of þe membre, scilicet vulue. And after þat lyne it aboue with hote tarre' [put a linen cloth into the part, that is to say, the vulva [vagina], according to its size. And afterward cover it with hot tar].[15]

A mother was expected to breast feed her child unless she was wealthy enough to hire a wet nurse to do so for her. *The Knowing of Woman's Kind in Childing* recommended that a new mother not breast-feed until she had recovered a little from the birth, the strain of which was believed to taint her milk (470–74). Should she employ a wet nurse, the woman should be young, healthy, sober, have had two children of her own and love her charge as if it were hers (477–82). The text suggests that a child be weaned at the age of one or two.

Medicine endeavoured to make what should be a joyous event as straightforward as possible, recommending intervention by the midwife and recipes for all eventualities that might arise in the birth process. Should all this fail, the woman was left to call upon God and a small band of saints whose motherhood was exemplary to all.

The Birthing Room

Gail McMurray Gibson suggests that an intimate community of women presided at the birth and post-partum confinement, or lying-in, of the new mother that took place 'in emphatically closed female space'.[16] This space, as Monica Green suggests, may have been accessible to male medical practitioners. Generally, it seems that women were surrounded by other women, usually local, who were often friends of the mother-to-be and mothers themselves. In her first confinement, Ellen de Rouclif was attended by her former servant, local girl, Maud de Herthill, who stayed with Ellen throughout her pregnancy, was present at the birth, and held her baby boy while his mother 'was taken to and

---

15   Ibid., p.167.
16   G. McMurray Gibson, 'Scene and Obscene: Seeing and Performing Late Medieval Childbirth', *Journal of Medieval and Early Modern Studies*, 29.1 (Winter 1999), 7–24 (p.9).

made ready for bed' by her friend, Cecily de Shipton, who had moved in with Ellen during the final month of her pregnancy.[17] At her second confinement, Ellen was cared for again by Cecily and by another local woman, Ellen Taliour of Skelton, herself a mother, who stayed on after the birth of Alice, first as her wetnurse and thereafter, when ill health forced her to cease feeding the child, as her nanny.[18] Emmot Norice, [Nurse] of Hoby, whose surname indicates that wet nursing was her profession, was hired to nurse Alice after the recent death of her own son.[19] Ellen de Rouclif gave birth in her own room presumably in her own sheets and linen. For many, less well-off women, the luxury of an entirely enclosed and private space may not have been available. Some may not have had access to clean bed linen for their confinements. In 1549 Elizabeth Truslay bequeathed the coverlet and sheet, initially to be used to cover her corpse before burial, to her parish for loan to any honest woman of St Mary Westout in Lewes, 'for theire need in tyme of their lying in child bedde then to be delivered unto the church agayne.'[20] Nor did English women have access to a specially designed birthing aid: the birthing stool as used by Italian women. English women, like their French and German counterparts, gave birth in bed.[21] Both Mary and her mother St Anne are depicted in childbed as in the Long Melford Nativity (Suffolk)[22] and *The Bedford Hours*, folio 32. For the majority, the marital bed was the locus in which the drama of childbirth was played out.

17 Goldberg, *Women in England*, pp.74, 72.
18 Ibid., p.73.
19 Ibid., pp.79 and 65.
20 W. H. Godfrey, ed., *Transcripts of Sussex Wills Volume III*, Sussex Record Society, vol XLIII (Lewes: Sussex Record Society, 1938), p.121.
21 R. Graves, *Born to Procreate: Women and Childbirth in France from the Middle Ages to the Eighteenth Century* (New York: Peter Lang, 2001), p.30.
22 G. McMurray Gibson, 'Saint Anne and the Religion of Childbed: Some East Anglian Texts and Talismans', in *Interpreting Cultural Symbols: Saint Anne in Late Medieval Society*, ed. by K. Ashley, K. and P. Sheingorn (Athens: The University of Georgia Press, 1990), pp.95–110 (pp.100–01).

'Notwithstanding she shall be saved in childbearing': Instruction from the Pulpit and the Churching of Women

Childbirth brought with it joy but also danger and pain. In John Myrc's *Festial*, the sermon for the Nativity of the Blessed Virgin Mary acknowledged that childbirth brought with it so much suffering that it is was considered a miracle that the mother 'ys not all tobroken and braydon lymemal yn hur burth-tyme' (*De Nativitate Beate Marie*, fol. 140a). The Church endeavoured to prepare women for the 'jesyne' or childbirth of this world that could so easily become passage for her and her child to the next, by ensuring that she was spiritually prepared. Myrc's *Instructions for Parish Priests* advised priests to provide communion to heavily pregnant women:

> Whenne here tyme ys neghe y-come,
> Bydde hem do thus alle & some.
> Teche hem to come & schryve hem clene,
> And also hosele hem bothe at ene, [take communion]
> For drede of perele that may be-falle,
> In here trauelynge that come shalle.
> (79–84)

Myrc recommended that the midwives attending the woman during her confinement should also be prepared for the death of mother, child or both. They should be equipped with clean water and be ready to baptise the child even if it is not fully out of the birth canal (91–93). Should the mother die, the midwife should perform a caesarean section (and if too timid to do so, at this point she might call upon the help of a man) in order that the living child might be baptised. If the midwife baptised the child, both the vessel was to be burned and the water thrown into the font (113–80). Myrc's instructed that any woman dying in childbirth could not be buried in the church but was relegated to the churchyard as long as the child had been extracted and baptised.[23]

---

23   Erbe, *Mirk's Festial*, p.298, *Qui Sunt Sepeliendi in Cimiterio*.

For those women who survived childbirth, the Church offered a ceremony called the Churching of Women. This service had its roots in the Jewish ritual of purification (Leviticus 12. 4–5), in which a woman was reintegrated into the synagogue thirty-three days after the birth of a son and sixty-six after that of a daughter. While the medieval Church's ritual disassociated itself from uncleanness, marketing the ceremony instead as a ritual of thanksgiving for the safe delivery of the child and mother from the perils of childbirth,[24] it still smacked of purification of the female body tainted by sexual activity and the fluids of childbirth.

A new mother was confined after childbirth for a month or so. At the end of this period, the midwives and gossips (the 'god-sibs' or appointed godmothers who assisted at the birth and presented the baby on behalf of the mother for baptism) along with female relatives and neighbours, accompanied the new mother to the church door and from there into the Church to stand near the altar.[25] Ellen de Rouclif was accompanied at her churching, some three weeks after the birth of her son, by her friend Cecily Shipton (who had been present at the birth), Ellen's sister-in-law, the baby's godmother, Margery de Rouclif, and another local woman, Isabel de Strensall, who was pregnant at the time.[26] At her churching after the birth of her daughter, Alice, Ellen was accompanied, once more, by Cecily Shipton, by a local woman Agnes de Frithe, and Robert Thewed of Rawcliffe (a friend of her husband, Gervase). A comment made by Osbern of Bokenham in his life of St

---

[24] Christian revision of the ceremony's purpose appears in a letter from Pope Gregory to St Augustine of Canterbury (601) as quoted by Bede: As to the interval that must elapse after childbirth before a woman may enter church, you are familiar with the Old Testament rule: that is, for a male child thirty-three days and for a female, sixty-six. But this is to be understood as an allegory, for were a woman to enter church and return thanks in the very hour of her delivery, she would do nothing wrong. Bede, *A History of the English Church and People*, ed. and trans., L. Sherley-Price (Harmondsworth: Penguin, 1955, reprint 1983), p.77.

[25] G. McMurray Gibson, 'Blessing from Sun and Moon: Churching as Women's Theater', in *Bodies and Disciplines: Intersections of Literature and History in Fifteenth-Century England*, ed. by B. Hanawalt and D. Wallace (Minneapolis: University of Minnesota Press, 1996), pp.139–54 (p.149).

[26] Goldberg, *Women in England*, pp.71–72.

Elizabeth of Hungary suggests that women wore their finery to the ceremony to which the newborn child might also be brought.[27]

The ritual comprised an exhortation, two psalms, the *Kyrie eleison*, the Lord's Prayer, verses and a prayer of thanksgiving, after which the woman took communion.[28] The *Sarum Missal*'s directions for the *Benedictio mulieris post partum*, indictates that the ritual took place before the church door and that, on its completion, the woman was sprinkled with holy water then formally lead by the priest, into the church by her right hand.[29] Gail McMurray Gibson describes how the new mother

> was brought veiled to the church to present the chrisom cloth of her baptized child [...] and a lighted candle that when blessed by the priest symbolized the woman's own restored and purified body. She then processed into the church to be ritually readmitted by the priesthood into the Mass and to the community of the faithful [...].[30]

The chrisom, or cloth tied over the anointed spot on its forehead where the baptised child had been marked with the sign of the cross, was burnt by the priest or kept for 'the uses of the church,' because it had been touched by the blessed water of the font, that was believed both powerful and holy and should be touched by no-one except the child.[31] It is likely that the woman would have offered her candle of thanksgiving at the Lady altar of the Church.[32]

---

27 Osbern of Bokenham praises Saint Elizabeth of Hungary for dressing without jewels or costly clothes simply for her own churching and for carrying her own child, suggesting that it was the fashion for many wealthy women to dress splendidly and for someone else to carry their offspring, *Legendys of Hooly Wummen*, ed., M. Sarjeantson, EETS OS 206 (Oxford: Oxford University Press, 1938, reprint 1971), p.266, lines 9793–9800.
28 *The Prayer Book Dictionary*, ed. by G. Harford, M. Stevenson *et al* (London: The Waverley Book Company, 1912), p.204.
29 Dickinson, *Missale ad Usum Insignis, Ordo Sponsalium*, column 849.
30 Gibson, 'Blessing from Sun and Moon', pp.144–45.
31 E. Duffy, *The Stripping of the Altars. Traditional Religion in England 1400–1580* (New Haven: Yale University Press, 1992), p.280.
32 T. Coletti, 'Genealogy, Sexuality, and Sacred Power: The Saint Anne Dedication of the Digby *Candelmas Day and the Killing of the Children of Israel*', *Journal of Medieval and Early Modern Studies*, 29.1 (Winter 1999), 25–59, (p.45).

The churching ceremony began with Psalm 120 (Douay–Rheims version), a psalm of thanksgiving, and 127, a declaration of the fertility of the righteous. The content of each was relevant to a post-parturient woman. Psalm 120 acknowledges the efficacy of God's protection that *'Non sinet nutare pedem tuum, non dormitabit, qui custodit te'* [He will not suffer your foot to stumble and he who watches over you will not sleep] (120. 3), a welcome safekeeping for a new mother coming to terms with the demands of a newborn baby. Psalm 127 promises that a husband and wife, who feared the Lord, shall be fertile *'sicut vitis fructifera, [...] Filii tui ut surculi olivarum circa mensam tuam'* [as a fruitful vine; your children around your table like the fresh shoots of the olive] (127. 3–4) and concludes with the blessing for continued fertility *'Ut videas filios filiorum tuorum'* [May you see your children's children] (127. 6). The prayer was explicitly one of thanksgiving for the mother having survived childbirth,

> O god, who has delivered this woman thy servant from the peril of childbirth, and hast made her to be devoted to thy service; grant that when the course of this life hath been faithfully finished, she may obtain eternal life and rest under the wings of thy mercy.[33]

The association of the ritual with thanksgiving and its disassociation from purification is undercut, however, by the fact that the post-parturient woman was excluded from the church until the ceremony has taken place, and by its conclusion in which the new mother is sprinkled with holy water, *'Asperges me, Domine, hyssopo* [Sprinkle me, Lord, with hyssop].' These words are taken from Psalm 50, in which the psalmist requests God's mercy and that God

> *Penitus lava me a culpa mea, et a peccato meo munda me.* [...] *Ecce, in culpa natus sum, et in peccato concepit me mater mea.* [...] *Asperge me hyssopo, et mundabor, lava me, et super nivem dealbabor.*

---

33 Warren, *Sarum Missal*, Part II, p.165. The Latin reads: *Deus, qui hanc famulam tuam de pariendi periculo liberasti, et eam in servitio tuo devotam esse fecisti; concede, ut temporali cursu fideliter peracto, sub alis misericordiae tuae vitam perpetuam et quietam consequatur.* Dickinson, *Missale ad Usum Insignis, Ordo Sponsalium*, column 849.

[Wash my wickedness from me and cleanse me from my sin. [...] For behold I was conceived in wickedness and my mother conceived me in sins [...] You shall sprinkle me with hyssop and I shall be cleansed. You shall wash me and I shall be made whiter than snow]. (Psalm 50. 4, 7, 9)

For those familiar with the Psalter, this blessing reiterated the connection between sex, childbirth and sin, the taint of which was only removed from the mother at her churching. Only after these words had been spoken did the woman enter the church, *'Deinde inducat eam sacerdos per manum dexteram in ecclesiam dicendo, "Ingredire in templum Dei; ut habeas vitam aeternam et vivas in saecula saeculorum"'* [Then the priest shall lead her by the right hand into the church saying, "Enter the house of God; so that you may have eternal life for ever and ever"].[34]

Her post-partum state precluded the mother from entering the church, so her child's baptism was held, either in her absence or delayed until the mother had undergone her churching ceremony. The midwife prepared the baby for its baptism, washing away the birth fluids with warm water, oil, salt or rose petals, and tied the umbilical cord.[35] The baby was brought to the church in a procession. The gossips, midwife, the other godparents (two godmothers and a godfather for a girl, two godfathers and a godmother for a boy) and the father, who were met at the church door by a priest and permitted entry only after stating the child's sex, name, the names of the godparents and confirming that the child had not been baptised already.[36]

Records tend to record the baptism of the sons and daughters of the wealthy and reveal that these ceremonies could be extravagant. In a letter dated *c.* 1482, giving directions for the christening most probably of his son, Sir William Stonor of Berkshire requested that his brothers, Tomas and Rokys, lead the child, Thomas Lyne carry the salt and Jon Doyly the basin while others carry gifts and torches.[37] The salt was required for placing in the child's mouth and invoking the pro-

---

34   Dickinson, *Missale ad Usum Insignis*, column 849.
35   Hanawalt, *Ties That Bound*, p.172.
36   Fleming, *Family and Household*, p.61.
37   *Kingsford's Stonor Letters and Papers 1290–1483*, ed. by C. Carpenter (Cambridge: Cambridge University Press, 1994), p.467.

tection of angels on him or her, while the basin may have been intended for the godparents to wash their hands in before they left the church in case any of the holy oils remained from contact with the child.[38] In that William was the first Stonor male heir to succeed as an adult since 1354, one can imagine the high hopes placed on the celebration of the baptism of his own son and heir.[39]

If the family could afford it, a feast was held for relatives, neighbours and friends to celebrate the baby's arrival, at which gifts were given to mother and child and by the parents to the guests.[40] In October 1351, some three weeks before Martinmas (11 November), Ellen and Gervase Rouclif baptised their son, John, the day after he was born, in the abbey of St Mary's, York. The godparents were family and friends who lived locally: his aunt, Margery de Rouclif, widow of Gervase's brother and Gervase's friends, John de Thornton and John de Melsa.[41] The feast to which godparents, friends and neighbours were invited, does not take place until after Ellen's churching that occurred three weeks later, on the feast day of St Martin. When their daughter, Alice, was born on the Saturday before the first Sunday in Passiontide, in 1353, she was christened either on that day or the day after, having one godmother, Alice de Beleby, wife of Richard de Warwyk, after whom she is named, and one godfather, Thomas Smyth of Clifton in York.[42] Isold, wife of William de Kirkeby of Bootham in York, carried the towel and ewer with which the godparents washed their hands.[43] The feast to celebrate Alice's arrival was delayed also until the day that Ellen's churching took place.[44]

On her reintegration into the Church, a new mother might hear childcare instruction disseminated from the pulpit. A mother's responsibility for her child's safety was brought to parishioners' attention regularly. In a canon of the Council of Canterbury (1236), priests were ordered to exhort mothers, every Sunday, not to sleep in the same bed

38 Duffy, *Stripping of the Altars*, pp.280–81.
39 Carpenter, *Kingsford's Stonor Letters*, p.7.
40 Fleming, *Family and Household*, p.62.
41 Goldberg, *Women in England*, pp.72, 75, 76.
42 Ibid., pp.62, 69.
43 Ibid., p.68.
44 Ibid., p.65.

with their infants because they might accidentally smother them; also infants were not to be left near fire or water without a guardian.[45] 'Overlaying' (suffocating the baby when in bed with an adult) was designated a venial sin, worthy of interrogation in the confessional, in Myrc's *Instructions for Parish Priests*.

Underpinning the advice given to mothers was the assumption that they loved their children. Examples of maternal love are found in sermons. One mother considered her child's wellbeing by taking 'a stree or a rusche and byddeth hym warme ith [...] for to hete the childes hondes' while another, in despair of her sick child, 'makyth a candell, and makyth a vowe in prayer'.[46] In addition to the provision of loving care, dispensing loving discipline was also the mother's duty. The author of *How the Good Wijf Tauȝte Hir Douȝtir* warned that sparing the rod spoiled the child:

> And if þi children been rebel, & wole not hem lowe [be humble]
> If ony of hem mys dooþ nouþer banne hem ne blowe,
> But take a smert rodde, & bete hem on a rowe
> Til þei crie mercy, & be of her gilt aknowe.
> (188–90)

Literature offers many examples of successful and joyous childbirth, no more so than the birth of Christ. Cycle drama presents the actual moment of delivery, and the N-Town cycle in particular makes the gynaecology of the Virgin Mary 'recurrent spectacle'.[47] It engages also with the loss of a child and the death in childbirth that proved a conclusion to many women's wifehood.

---

45 R. Blumenfeld-Kosinski, *Not of Woman Born: Representations of Caesarean Birth in Medieval and Renaissance Culture* (Ithaca: Cornell University Press, 1990), p.13.
46 G. R. Owst, *Literature and Pulpit in Medieval England* (Oxford: Basil Blackwell, 1961), pp.34–35.
47 Gibson, 'Scene and Obscene', p.17.

'A, hyr body is grete and she with childe!' The Drama of the Pregnancy and Childbirth of the Virgin Mary

The quotation is Joseph's response in the Towneley *Annunciation* to his wife's altered physique. Mary's body reacts to pregnancy in the usual way, with a swelling womb and thickening waist. Post partum, Mary's breasts produce milk and she nurses her son yet her motherhood is achieved through virginal conception and a painless labour that leaves her hymen intact. Herein lies what Teresa Coletti has called the paradox of Mary's body.[48] Her motherhood is both similar to and yet radically different from that of other women and quite how women responded to this remains a vexed question. There are those who, Gerda Lerner suggests, see in Mary, a figure to whom no female can aspire since virginal conception and birth is impossible for mortal women[49] and in the medieval Marian cult, a negative impact that served to emphasise 'the weakness, inferiority and subordination of real females'.[50] Medieval representation of the Virgin Mary and response to it is complex. Mary is a polysemic figure, capable of sustaining many different meanings and interpretations simultaneously. While her inviolate virginity is indicative of her sanctity and otherness, aspects of her life validate ordinary women's experiences. Mary bears, cares for, nurses and protects a child, whose untimely death she witnesses and laments, as evoked in the *Planctus Mariae* lyrics. Of medieval drama Teresa Coletti observes, that while it emphasises Mary's difference, at the same time it 'invokes roles for Mary that directly link her to historical women'.[51] We have seen already in the *Mary Play* that Mary and Joseph participate in a

---

48   T. Coletti, 'Purity and Danger: The Paradox of Mary's Body and the Engendering of the infancy Narrative in the English Mystery Cycles', in Lomperis and Stanbury, *Feminist Approaches to the Body*, pp.65–95.

49   G. Lerner, *The Creation of Feminist Consciousness From the Middle Ages to Eighteen-Seventy* (Oxford: Oxford University Press, 1993), p.128.

50   *Religion and Sexism: Images of Women in the Jewish and Christian Traditions*, ed. by R. Radford Reuther (New York: Simon and Schuster, 1974), p.246.

51   Coletti, 'Purity and Danger', p.82.

wedding ceremony based upon the Sarum *Ordo Sponsalium*. The Infancy plays of the English mystery cycles demonstrate how Mary's pregnancy and childbearing is subject to the practices advocated by social custom and medical texts.

Although Mary conceives very differently her actual pregnancy replicates that of all women. As is patently obvious to Joseph, his wife's body displays the tell-tale signs of the child growing in her womb; 'A, hyr body is grete and she with childe!' (Towneley *Annunciation*, 158), 'Hir sidis shewes she is with childe' (York *Joseph's Trouble about Mary*, 102), 'þi wombe to huʒe doth stonde!' (N-Town *Joseph's Return*, 26), 'Ye be with child soo wondurs grett' (Coventry *Shearmen and Tailors' Pageant*, 111), 'Now hasse shee gotten her, as I see, / a great bellye' (Chester *Nativity*, 130–31).[52] Although Joseph comments on his wife's swelling body, I think that we are to understand that he does not overstep the mark in the delicacy of his observations. Joseph simply states the obvious, unlike the foolhardy John Paston II, whose comments regarding the Duchess of Norfolk's pregnant body apparently upset her Ladyship. Lady Brandon, the wife of one of the Duke's retainers, records that John commented 'my lady was large and grete [...] [the child] sholde haue rome jnow to goo owt att'.[53] John explains to his brother that what he meant to say, was that her Ladyship was not overlaced to the detriment and constriction of the baby, something that is to be avoided from the seventh month onwards according to *The Knowing of Woman's Kind in Childing* (271–81). Had John Paston actually spoken as recorded by Lady Brandon, his remark would have strayed too low below the belt in its focus on the Duchess' private parts and would have broken a cultural taboo.

The N-Town playwright evokes the cravings that pregnant women experience in his inclusion of the miracle, found in the *Gospel of Pseudo-Matthew* and the 'Cherry Tree Carol', of the cherry tree that

52 M. Stevens and A. C. Cawley, eds., *The Towneley Plays*, Volume One: Introduction and Text, EETS SS 13 (London: Oxford University Press, 1994), R. Beadle, ed., *The York Plays* (London: Arnold, 1982), Hardin Craig, ed., *Two Coventry Corpus Christi Plays*, EETS ES 87 (London: Oxford University Press, 1957), R. M. Lumiansky and D. Mills, eds., *The Chester Mystery Cycle*, Volume One: Text, EETS SS 3 (London: Oxford University Press, 1974).
53 Davis, *Paston Letters*, I, letter 450.

bends its branches so that Mary can eat its fruit. Rosemary Woolf believes its inclusion is illustrative of Mary's innocence (the tree itself bows when Mary prays to God to enable her to taste some)[54] but I suggest that Mary's desire for the fruit is evocative also, of the sudden desire for strange or out of season foods experienced by some mothers-to-be. In February 1454, a wearily pregnant Margaret Paston craved dates and cinnamon, that she requested her husband to send straight away, signing off her letter, 'Be youre gronyng wyff'.[55]

In the Chester *Nativity* the fatigue of a woman in the final stages of pregnancy and desirous of its conclusion is heard when Mary asks Joseph's help in dismounting from the donkey, 'Helpe me downe, my leeffe fere, / for I hope my tyme bee neere' (461–62). Mary understands that the birth is imminent. In the York *Nativity* this is a matter of intuition, 'Sir, witte ȝe wele þe tyme is nere / He will be borne' (34–55) while in the N-Town *Birth of Christ* Mary feels the baby move, 'Betwyn myn sydys I fele he styrth' (96). Further, in N-Town, Joseph is concerned for his wife's wellbeing. Joseph recognises the danger of physical exertion and emotional stress to a heavily pregnant woman, against which *The Knowing of Woman's Kind in Childing* warned,

> My spowse, ȝe be with childe, I fere ȝow to kary,
> For mesemyth it were werkys wylde.
> But ȝow to plese right fayn wold I.
> ȝitt women ben ethe to greve whan þei be with childe.
> (N-Town *Birth of Christ*, 20–21)

The mother of God's 'jesyne' takes place in 'an hous þat is desolat, withowty[n] any wall' (N-Town *Birth of Christ*, 101), a stable (Chester *Nativity* 458) that, in York, is derelict and whose 'walles are doune on ilke a side, / Þe ruffe is rayued [torn open]' (*Nativity* 17–18) or in some unspecified place on the way to Bethlehem (Coventry *Shearmen and Tailors'*, 188). Although her birthing room leaves much to be desired, it replicates the exclusion from the comings and goings of society as it carries on its daily business, experienced by many parturient women.

---

54   R. Woolf, *The English Mystery Plays* (Berkeley, California: University of California Press, 1972, reprint 1980), p.176.
55   Davis, *Paston Letters*, I, letter 151.

Christ's actual birth is portrayed in the York, N-Town, Coventry and Chester cycle plays. This birth was understood to have been like no other; Mary's virginity remained intact and she suffered no pain. Of course, all of the Nativity plays emphasise the unique difference in kind of Mary's childbirth. In the York Tilethatchers' *Nativity* Mary tells the audience that she feels 'all cladde in comforte clere' (51) and calmly states 'Nowe borne is he' (56). Mary emphasises the gap between her own experience and that of other women in conversation with the three Kings,

> [...] I consayued my sone sartayne
> Withouten misse of man in mynde,
> And bare hym here withouten payne,
> Where women are wonte to be pynde.
> (York *Herod and the Magi*, 347–50)

In N-Town Joseph affirms his wife's unique experience of childbirth, 'Modyr on erth was nevyr non clere / With-owth sche had in byrth travayle' (203–04). In Chester Mary asserts that 'Payne felte I non this night' (505). In each of these plays childbirth is painless, instantaneous and accompanied by bright light, all features of the miraculous nature of Mary's delivery remarked upon by Bridget of Sweden in her vision as she witnesses the Nativity:

> Then she beyng thus in prayer, I sawe the chylde in her wombe meve and styrre hymselfe and sothenly in a moment and in the twynklynge off an ey she had borne her chylde, [...] And that maner off the byrth was so sothenly and so wysely doone that I myght not discerne nor perceyve how or what membyr off her body she had borne her chylde wythall.[56]

Bridget, herself a mother of eight, notices how unlike that of other mothers immediately after the birth Mary's body returns miraculously to its pre-parturient state, 'Then the wombe of the Vyrgyn that was

---

56   All quotations from *The Revelations* of Bridget of Sweden, are from the unedited, Middle English collection that extracted and rearranged individual revelations to construct a life of the Virgin as told by her to Bridget, as found in the late fifteenth-century MS Rawlinson C. 41, fols 12v–16. Extracts are published in Barratt, *Women's Writing in Middle English*, Chapter XII, 38–49 (pp.87–88).

very grete afore the byrth, yt swagyd and wythdrewe inwarde agayn to the state that yt was in afore she conceyvyd' (*Revelations*, Chapter xii, 55–58).

Although the nature of Mary's childbearing is different in kind from all other women, the concern expressed by her husband is not. Joseph desires that Mary be accompanied by the kind of women who would normally attend a parturient mother. Through their misconcepttion that Mary's delivery will be like that of any other woman, the characters with privileged entry into the childbirthing space emphasise the deviancy of Mary's parturition. In their attempts to apply to Mary's labour the contemporary social and medical norms of childbirth, these norms are revealed and the audience permitted access to this usually curtained-off place, the secrets of the parturient body and the ministrations of the women who directed the drama of childbirth.

The Chester and N-Town playwrights incorporate the apocryphal narrative, found in the *Protevangelion* and the *Pseudo-Matthew* of midwives, Zelomi and Salome, who attend Mary. They do so in a manner that brings Mary's experience closer to that of the women in the audience, and underlines the unique purity of the Mother of God. Zelomi believes, without question, that Mary's virginity has been untouched by giving birth. The doubting Salome attempts to disprove this by examining Mary, and her hand withers for her impiety. It is restored to health only after she acknowledges Mary's undamaged virginity and worships the Christ child. While Rosemary Woolf is surely correct in suggesting that this story is an illustration of scepticism rebuked,[57] in the hands of the playwrights, it is also opportunity to present Mary's childbirth in terms of contemporary social practice, as far as her unique somatic experience permits, emphasising its similarities and crucial differences.

No doubt, like many fathers in the audience, in the Coventry *Shearmen and Tailors'*, Chester *Nativity* and N-Town *Birth*, Joseph assumes that a labouring mother should not be left alone and that the birth should be overseen by midwives for whom he goes off in search. The Chester and N-Town Josephs are very concerned about social propriety, acknowledging that childbirth is women's drama and

---

57   Woolf, *English Mystery Plays*, p.177.

that the expectation is that women will oversee this event. Although he recognises that Mary's delivery will be special, the Chester Joseph sets out to seek midwives 'for usage here of this cittye / and manners sake' (473–74) for whose services he intends to pay (484). In N-Town Joseph understands that 'It is not conuenyent a man to be / þer women gon in travalynge' (133–34) and so he goes in search of midwives to comfort his wife (172). He is concerned that Mary has food and drink, should she require it, and worries about the pain experienced in childbirth that can induce fainting, 'Travelynge women in care be bownde / With grete throwys whan þei do grone; / God helpe my wyff þat sche not swownde' (130–32), especially, as warned of in the *Knowing of Woman's Kind in Childing*, because his wife 'is so ȝenge' (137). A fear of childbirth can be heard in Joseph's self-mocking admission, 'I drede me sore of þat fare food!' (145).

In the Coventry play the midwives never materialise but they do so in Chester and N-Town. They are proud of their professional skill that is readily acknowledged by others; Tebell (the Chester Zelome) promises Joseph that 'Wee will doe all that ever wee maye. / For too such middwives, I dare well saye, / are not in this cyttye' (486–88). The N-Town Salome speaks of their willingness to help all women whatever the circumstances (148–49) and concedes 'all men me knowe [her] / For a mydwyff of wurthy fame' (150–51) while Zelomye too is a renowned midwife (154). Gail McMurray Gibson may well be correct in interpreting Salome's comment 'Whan women travayl, grace doth growe; / þer as I come I had nevyr shame' (152–53) as meaning that, because female, Salome is not prohibited from the birthing space that for her holds not shame but grace.[58] I suggest that this remark conveys also Salome's pride in her obstetrical skills: she has never suffered dishonour in the birthing room by losing either mother or child.

Because this is no ordinary birth, intervention by the midwives is unnecessary. Mary gives birth alone, instantaneously, unaided and without pain. Mary suffers none of the usual physical effects of the strain of parturition, as revealed to Bridget of Sweden, 'In thys she nevyr chaunged her colour nor was anythyng weyke or seyke nor

---

58   Gibson, 'Scene and Obscene', p.19.

lakkyd anythyng off her bodyly strenght, as other women doo in tyme off byrth' (*Revelations*, Chapter xiii, 84–86). The more usual physical symptoms of labour are to be found in the Towneley *Second Shepherds' Play*. This cycle is unusual in that it has no Nativity play. In its place is a parody of Christ's birth, played out between Mak (the Joseph stand-in) and his wife Gyll (who is more Eve than Mary). The couple attempt to hide a sheep, that Mak has stolen, by pretending that the animal is really the son to which the overly fertile Gyll, who Mak moans produces one or two children annually (350–51), has given birth during the night. Gyll swaddles the sheep and lays it the cradle beside her bed. Swaddling, or the wrapping up of child's limbs immediately after birth, was commonplace during the Middle Ages and believed to provide warmth, comfort and protection for the new born. Bridget of Sweden reveals something about the manner of swaddling. Bridget describes how Mary swaddles her son first in linen and then woollen clothes, 'byndyng and swathynge hys lytyl blyssyd body, hys armys and hys leggis, with the swathynge bonde whych was sewde in fowr partis upon the upper wolen clowth' (*Revelations*, Chapter xiii, 80–82). The swaddling bands are sewn to the child's outer garment, thus keeping its limbs immobile. Margery Kempe indicates how some women used what was to hand for this process, when she records how, in her vision of helping Mary after the birth of Christ, she 'beggyd owyr Lady fayr whyte clothys and kerchys for to swathyn in hir sone whan he wer born' (*Book*, Chapter 6, 580–82). Like other new mothers, Mary is concerned for her son's well being, swaddling him with what she has, 'And I sall happe þe, myn owne dere childe. / With such clothes as we haue here' (York *Nativity*, 120–21).

Gyll enacts the part of the newly delivered mother who has been in labour all night until daybreak, bemoaning the pain 'A, my medyll!' (772) that causes her to 'grone, / And cry outt by the wall / On Mary and Iohn / For sore' (639–42). The manner in which Mary has given birth, however, is outside the midwives' experience and so they proceed as if Mary were like Gyll, or any other woman. N-Town provides the longest and most detailed spectacle of events in the birthing chamber.

Joseph is invited into the female space of confinement. Men enter Gyll's parodic lying-in space too. Unlike the three shepherds looking for their lost sheep, whose noisy disruption Mak tries to quell, 'Ye do wrang, I you warne, / That thus commys before / To a woman that has farne–' (768–70), Joseph is a silent onlooker. He is upstaged, quite appropriately according to social decorum, by the new mother and the ministrations of the midwives. The N-Town Joseph understands a particular etiquette governs this locus and assumes that this extends to the behaviour expected from the mother-to-be. Believing Mary in labour, Joseph considers her joyous laughter inappropriate and that it will cause offence to the midwives, who Joseph fears will leave. He counsels his wife to be grave (188), an emotion more becoming to modest, female behaviour, more suitable for the serious and life-threatening business of giving birth and one that Joseph hopes will 'wynnyth all þe mydwyuis good diligens' (189). In contrast, the midwives make no comment regarding Mary's laughter: patriarchal rules governing desired female behaviour simply do not apply within this female space where a woman can behave as suits her best. They are interested, however, in what has already taken place within their domain.

In N-Town Zelomye assumes that Mary must have received the help of some unidentified midwife and desires to know the identity of one who would have been her professional rival in the city (215). In the same way that Mary submitted to a medieval wedding ceremony, like all new mothers, she submits to post-partum physical examination in which the midwife ascertains if any further procedures or medicines are required. In N-Town Mary undergoes two intimate examinations. In the first, having invited Zelomye to 'Tast with ȝoure hand ȝoureself alon' (225), Zelome examines her *Hic palpat Zelomye Beatam Virginem* [At this point Zelomye strokes the Blessed Virgin]. Zelomye explains to Mary that by examining her, Zelomye can assess if Mary requires analgesic medicine and reassures her that she has the skill to 'ȝow comforte and helpe ryght wele / As other women yf ȝe haue pyn' (220–21). What commences as an assessment of the damage sustained in childbirth, leads to the discovery of the state of her cervix: Mary is still a virgin, as she claims, because her hymen is intact. Salome does not believe her colleague's findings and she too is invited to 'Towche with ȝoure hand and wele a-say' (251). As she touches Mary her hand withers as punishment for her disbelief of Mary's post-partum virginity.

In Chester Mary is subject to only one examination, since Tebell believes immediately that this is no ordinary childbirth (529–30). The stage direction instructs Salome, '*Tunc Salome tentabit tangere Mariam in sexu secreto*' [Then Salome tests by touching Mary in her secret sexual place] and, immediately, her hand withers. This moment might be dramatised by lifting Mary's robe, perhaps done with the midwife's back to the audience shielding Mary from the audience's view. Something more explicit should not be discounted, as the N-Town Zelomye proclaims, 'Here opynly I fele and se: / A fayr chylde of a maydon is born' (228–29).

N-Town lays bare the probing of post-parturient women that is normally the business of women. Joseph is extraneous to the female community in the birthing room and remains appropriately silent throughout this procedure. The N-Town Zelomye makes explicit how Mary differs from other women and, as the Christ child 'nedeth no waschynge as other don: / Ful clene and pure forsoth is he, / Withoutyn spott or ony polucyon' (230–33), confirms the absence of the bodily fluids that usually accompany birth. Although a virgin, Mary begins to lactate (235–36) and her body behaves in a manner outside of Zelomye's experience. The N-Town *Mary Play* was not alone in presenting the Virgin breast feeding, since it was an image popular in statuary and in lyric poetry,

> As she him took all in her lap.
> He took that maiden by the pap.
> And took thereof a right good nap [grip].
> And sucked his fill of that licour.[59]

Mary's lactation causes the midwife readily to acknowledge that a miracle has taken place. In contrast, Salome doubts what experience and medical knowledge tell her is impossible: that a virgin can give birth, that this is done painlessly, and that a virgin can lactate. Invited by Mary to examine her intimately, Salome does so, '*Hic tangit Salomee Mari[am]*' and in the process her hand withers as it makes contact with the uncorrupted flesh of one whose faith was absolute and unquestioning from the moment of the Annunciation. It is only restored

---

59 F. M. M. Comper, ed., *Spiritual Songs from English MSS. Of Fourteenth to Sixteenth Centuries* (London: Macmillan, 1936), p.27.

when she acknowledges the miraculous, touches the clothes in which Christ is laid and worships the child born in this unique fashion.

In a custom familiar to a late medieval audience, the departure of the midwives is followed by the sequence of visits and gift-giving in celebration of the safe arrival of a new baby. Some of the gifts given by the shepherds, such as the pan pipes, hat and mittens (Coventry *Shearmen and Tailors'*), the tin bell, two hazelnuts on a string and horn spoon (York) and the farthing for Mak and Gyll's new 'baby' (Towneley *Second Shepherds' Play*), recall the kinds of rattles, clothes, keepsakes and monies given to new born babies both then and now. Spiritually significant in symbolising Christ's earthly power and death the gold, frankincense and myrrh given by the three Kings are evocative also of the gifts given by the wealthy.

The spiritually misguided attempt by Joseph and the midwives to manage Mary's deviant childbearing body in the N-Town *Nativity*, reveals the social customs and medical knowledge that governed the birthing chamber and the birthing body. How the audience responded to this probing of the most holy orifice can only be surmised. Probably, some were heartily amused at one cross-dressed actor examining another, for a marker of virginity that he never could possess. Others might have been shocked at such an undignified examination of Mary's and God's privity. Some mothers in the audience might well have felt envy at Mary's pain-free childbirth. In the same way that the fictitious Gyll calls upon Mary in her pretended labour, historical record reveals that other women identified with her childbearing, different in kind as it was to their own. A mother bequeathed to her daughter a belt, believed associated with Mary, with a view to helping her in any future labour that she might experience:

> by the will dated August 26, 1463, Eufemia Langton, wife of Sir John Langton of Farnley, near Leeds, bequeathed to Margaret Meyryng, her daughter, a silver-gilt cross, an Agnes Dei, and *zonam Beatae Mariae Virginis*.[60]

Another Marian belt housed at Westminster was that 'which women with cheild were wont to girdle with'[61] and which Elizabeth of York,

---

60 Waterton, *Pietas Mariana*, pp.90–91.
61 Duffy, *Stripping of the Altars*, p.384.

Queen of Henry VII, paid to use to ease her labour pains.[62] In the book of her privy-purse expenses, the following entry occurs on the 13 December 1502, 'Item. to a monke that brought oure Ladye gyrdelle to the quene in rewarde, vis. viiid'.[63] In spite of the many cultural productions that stressed the difference in kind between Mary's mothering and that of other women, women chose to see similarity. This is no better evidenced than in women's reception and re-appropriation of the ceremony designed to re-integrate them into the Church after their childbirth.

The Churching of the Virgin Mary

Not only did women identify with Mary's parturition, they identified also with her as a new mother undergoing a ritual to reintegrate her into the spiritual life of her community. All four of the English mystery cycles contain a pageant devoted to Mary's purification in the Temple. Both Gail McMurray Gibson and Theresa Coletti suggest that medieval women recognised echoes of the private and personal ceremony of the Churching of Women in the public and corporate enactments of Mary's Purification, in cycle drama and in the civic processions, held annually on 2 February, the feast of Candlemas held forty days after the Nativity in commemoration of Mary's Purification.[64]

The *Purification* pageants dramatise Mary's participation in a ceremony required of new mothers in Jewish tradition and to which the medieval Churching of Women is related. The plays' characters, use of candles and processional staging recall also civic Candlemas celebrations. Evidence in a fourteenth-century record from Beverley reveals the form that the Candlemas celebrations took there. A procession of

---

62 B. Anderson and J. Zinsser, *A History of Their Own*, volume I (London: Penguin, 1990), p.294.
63 Waterton, *Pietas Mariana*, p.91.
64 Gibson, 'Blessing from Sun and Moon', pp.139–40; T. Coletti, 'Genealogy, Sexuality', 25–59.

all of the members (male and female) of the Guild of Saint Mary, moved through the streets to the parish church with musical accompaniment, led by one of the members dressed as the Virgin Mary as a queen, carrying her son in her arms, followed by Joseph, Simeon and angels carrying twenty-four thick wax candles.[65]

Mary participates in the purification ritual even though, as Joseph points out, this is unnecessary as she remains pure post partum (N-Town, 103–10, York, 191–215, Chester, 119–30) but she does so, since she is eager to undergo a ceremony required of and experienced by all other women, 'As other women doith in feer' (York *Purification*, 196). In Chester Joseph carries virgin wax while in N-Town Mary, Joseph, Symeon and the prophetess Anna carry candles and process up to the altar upon which the Christ child is laid, actions evocative of to the offering of the new mother's candle of thanksgiving at the Lady altar in the Churching of Women ceremony.

The stage directions in the *Candlemes Day and the Kyllyng of þe Children of Israelle* play[66] also evoke the ritual of the Churching of Women. In *Candlemes Day* Anna is accompanied by a number of virgins (originally five in the list of players), each of whom holds a candle. Singing in praise of the Christ child whom Simeon carries, they all process around the temple. When the ceremony is concluded, Symeon acknowledges that Mary 'The lawes […] ful welle ye han obbeyed / In this tempille, with hert and mende' (*Candlemes Day*, 519–20). Coletti asserts that the Digby's play's Candlemas episode 'doubles as a churching procession, in which the newly delivered mother went to church for her purification in the company of women'.[67] The correspondences are indeed many. Mary goes to the Temple for her reintegration into the religious practice of her peers as a post-parturient woman sought reintegration into the Church. Mary is met by Simeon and the new mother bringing her baby was met by the priest. Mary carries a candle

---

65   A. H. Nelson, *The Medieval English Stage* (Chicago: The University of Chicago Press, 1974), p.88.
66   *The Late Medieval Religious Plays of Bodeleian MSS Digby and E Museo 160*, ed. by D. C. Baker, J. L. Murphy and L. B. Hall, EETS 283 (Oxford: Oxford University Press, 1982).
67   Coletti, 'Genealogy, Sexuality', p.31.

and is usually, although not exclusively, accompanied by women; the prophetess Anna, virgins and, in the civic procession at Beverley, their number is swelled by the burghers' wives – the majority of who would have been mothers themselves – and probably local midwives who administered to them during their confinements. An ordinary mother was surrounded by the same supportive group of women at her Churching. The focus of Mary's Purification was the new mother and childbearing, as is confirmed in Anna's urging the maidens to follow her, 'and shewe ye summe plesur as ye can, / In the worship of Jhesu, Our Lady, and seynt Anne,' (549–50) the latter of whom was revered especially for her three marriages and the Holy dynasty that stemmed from them. The Digby *Candlemes Day* may not have been the only play written for a Candlemas performance. The existence of another, stand-alone Candlemas play may lie behind the entry in the York *Ordo Paginarum* of 1415. Played by a religious house, formerly the House of St Leonard (now Masons), the entry lists the *dramatis personae* as Mary with the boy, Joseph, Anna, the midwife with the young doves, Simon receiving the child into his arms, and the sons of Simeon.[68] The presence of a midwife and so many children, suggest that this play too encouraged connection between Mary's Purification and the Churching of Women.

The N-Town *Purification* identifies yet another connection between Mary's Purification and the Churching of Women. When Joseph makes an offering of five pence to the priest (178) (in addition to the two doves that appear in all other versions of the Purification plays), he pays the equivalent of what was a customary fee for a woman's churching. The 1482–83 accounts of the parish priest of Hornsea, record the following monies obtained specifically from individual and group churchings:

> Item, for the purification of William Hall's wife, 1½d.
> Item, for the purification of William Pellow's wife, 1½d.
> Item, on the day of the purification of John Watson's wife, 1½d.
> Item, for the purification of six different women, 9d.
> Item, for the purification of Thomas Wheytley's [wife] 1½d.
> Item, for the purification of Henry Schomaker's wife, 1½d.

68   Beadle, *York Plays*, p. 435.

Item, for the purification of John Maior's wife, 1½d.
Item, for the purification of six different women, 8d.[69]

In his giving of monies, Joseph replicates the behaviour of the grateful fathers in fifteenth-century Hornsea but, in his donation of five pence, Mary's husband is more generous.

We have testamentary evidence that real women participated willingly in the ceremony of churching. Rather than dwelling upon the cleansing of the defiled, post-partum female body upon which the male-produced text focuses, women celebrated its power in bringing life into the world along with that of the attending midwives who assisted in the process.[70] For women the ceremony was neither clandestine nor an occasion for embarrassment about the post-partum body. It was quite the contrary.

Ellen de Rouclif chose to be churched after both of her deliveries, accompanied, on each occasion, by her close friend, Cecily, who shared the events of the birthing room with her, and other local women who were significant to the new mother. Margery Kempe attended both her local Candlemas procession and the private churchings of local women (Chapter 82). As one would expect, royal churchings were extravagant affairs. The *Liber Regie Capelle* (*c*. 1449) stipulated that the queen, dressed in the most elaborate and costly garments, should be lead by two and followed by her female attendants in procession from her state bed to the church door and to the altar, and that a duke should carry a golden candelabrum representing the queen's purified body.[71] In 1465, sixty female attendants, many priests carrying relics, and scholars singing and carrying lights accompanied Queen Elizabeth Woodville at her churching.[72]

Women did indeed detect parallels between their own private ritual and Mary's Purification. Margery Kempe leaves us evidence of the connection that she made between Mary's purification and the

69 Goldberg, *Women in England*, p.81.
70 This has been argued by Gibson, 'Blessing from Sun and Moon', p. 149 and B. R. Lee, 'The Purification of Women After Childbirth: A Window Onto Medieval Perceptions of Women', *Florilegium*, 14 (1995–96), 43–55.
71 Gibson, 'Blessing from Sun and Moon', p.148.
72 Ibid., p.147.

private churching of ordinary women. In what commences as her recollection of the meditation in which she stands alongside Mary at her Purification, Margery moves swiftly and seamlessly into how she connected Mary's Purification and private ceremonies,

> whan sche saw women ben purifyid of her childeryn. Sche thowt in hir sowle that sche saw owr Lady ben purifiid, and had hy contemplacyon in the beheldyng of the women wheche comyn to offeryn wyth the women that weryn purifiid. (*Book*, Chapter 82, 6687–90)

Margery calls the ceremony by the term 'purification' but, in the mind of this woman at least, it is reclaimed as women's time for celebration of the power of the female body to reproduce, the apogee of which was Mary's own childbearing. Medieval women clearly responded to a perceived similarity between their own childbearing and that of Mary, rather than the gulf so emphasised by celibate churchmen. In participating in a churching ritual, the one who had recently brought another Christian soul into the world overtly linked her childbearing and her female companions' motherhood with that of their most celebrated figurehead, the Mother of God. This is not marked by the patriarchal exchange of money between the father and the church, but by a matriarchal one: a candle given from one mother to another, placed either before an image of the Virgin Mary or on her altar in the Lady Chapel. Eamon Duffy suggests that the altar of the Lady Chapel of Ranworth Church, in Norfolk, was used in precisely this way:

> It was the custom for women when they came to be churched to offer a candle in thanksgiving their delivery before the main image of the Blessed Virgin, or at the Lady altar. At Ranworth this south altar [behind which were located the images of the Holy kindred] was the Lady altar, and it was here in all probability that women would have brought their babies and their offerings.[73]

The woman identified her own successful childbearing with that of the Virgin Mary and St Anne, ritually acting out this connection, in a sacred space surrounded by the women, many of them mothers themselves, who had helped her through her confinement. One can only contemplate how much more emphatic the celebration of women's power might be

---

73 Duffy, 'Holy Maydens, Holy Wyfes', p.196.

in the group churchings that took place at Hastings and elsewhere, of women who had given birth at a similar time. Evidence suggests that what medieval women took from the Virgin was not only protection in their hour of greatest need, while in labour, but also power by association. Men might understand the churching of women as stemming from the ritual purification of the pollution of the female sexualised body after childbed. Women chose to interpret the ritual differently, in a manner that celebrated their physicality and sexuality. As Gail McMurray Gibson argues,

> we may well conclude that the meaning of the purification ritual for the women who were churched must have been very different from the meaning projected by the celibate male elite who presided at the altar. [...] The men remained literally marginal, on the outskirts of the ceremony and its meaning.[74]

The new mother and her gossips were able to re-write the male text of the impure and polluted, post-partum female body, and imbue both it and the women who helped other women in their childbearing, with a power to be celebrated.

It is telling that, rather than burying the memory of their body's pollution in childbirth, the memory of their own and other women's churchings were retained and formed one means by which women measured time. This is no better illustrated than in the legal depositions where female witnesses used their own pregnancies, confinements and churchings in order to calculate Alice de Rouclif's date of birth. Among them, Cecily de Shupton knew Alice's date of birth because she was present at it, Agnes de Fritheby recollected that she was present at Alice's mother's churching, and Agnes the Ald and Emmot Norice remembered Alice's date of birth because they both had sad experiences of motherhood engraved upon their memories, each having lost a son shortly before Alice was born, which enabled Emmot to become Alice's wet nurse.[75] Women's time was measured primarily by the memory of

---

74 Gibson, 'Blessing from Sun and Moon', p.149.
75 Alice de Tange deposed that 'exactly a fortnight before the day of Alice's birth this witness gave birth to a son at Rawcliffe, now dead who had he lived would not have completed twelve years of age before next Lent' while Emmot Norice stated that she gave birth to a son born a week after the Michaelmas before that

their own and others' parturition, successful or otherwise, and this perception of time ran alongside those temporal markers used traditionally in a patriarchal world; the calendar, the seasons and the church year.

The Lottery of Motherhood

Inevitably, medieval literature depicts wives who die in childbirth. Thomas Malory's *Book of Sir Tristram De Lyones* (1469), opens with the death of Elyzabeth, wife of king Melyodas of Lyones.[76] When Elyzabeth was heavily pregnant, Melyodas was taken prisoner by an unnamed lady whose love he did not requite. Discovering her husband's absence Elyzabeth, 'nyghe oute of hir wytte,' rushed off to find him (*Sir Tristram*, VIII, I). As the *Knowing of Woman's Kind in Childing* warned, the over exertion and emotional distress this late in pregnancy brought on her labour pains when she was deep in the forest, with only a gentlewoman to help. The child, Tristram, was born after a difficult labour with 'many grimly throwys' and Elyzabeth became fatally cold. On her deathbed, the queen acknowledged that her death might have been prevented had she not rushed after her husband, and if those skilled in midwifery had been present, 'I muste dye here for his sake for defawte of good helpe' (*Sir Tristram*, VIII, I).

Literature leaves us evidence that the experience of motherhood was not as fulfilling for all as they might hope. Not all women successfully conceived, and if they did this was no guarantee that they would give birth to a healthy baby. This sadness is nowhere better illustrated than in the commissioning of Osbern of Bokenham to write the *Vita S. Annae matris S. Mariae* (1447), by Katherine Denston, wife

---

Saturday [before the first Sunday in Passiontide: Alice's birthday]. Her son died [...] the Friday before that Saturday'. Goldberg, *Women in England*, p.64.

76 *Malory Works*, ed. by E. Vinaver (Oxford: Oxford University Press, 1983), pp.227–511.

171

of John and half-sister of John Clopton of Long Melford, in Suffolk.[77] By 1500 Anne had become an extremely popular name, especially for heirs to noble houses, as Marina Warner explains, in the hope that these girls would be 'greatly fruitful, too, to found unshakeable, prolific dynasties: Anne's liturgical titles include *Stirps beata* (Blessed stock) and *Radix sancta* (Holy Root); her patronage implied fertility to a degree Mary's single conception could not'.[78] Her concern to produce an heir and continue the family line, and the belief in Anne's efficacy as a childbearing saint, is suggested in the supplication to Anne with which Bokenham concludes the life:

> Prouide, lady, eek þat Ion denstone
> & Kateryne his wyf, if it plese þe grace
> Of god aboue, thorgh þi merytes a sone
> Of her body mow haue or they hens pace,
> As they a dowghter han, yung & fayre of face,
> Wyche is anne clepyde in worshype, lady, of þe
> & aftyr to blysse eterne conuey hem alle thre.
> A.M.E.N. lorde for charyte.
> (*Vita S. Annae*, 2092–99)

For Gail McMurray Gibson, Bokenham's instruction from his patroness was clear,

> Bokenham wrote for Katherine Denston an incantational text invoking childbirthing grace and protection, invoking from the saint of long-sought childbirth the saint who had been finally glorified with triumph over the womb – safe delivery of the male issue that Katherine (alas, fruitlessly) hoped would continue the name of Denston and the kin of Clopton.[79]

Coming from a family especially concerned with dynasty, Katherine responded to Anne as an exemplar of lineage, as a Mother saint, matri-

---

77 *Legendys of Hooly Wummen*, ed. by M. Sarjeantson, EETS OS 206 (Oxford: Oxford University Press, 1938, reprint 1971). For a translation see S. Delany, *A Legend of Holy Women: Osbern Bokenham Legends of Holy Women* (Notre Dame: University of Notre Dame Press, 1992), pp.29–42.
78 M. Warner, *From the Beast to the Blonde: On Fairy Tales and Their Tellers* (London: Vintage, 1995), p.88.
79 Gibson, *Theater of Devotion*, p.107.

arch and protectoress of childbirth. Katherine's motivation for appealing to St Anne may be found in the life experiences of those women close to Katherine. In 1420 her mother, Margaret, had died young while Katherine was still a child, followed by her stepmother who died giving birth to her stepsister.[80] Her devotion to the Mother of Mary suggests that Anne's association with childbirth spoke to Katherine, who perceived a similarity between her own and St Anne's wanting and waiting for a child. Unlike St Anne, Katherine never had the longed for child – a son and heir – but did produce a girl who she dutifully named Anne, in honour of the saint.

Other women saw their children die before them. The grief felt by such mothers is poignantly expressed in many lyrics in which Mary laments her son's death on the Cross. In one fifteenth-century lyric, Mary complains to other mothers that while she has seen her son crucified, they take joy in their children who,

> [...] Ye daunce upon youre knee,
> With laghing, kissing and mery chere: [...]
> Thy childis capps thou castest upon.
> Thou pikest his heere [trims his hair], beholdest his ble, [...]
> O! woman, a chaplet chosen thou has:
> Thy childe to were it dose thee liking.
> Thou pinnest it on – grete joye thou mas.[81]

The lyric speaks of the loving actions of ordinary mothers; who show affection to their children, dress them up, play with them and enjoy their company. Grief is heard also in the lamentation of those whose sons are killed by Herod's soldiers in the *Slaughter of the Innocents* pageants found in many of the cycle plays. One mother sees only a future of such sorrow that her life will become worthless, while another laments the pains of pregnancy, 'fourty wekys gronynge,' that have resulted in no more than the pain at the loss of the child whom she fed at her breast (N-Town *Slaughter of the Innocents*, 94–96, 100–04). In a demonstration of the strength of their maternal love, the women in the York *Slaughter*

---

80 Gibson, 'Saint Anne and the Religion of Childbed', p.104.
81 Davis, *Medieval English Lyrics*, number 112, pp.210–11.

attempt vainly to fight back. Again the lament is heard by the mother whose life becomes empty and meaningless, at the death of her child,

> Allas þat we wer wroghte
> In worlde women to be,
> Þe barne þat wee dere bought
> Þus in oure sighte to see
> Disputuously spill.
> (226–30)

In the Digby *Candlemes,* the *prima mulier* cries out 'Alas, alasse, good gossypes! / This is a sorowfulle peyn' (315), to the women who were involved in his delivery and her purification. The untimely death of a child is both a personal grief of the mother and a collective loss, shared by the whole female community. Their only retribution is to fight back *en masse* against the one unarmed male on stage, Watkyn, with the only weapons that are at hand; their distaffs. They beat Watkyn with female symbols that are powerless against male violence and cannot bring back their dead sons. The loss of a child was no casual matter and some mothers were willing to sacrifice themselves attempting to save that of their children. On 9 August 1298, Alice and John Trivaler's shop caught on fire and in running back into the burning building to save their trapped son, Alice 'was overcome by the greatness of the fire and choked'.[82]

Although largely women's business, childbearing in the Middle Ages was directed by male texts; books on gynaecology and women's health, instruction in motherhood from the pulpit, a special ceremony to reintegrate the parturient body into that of the church. The various dramatisations of the Virgin Mary's childbirth and purification show the influence of the medical texts, religious ceremonial and social practice that informed childbirth. Replicating the somatic changes brought about by pregnancy, the plays dramatise how Mary's body alters during pregnancy; her womb swells, she experiences cravings and, post-partum, she lactates. Like those women fortunate enough to have a space of their own, Mary gives birth in a private birthing space

---

[82] *Records of Medieval Oxford, Coroners' Inquests, the Walls of Oxford, Etc.*, ed. by H. E. Salter (Oxford: Oxford Chronicle Company, 1912), p.7.

into which her concerned husband brings the midwives who officiated over medieval parturition. They endeavour to minister to this new mother as they would any other woman. Like all recently delivered mothers, Mary is subject to a post-partum examination, although, of course, the midwives' findings are miraculous. When playwrights dramatised the Mary's purification, they conceived of it in terms of the churching in which medieval women participated after their successful parturition. Like any new born baby, Mary's son is given presents and his birth celebrated by visitors who come to see and welcome the new arrival. The male text constructed the parturient body as something at best, to be secluded and kept at a respectful distance and, at worst, something whose pollution by the fluids crucial to pregnancy and childbirth required special ritual cleansing. Evidence from Margery Kempe's *Book* demonstrates that, despite the difference that clerics stressed between Mary's and ordinary women's childbearing, women perceived a similarity. Through obedient participation in the male conceived and regulated ceremony of Churching, women were able to re-write the male text of the impure and polluted, post-partum female body and celebrate the power of this aspect of wifedom.

Chapter Five
Hardworking Housewife and Garrulous Shrew

A married a couple had to learn to live together and make the best of things since once a licit marriage had been contracted a spouse could not be set aside easily. Marriages might be annulled, that is declared never to have existed, if either spouse was found subsequently to have failed any of the criteria of eligibility. Impotence was grounds on which to annul a marriage but this came with a caveat: if either partner was found to be fertile at a later date the marriage could be reinstated. This occurred in the case of John Poynant (1378–80) whose marriage to his wife was annulled on the grounds of his impotence, but when he subsequently remarried and impregnated his second wife, the church court rescinded this second marriage along with that of his first wife who had taken another husband, commanding John and his first wife to resume married life together.[1] What happened either to the second wife and their child or the second husband is not recorded. Church court records testify to the frequency with which the validity of marriage was examined where a prior marriage was believed to have existed as in the case of Alice Marshall who, in 1489, was living as wife of Richard Bisshop while she had another husband living.[2] Unfortunately the court's ruling has not survived. A couple might be granted a judicial separation *a mensa et thoro* (from table and bed) on the grounds of heresy, adultery and cruelty or mistreatment, but the couple might not remarry.[3] Invalidity, but not incompatibility, might secure a licit, permanent dissolution of a marriage, leaving each spouse free to form a new union. The best that the Church could offer as a salve for disharmony was a separation that prohibited either of the spouses from

---

1   Brundage, *Law, Sex and Christian Society*, p.512.
2   Goldberg, *Women in England*, p.135.
3   Cosgrove, 'Consent, Consummation and Indissolubility', p.96.

remarrying, since their initial union, however disharmonious, still existed in the eyes of Church and God.

Disharmony might be avoided if spouses listened to advice given in the sermons and conduct books that defined what patriarchy did and did not want of its wives. Additionally, women might follow the example of the Madonna whose chastity, silence and obedience were fêted throughout Christendom and who represented the epitome of the good wife and mother. Proverbs defines the obverse of the *mulier fortis* and identifies behaviour that a wife should avoid:

> *Et ecce mulier occurrit illi ornatu meretricio praeparata ad capiendas animas garrula et vaga quietis inpatiens nec valens in domo consistere pedibus suis nunc foris in plateis nunc iuxta angulos insidians.*
> [And behold there met him a woman with the attire of an harlot and subtle of heart and she is loud and stubborn her feet abide not in her house now is she without now in the streets now she lies in wait at every corner].
> (Proverbs 7. 10–12)

This definition of wifely misconduct is repeated and is one to which lurid details accrete to form a damning catalogue of faults inherent in women, as cited in *De Coniuge non Ducenda*,

> By nature woman's quick to chide,
> Deceitful, jealous, full of pride; [...]
> A woman will receive all males:
> No prick against her lust prevails. [...]
> Her tongue's a sword: its cutting blow
> Like lightning brings her husband low. [...]
> The wife's demands are always met;
> If not, she'll quarrel, rage and fret.[4]

The disobedient housewife is garrulous, lascivious and a rod to her husband's back. She recalls Eve rather than Mary in her behaviour.

This chapter explores the way in which late medieval literary wives reflect what it is that men wanted from them and the behaviour that men most feared. Once more, in listening to both good and bad wives talking back, one can hear what it is that women wanted from and found in the role of spouse and the behaviour that they expected

---

4   Blamires, *Woman Defamed*, pp.127–28.

from their husbands. We begin with the conduct books that define the parameters of good and bad wifehood.

'Housewijfli þou schalt goon on þe worke day': Wifely instruction in Conduct Books

The advice found in conduct books reflected the interests of the social groups for whom they were produced. While the basic tenets and virtues required of wifedom are acquired at the mother's knee, conduct books share a presumption that perfecting the role continues once a woman is married, and that its subtle nuances are learned through the tutoring of her husband.

It is fortuitous that one conduct book that has survived was written by a father for his daughters of marriageable age. In the absence of their mother's guidance, the purpose of Geoffrey La Tour-Landry's *Book of the Knight* was to instruct his daughters in those qualities required of a lady who would become someone's wife and mother. Sifting through the *Book*'s exemplary tales, much can be gleaned about the behaviour desired of an aristocratic wife.

The tale of how the King of England chose his spouse reveals the importance of assured, habitual good manners and demure personal conduct:

> y wyll take none for fairnesse nor plesaunce, But y wyll haue her that is of demure manere, ferme in estat and countenaunce, and of goodly behauing. [...] And there nis not in this world gretter richesse thanne to haue a wyff ferme in her estate, behauing, and of good maners.
> (Chapter XII, p.17)

Her social position required the King's, and indeed any aristocrat's wife to behave accordingly – something to be learned very early on by the daughters of a knight who will marry into their own social class. Keeping up appearances was paramount. Appropriate wifely behaviour for aristocratic ladies was to impress with one's piety and modesty.

A lady did not gad unaccompanied about the countryside to jousts, pilgrimages and feasts (Chapter XXV). Nor did she dress in the fashion of 'unthrifti women that bene euell women of her body' (Chapter XXI, p.30). Complaints about the excessive nature of women's dress were commonplace. St Paul advised women to dress respectably and modestly, and to avoid extravagance in hair decoration and material for their dresses (I Timothy 2. 9–10). Such items were indicative of vanity and pride. Margery Kempe's regret about the clothes that she wore as a younger wife reveals how censure of their dress was internalised by some women,

> sche wold not leevyn hir pride ne hir pompows aray [...]. And yet sche wyst ful wel that men seyden hir ful mech velany, for sche weryd gold pypys on hir hevyd, and hir hodys with the typettys were daggyd. Hir clokys also wer daggyd and leyd with dyvers colowrs betwen the daggys, that it schuld be the mor staryng to mennys sygth and hirself the mor ben worshepd.
> (*Book*, Chapter 1, 255, 257–62)

Margery readily admits that in the pride and vanity of youth she used to wear the height of fashion to impress those around her, and that this was behaviour for which many criticised her.

In La-Tour Landry's *Book*, the tale of the King of England reveals another quality to be fostered in preparation for wifehood: the ability to be measured in speech. La Tour-Landry advised his daughters, 'y praie you haue not mani wordes, for who so usithe to speke moche, he saithe not euer trouthe; and ther for ansuerith atte leyser, and understonde what is saide to you or ye ansuere' (Chapter XII, p.17). One can imagine the noise produced by the teenage chattering of the three motherless girls that inspired the Knight to advise that silence is golden. In advocating that a woman be measured in speech, the Knight of La Tour-Landry suggests that his daughters acquire a virtue for which the Virgin Mary was famed. The Knight explains that an aspect of Mary's virtue was her silence, which she maintained at the Annunciation until she was fully apprised of the situation in which she found herself and asked Gabriel, 'the ende of the faytte or dede the whiche he dyd announce to her'.[5] Mary's silence

---

5   Wright, *Book of the Knight*, pp.148–49.

was praised from the pulpit by Dr William Lichfield, Divine of All Hallows the Great in London, in a manner that contrasted her behaviour with Eve:

> Eve, oure oldest moder in paradise, held long tale with the eddre, and told hym qwhat god had seyd to hire and to hir husband of etyng of the apple; and bi hire talkyng the fend understod hire febylnes and hire unstabilnes, and fond therby a way to bryng hir to confusioun. Our Lady seynt Mary did on an othere wyse. Sche tolde the aungel no tale, bot asked hym discretly thing that she knew not hireself. ffolow therfore our lady in discret spekyng and heryng, and not cakelinge Eve that both spake and herd unwisely.⁶

As a medieval audience knew, the garrulous Eve met a fate worthy of a woman who could not hold her tongue.

Much of La Tour-Landry's counsel reveals the double standard prevalent in late medieval society. The wicked man could benefit from a good wife (Chapter CI) but not *vice versa*. A gentlewoman should have a gentle heart (that is be devoid of anger) (Chapter XIV) and should not be jealous (Chapter XVII), but the jealous husband should not be loved any the less because 'he dothe it for the feruent loue that he hathe to her' (Chapter XVII, p.25). Although the Knight maintained that modesty was more prized than good looks, the text warned that a wife may lose her husband's love if she lost her beauty (Chapter XVII). Should she discover that her husband was having an affair, the good wife had to put up with this, accept his behaviour without criticism and win back his love: the moral being 'a woman may chastise her husbonde, and make hym do well, with fairnesse rather thanne with rudenesse' (Chapter XVII, p.24). Most importantly, the good wife was obedient (Chapters XVIII and XIX) and retained her good name by keeping her body 'vndefouled and in clennesse' (Chapter CXVI, p.157). The *Book of the Knight* emphasised the punishments for adultery (in his book it is invariably the woman who is the culprit) and the dangers of bigamy and intercourse within the forbidden degrees of consanguinity/affinity. The Knight's daughters were untutored, however, in the regulation of the when, where and how of spiritually-safe sex, nor were they reminded that they might legitimately demand payment

6   Owst, *Literature and Pulpit*, p.387.

of the marital debt. The short moral tales demonstrate that bad wives (those who are deceitful and sexually profligate) are invariably punished, and good wives (who are demure and sexually chaste) are rewarded with their husband's trust and love.

How the Good Wijf Tauȝte hir Douȝtir suggests that women from other social classes were deemed to require marital instruction also. That the narrative voice is that of the goodwife indicates that patriarchy felt that such instruction should come from the mother, even if this could not always be the case as with the Knight of La Tour-Landry or indeed with girls who have been separated from their mothers by going into service. The text advocates a patriarchal construction of wifedom similar to that of La Tour-Landry, in terms of the virtues required: a wife should be chaste, silent and obedient, as well as modest so that she 'Fare not as a gigge, [...] Lauȝe þou not to loude' (55–56). Again we hear the exhortation to answer one's husband meekly (41), be well-mannered (53) and not gad about town (67). These are precisely the faults of which Alisoun of Bath's husbands rightly accuse her. Preservation of the family name and reputation was as important to the middle classes as it was for the aristocracy. There was a difference, however, in what was expected in terms of work between the wife of a rural knight and that of an urban freeman. In *How the Good Wijf Tauȝte hir Douȝtir* there is much emphasis on the practical skills of housekeeping where the wife, by virtue of her economic position, is much more hands-on in the daily running of a home and business where every penny counts. The text affirms that the wife of an urban freeman should be industrious, working herself when finances require this (116–17), should run the household efficiently and fairly, especially in her husband's absence when it is she who is left in charge to lock up and pay the wages which she should do on time (103–32).

Childcare was considered the wife's responsibility. A wife should discipline her children. A wise mother should save for her daughters' bottom drawer, from the moment that they are born, in order that her daughters might marry as soon as they can (188–200). Wives should avoid wasting money in taverns and getting drunk too often (67–79), should behave appropriately when out in public and avoid extravagance (174–75). Only if the family was wealthy enough, should the wife be hospitable and give alms (167–73). Missing from the *Good Wijf* is the expectation that a wife will be of noble birth, beautiful and have praiseworthy good manners. Such attributes are of secondary importance to a husband whose economic position required a wife who is no stranger to hard work.

In his *Instructions to his Son*, Peter Idley praised the good wife in a fashion not dissimilar to the Merchant's ironic encomium at the start of his tale:

> I reporte me to you that be maried:
> Wher is ther ony so glorius a lyffe!
> All thyng is wele and no thyng myscaried;
> No defaute is founde in the good wyffe.
> Betwene wedded folk is neuer striffe,
> But 'ye' and 'nay,' ther is non othir –
> They lieve in rest as shippe without Rother.
> (I, 526–32)

One wonders about his own two marriages: to Thomas' mother, Elizabeth Drayton (of Drayton in Oxfordshire) in around 1447 and then Anne Creting. Towards the close of Book I, Idley discusses marriage in a section devoted to *De vxore diligenda* (I, 1226–88). *De vxore* opens with an exhortation that Thomas should love his wife as 'hertely' (I, 1227) as he can. Idley's focus is on the affective aspect of the marital relationship. Loving one's wife and being considerate when speaking to her, is the key to Idley's philosophy of marriage. His father explains to Thomas that a good wife may be constructed, and that this is achieved primarily through how her husband addresses her. If Thomas speaks gently, his wife will love him more than any other man, fear him, not wish to offend him, and will look after his goods, neither wasting them nor spending his money (I, 1229–32). All this will be achieved by speaking to her kindly. If Thomas is 'croked and crabbed of speche / Lordly of countenauns and comberous to please' (I, 1233–34), however, he will end up in great distress and lose his wife's love. Behind Idley's advice may be detected past accusations of unkind speech and overbearing authority, thrown at him by one, or even both, of his wives. A husband's raised voice and assertion of his authority was not inclined to forge an affectionate relationship with his wife. One can hear the Wife of Bath voicing such a complaint.

Idley advises Thomas to treat his wife well because he and she are one flesh, and to despise her is to despise himself. In case Thomas had not learned the lesson, his father reiterated that the husband constructed a wife in his own image, 'Euer a good man maketh a good wyffe' (I, 1246). He advised Thomas to recall that God made Eve to be Adam's helper, and the words of St Paul to the Ephesians, in which Paul advised men to love their wives as Christ did his Church (I, 1247–57). House, land and other goods are given by parents and friends but wives are God given. Idley instructs that where love lasts and is constant, '[…] God euer sendeth / Prosperite and welthe and good encrese' (I, 1265–66), desirable outcomes of marriage for those like Idley with land to settle on their heirs. Idley advised that Thomas should 'lerne, sone, to lieue in peas' (I, 1267) and if he should find some fault in his wife, to remember that no-one, except God, is perfect (I, 1268–74). Although he tells Thomas that marriage is a union in which the woman is the man's helper whose status is 'not to be to lowe ne to ouer hye' (II, 1629), Idley does not wish Thomas to understand the relationship between the sexes as one of equality. Father warns son against giving women the upper hand because if he does, Thomas will find his wife 'contrarie' (I, 1281). Peter advises Thomas that, occasionally, the husband should acquiesce to his wife's wishes, in order for a quiet life:

> I wold in no wyse women displease;
> ffor I am bounde and may not flee.
> Women beith goode, whoso can hem please.
> Well y woote sufferaunce doth ease.
> (I, 1283–86)

Like the Wife of Bath, Idley too makes reference to the competition for the Dunmow Flitch. What is used by Chaucer's creation as a criticism of the quality of bacon or sexual satisfaction that Alisoun received from her first three husbands, is employed by Idley in more general terms, to advise that in his experience, married life is not perfect and that one should adjust one's expectations accordingly, since 'Beif and moton woll serue well ynowe' (II, 2204).[7] Idley mentions sex and father warns son to make sure that his wife has nothing to complain about in this department since, as we have heard already, Idley's opinion of woman's sexual voracity is that it drives her 'with hir croked instrument to encrees and multeplie' (II, 1790).

Peter Idley emphasises the importance of asserting one's authority over one's wife, who will be libidinous by nature, in order to mould her into the *mulier fortis* of Proverbs 31. Idley advocates the kid glove approach. We cannot know if Thomas followed his father's advice but we do know that he married a girl called Alice and that they had a son called Richard. Alice's experience of married life with Thomas cannot have been so terrible, as she married for a second time after Thomas' death, to a William Poche.[8]

How the Wise Man tauȝt His Son[9] is aimed, as was the *Goodwife*, at young, urban-dwellers but in this case at men who were apprenticed or indentured in trades, possibly outside of the family home and the father's sphere of influence. The son is assumed to work for a living (36) and is encouraged to be terribly conscious of his standing in the community. Contrary to what one might expect of a social group without the advantage of inherited wealth, the son is advised not to marry for money (73–74, 93–96). He should find out all he can about a prospective bride and choose someone who is biddable, 'And take good hede, [...] þat sche be meeke, curteis, and wijs' (76–77). That she is poor is irrelevant, as she will be unafraid of hard work, 'And sche wole do þee more good seruice / þan a riccher, whanne þou hast neede' (79–80). As in Idley's *Instructions* so too *How The Wise Man tauȝt His Son* suggests that a good wife may be constructed primarily through the husband's speech and the manner in he speaks to her:

---

7 History has proven Idley's advice not to travel the distance between Oxfordshire and Essex to have been sound. In 1467 the flitch was won by Stephen Samuel of Little Easton and in 1510 the winner was Thomas Fuller of Coggeshall, men who, like the 1445 winner, Richard Wright, lived within easy travelling distance of Little Dunmow, *Little Dunmow Priory*, [n.p].
8 D'Evelyn, *Peter Idley*, p.33.
9 Furnivall, *Babees Book*, pp.48–52.

> Neiþer calle hir bi no vilouns name;
> And if þou do, þou art not wijs,
> To calle hir foule it is þi schame; [...]
> But softe & faire a man may tame
> Boþe herte and hynde, bucke & do.
> (98–100, 103–04)

Cursing and shouting will achieve nothing; take the 'softly, softly' approach. If she was meek and served her husband well, a wife should be cherished (82–83).

Repeatedly texts demand that wives are obedient to their husbands. No woman was exempt. Even if she were royalty, a wife was expected to acquiesce to her husband. It is an expectation that caused marital strife. In the mid-thirteenth century, the Franciscan friar and Oxford lecturer, Adam Marsh, wrote with frank advice to Eleanor de Montfort, sister of Henry III and wife of Simon de Montfort. The content of Marsh's letter concerns shortness of temper and in it he warned Eleanor about the 'demonaical furors of wrath that do not shrink from disturbing the most loving peace of marriage, "For wrath killeth the foolish man, and envy slayeth the silly one"' (Job 5. 2).[10] Marsh advised Eleanor to emulate 'the most placid grace of the most pious Virgin Mary'.[11]

Medieval literature is replete with good wives, peasant and aristocratic alike, who are faithful, obedient, who produce the desired heir, and care for husband and children with admirable selflessness and industry. Chaucer gives the example of the saintly Griselda who concedes to Walter's every command, who is an able ruler in his absence and a devoted mother whose vow of marital obedience is tested beyond many readers', although not her own, endurance. The bewitched heroines in the Wife of Bath's tale and Dame Ragnell similarly obey the knights whom they marry. For illustration of selfless motherhood, one can look to Custance who cares for and comforts her baby son when they become refugees:

---

10   Gies and Gies, *Women in the Middle Ages*, p.132.
11   Ibid., p.134.

> 'Pees, litel sone, I wol do thee noon harm.'
> With that hir coverchief of hir heed she breyde,
> And over his litel eyen she it leyde,
> And in hir arm she lulleth it ful faste.
> (*Man of Law's Tale*, 836–39)

Custance prays to a saint synonymous with motherhood and its pain and sorrow, when she calls on the *Mater Dolorosa* (641). She does so when, as the mother of a child about to be falsely and maliciously banished from his heritage, she most needs pity and aid for her child's plight (855–56). Custance's prayer aligns her own motherhood with that of the maternal exemplar *par excellence*: the Virgin Mary, in this instance the aspect of Mary's mothering that recognises the pain that a mother feels at her child's suffering.

There are many examples of wives who behave badly. The sexual misconduct of Alisoun of Bath and May, and that to which Margery Kempe admits she was tempted, illustrates perfectly male assumptions regarding female lasciviousness. Alisoun of Bath and Margery Kempe wander quite unchecked outside of the domestic sphere, attending unchaperoned precisely the kinds of public gatherings against which La Tour-Landry and Idley warned. Both women dress themselves in finery and display the worldly vanity that churchmen criticised. The Wife of Bath and Margery exhibit the verbosity so criticised by La Tour-Landry.

In the interest of balance, the wives who feature in this chapter fall at either end of the spectrum: the virtuous, anonymous wives who are the protagonists of *The Wright's Chaste Wife* by Adam of Cobsam (fl. 1462) and the *Ballad of a Tyrannical Husband*, and the garrulous and obstinate Mrs Noah of the cycle plays. Unquestionably the portrayals of these women deal in the stereotypes of the good and bad wife. Of greater interest is the way in which we can detect women's understanding of what it was to be a good or bad wife by listening to them speak both within and against the ideology that their voices were designed to convey. In as much as these portrayals reveal what it means to be a good wife, we hear also what women considered the attributes of a good husband.

'A wife for to wedde & haue
That might hys goodes kepe & saue'

The *mulier fortis* of Proverbs 31 is trustworthy and her husband profits materially through her industry, particularly spinning, weaving, gathering food and time management. The anonymous girl who becomes the wife of a hardworking carpenter in Adam of Cobsam's tale, *The Wright's Chaste Wife* (1462) is just such a *mulier fortis*.[12] The tale deals with working people and centres around the attempted purchase of sexual gratification and an intelligent wife who outwits the men of the tale. It is not a fabliau and Cobsam's story is unlike that told by Chaucer's Miller. In the *Miller's Tale*, the carpenter's absence from home while employed in building work permits the development of the affair between his wife, Alison and the student-lodger, Nicholas. Contrary to fabliaux tradition, in the *Wright's Chaste Wife* the woman's scheming is employed in order to remain sexually faithful to her husband. This text, with its inversion of fabliaux expectations, is of particular interest to a discussion of wifehood on two counts; firstly there is compelling evidence to suggest that Cobsam has reproduced a tale originally narrated by a female voice and secondly women especially appear to have enjoyed this story and to have told it to younger girls who learned the skills of womanhood as they worked at their spinning. Barbara Hanawalt suggests that female authorship and narratorship for the tale is detectable in a number of ways; through its limited use of Cobsam's voice (confined to framing a pre-existing story), in the story's setting in a space entirely dominated by the wife, the tale's preoccupation with the female work of weaving, the importance to the plot of gender inversions and the two wives'

---

12 *The Wright's Chaste Wife*, ed. by F. J. Furnivall, EETS OS 12 (London: N. Trübner, 1865), pp.1–20, lines 28–29. More recently the work has been edited by Eve Salisbury in *The Trials and Joys of Marriage* (Michigan: Medieval Institute Publications, 2002).

collusion at the story's denouement.[13] The *Wright's Chaste Wife* offers a female perspective of ideal wifehood.

Marrying later in life, the carpenter wishes primarily for a wife who is a good economist able to enhance his material wealth. He marries a widow's daughter after which he is employed for two or three months by his local Lord to build a timber hall (105). The couple's separation is not unusual. Hanawalt cites many historical instances of spouses separated through the husband's business commitments, indicating that it was quite common among London merchants and craftsmen to leave their wives at home to manage the business in their absence.[14] Business takes Alisoun of Bath's fourth husband to the capital throughout Lent. While this period of separation gave Alisoun opportunity to court Jankyn, the wright is more fortunate for it permits his wife to capitalise, literally, on her virtues that are those promoted in *How the Good Wijf Tauȝte hir Douȝtir*. Not only is the wright's bride economically capable and can 'hys goodes kepe & saue' (29) but she is also famed for being 'stabylle & trewe, / Meke of maners, and feyre of hewe' (34–35). The carpenter is assured of her chastity as his bride came with a dowry of a chastity indicator, in the form of a rose garland that retains its colour as long as the wife remains faithful to her husband. In as much as the tale praises the virtues of this young wife it reveals also the persistence of male distrust of female sexuality. Even though he owns the garland, in a belt and braces measure, the carpenter uses his skill to construct a trap to outwit the men who, he assumes, will inevitably attempt the corruption of his young, and undoubtedly willing, wife.

Contrary to fabliaux expectations, this story reveals how a loyal and faithful wife uses the tools traditional to female industry, and not a little gender role reversal, to enhance her husband's wealth and her own prestige. The tale demonstrates that it is men, rather than women, who are sexually profligate. When the carpenter tells the lord about the properties of the garland, the lord decides to test its efficacy and

---

13   The story's female ancestry and female transmission is suggested by Barbara Hanawalt, *'Of Good and Ill Repute': Gender and Social Control in Medieval England* (Oxford: Oxford University Press, 1998), pp.94–96.
14   Ibid., pp.90–92.

the fidelity of the new wife. When the lord arrives at the couple's home the wife's first thoughts are for her husband's well-being, 'Syr, howe faryth my swete spowse / That hewyth vppon youre tre?' (137–38) and it is the lord who broaches the subject of adultery. His intentions are anything but the innocent curiosity that R. H. Llewellyn[15] identifies as his motivation and the lord moves swiftly and seamlessly from the courtly lover's complaint, that without her love his heart will burst, to the desire for sex familiar in fabliaux tradition. The lord wishes to 'pley with thee in some preuy place' (146), both in some hidden location and in her vagina, but it is in another pit entirely in which he finds himself. The carpenter's wife attempts to dissuade the lord from his desire because her husband will learn of it through the garland's condition until the lord offers her forty marks 'that schalle do the good' (159). The sensible wife wants to see the colour of his money before she will go any further and the lord duly hands over the coins. The Wife convinces him to enter the room with a secret trapdoor constructed by her husband, and the lord falls over forty feet beneath the floor. He remains here until her husband returns but, in the meantime, the young wife very cleverly humiliates him by practising gender-role inversion.

In this poem the man, and a lord to boot, is rendered utterly dependent upon a working woman to supply him with the food required for survival. This he obtains only if he carries out women's work: beating flax to separate its fibres. More accustomed to wielding a sword, symbolic of his class and gender status, the lord is unmanned as he is forced to use a female, working-class version of this: a 'swyngylle' (216) or wooden implement resembling a sword, used for beating raw flax or hemp. This mock phallic symbol parodies the power and authority that he formerly held. Threats of violence are futile in this world, ruled by a woman who holds all the power and is, literally, on top of her gender and class superior who lies imprisoned below in the pit.

The steward notices his lord's absence and, enquiring after him, gets into conversation with the carpenter. Intrigued by the story of the

15   R. H. Llewellyn, '"The Wright's Chaste Wife" Disinterred', *Southern Folklore Quarterly*, 16 (1952), 251–54 (p.252).

man's garland he too follows his lord to the carpenter's house. The steward makes no bones about his desire; he puts his arms around the wife's neck and states that he wants to sleep with her (285). The steward is parted from the twenty marks that he offers and he also ends up in the pit. In order to survive, he too must work but is very reluctant to do so. The wife upbraids him, 'As a man buxome and bayne / Thowe shalt rubbe, rele, and spynne' (348–49). In demanding that he be obedient and 'bayne' or compliant, the wife requires and exacts from the steward what is promised uniquely by the woman in the church marriage service. The steward too is forced to wield a swingling stick to earn his keep.

The local parish church's proctor (its administrator and lawyer who sat in the ecclesiastical courts) hears from the carpenter about his magic garland. He too goes to visit the young woman with the intention of committing adultery. Like the lord, the proctor wishes to play within the wife's secret sexual place (431) and attempts to secure this by the skilful pleading that one might expect from an advocate. His words fall on deaf ears and he meets the same fate as the lord and his steward, parting with twenty marks for the privilege of falling through the trap door. Like the other men, he is very reluctant to work for his keep. He admits that what the wife wants him to do is woman's work and consequently outside his experience, 'For I lernyd neuer in londe / For to haue a swyngelle in hond / By day nor be nyght' (475–77). Unlike the lord and the steward who require no tuition in their task that is reliant on brute force, the proctor is given a job that involves greater manual dexterity. He is given a distaff or wooden board with a fork or ornate comb on the tip, to which the beaten flax is tied and from which the spinner draws as she spins the thread. He is required to wind the flax fibres made by the Lord and steward around the distaff, ready for its spinning into linen. The poem makes clear that the proctor can wind the distaff, usually a task carried out by unmarried women according to the wife (505–06), only after instruction from her, 'As ye haue taute me' (513). He then begins to spin 'wele and Fyne' according to the narrator, although the lord is concerned about the quality of his thread, 'þou spynnest to grete' (517). The lord is worried about the appearance of thick and thin spots, known as slubs, which give an uneven appearance to the spun thread of inexperienced spinners. The men's conversation reveals that women's work is not as easy as they had assumed and that the level of expertise required to produce the fine textured clothes worn by a lord, steward and church official, is not acquired after only one lesson.

When the carpenter returns home he discovers that his enterprising wife has set up a cottage industry, in which three men are working for their keep under her very strict commandment, and that this is to his profit. The wife does well at her commercial enterprise and brings into the family coffers eighty marks (£53 20s. 7d.) in the space of the two or three months of her husband's absence. The wife has made no insignificant contribution to the household finances, has had processed the raw materials required in spinning for the cost of food alone and all is achieved with minimal disruption to her own housework since she 'went in to her lofte, / Sche satte and dyd here dede' (203–04).

If we assign the tasks in the order in which the men arrive at the house, the lord 'knockyd lyne,' bundling up the flax ready for the steward to beat it and separate the fibres from the pulp, and the proctor to wind the yarn on a reel and spin (526–29). When he sees his lord trapped beneath the floor performing women's work, the carpenter is appalled. Since the garland has not faded there is none of the suspicion of his wife's adultery that one expects at the dénouement of a fabliau. He is so distressed at the class and gender inversion that his lord has suffered, that the carpenter never even asks the nature of the crime for which the lord begs his mercy (551) and simply wants him released. The carpenter does not display the same urgency about the steward and proctor, since neither is his lord or employer.

His wife refuses their release until the lord's wife comes and discovers 'Howe þey would haue done wyth *me*' (563, italics my own). The carpenter's wife's grudge is equal against all three, for lust is no respecter of social class and is a sin of which men of all ranks can equally be guilty. On each occasion it was the man who attempted to initiate adultery but the carpenter never queries the motivation of the three men in his cellar: it is satisfaction enough that his wife has not slept with any of them. For the carpenter to have asked why they were under his floor would be to dispel the commonly held belief that it is women who are lecherous and the initiators of adultery. The wife, however, offers an alternative truth: that it is men, and not women, who are drawn to adultery. She disseminates her subversive text to a receptive audience: the other wife also injured by the lord's conduct, for who the carpenter's wife insists on sending and to the conjectural, extra-textual audience of women gathered about their spinning, listening to a female narrator telling this story. It is the lord's wife who asks the men why they are imprisoned in the carpenter's cellar. Since the captives offer no explanation, this is supplied by the carpenter's wife, in a matter-of-fact response, 'Alle they would haue leyne me by, / Everych in ther manere, / Gold and syluer they me brought' (587–88). The wife admits that she took their money but argues that she is blameless because she never intended to sell her body and commit adultery. The lady's response is revealing. She expresses neither shock nor outrage at her husband's attempt at adultery, but laughs and enjoys his discomfort (601). The wives' reaction suggests that their lust and infidelity is no more than what women expect from men. In revenge they collude in the men's humiliation. What does surprise the lord's wife is that her husband has participated in women's work. Although she too is a busy woman, her husband has never done anything that might be considered female work. In this the carpenter's wife's tale reveals yet another truth, that women's work is 'gret trauayle and peyne' (579), the reality of which the three captives are forced to acknowledge. In recompense for her treatment by the three men, and the alternative narratives that she relates about gendered sexuality and women's work, the lady gives all of the money to the carpenter's wife. She has earned it. In a swipe against the presumption of women's sexual misbehaviour, the narrator acknowledges that all women are sisters of the wright's chaste wife since 'trewe bene good women alle / That nowe bene on lyve' (638–39).

Another hardworking wife is described in the anonymous *Ballad of a Tyrannical Husband*[16] that survives in a manuscript from around 1500. In the ballad husband and wife's work is delineated clearly:

> The goodman an hys lade to the plow be gone,
> The goodwyfe had meche to doo, and servant had she none,

---

16   *Ballad of a Tyrannical Husband* in Salisbury, *Trials and Joys of Marriage* and online at http://www.lib.rochester.edu/camelot/teams/thtxt.htm

Many smale chyldern to kepe besyd hyrselfe alone,
She dyde mor then sho myght withyn her owne wone.
(21–24)

The farmer's wife is the epitome of the *mulier fortis*. She has children who she looks after day and night, as well as finding time to milk the cows, make butter and cheese, feed the fowl, bake, brew, cook and make linen and woollen cloth; beat flax, comb it with a hatchel, tease and card wool, and then spin it (42–60). Once again, the enhancement of her husband's goods is accepted as part and parcel of a wife's duties, 'Soo I loke to owr good withowt and withyn' (73). *The Boke of Husbandry* (1523) by Anthony Fitzherbert assumes a similar level of industry from a wife,

> And when you are up and ready, then first sweep the house, set the table, and put everything in your house in good order. Milk your cows, suckle your calves, get your children up, and dress them, and provide your husband's breakfast, dinner, supper, and for your children and servants and take your place with them. Send your corn and malt to the mill so that you can bake and brew whenever there is need [...].[17]

In addition, Fitzherbert considered it woman's work to make butter and cheese, feed the pigs and poultry, grow vegetables, sow flax and hemp that she will manufacture into the family's bed linen and clothes, and help her husband with farming tasks when required. The work of keeping the family fed and clothed might be supplemented by commercial enterprise. Margery Kempe set up a brewing business of her own (Chapter 2) that survived for nearly four years. When this failed, she ran a milling business for a brief time. Jeremy Goldberg has found that wives in medieval urban centres participated in a variety of trades including all aspects the textile industry, brewing, baking, poultry sales, regrating (buying goods to sell on again quickly in the locality), cheese and butter manufacture.[18]

Although busy from morning until night, her tyrannical husband (72) deems his wife's work of less value and physically easier than his

---

17   *English Historical Documents*, V, ed. by C. H. Williams (London: Eyre and Spottiswode, 1967) and translated in Goldberg, *Women in England*, pp.167–68.
18   Goldberg, *Women in England*, Chapter VI, 'Work in the Town'.

own. When his food is not on the table on his return from the fields, the husband accuses his wife of being too slow 'Alle thys wold a good howsewyfe do long ar het were prime' (78). In turn, the wife accuses her husband of ingratitude for her household economy:

> Yet I have not a feyr word whan that I have done.
> Soo I loke to owr good withowt and withyn,
> That ther be none awey noder mor nor myn,
> Glade to ples yow to pay, lest any bate begyn.
> (72–75)

They agree to swap tasks with the wife going to plough and the husband to run the household. The wife prepares much beforehand, making the butter and curing the meat. She attempts to advise her husband in her duties; look after the children properly and do not let them cry, avoid over stoking the kiln fire (where malt is dried for brewing), look after the geese (presumably being fattened for winter). He is arrogant in his reply, 'Teche me no more howsewyfre, for I can inowe' (108), for he assumes that housework is not mentally taxing. Sadly, the poem breaks off after the first fitt and we never learn how the experiment concludes. It is possible that the wife failed to plough a straight furrow and returned to her domestic labour, more willing to be horrendously overworked indoors than physically exhausted outside. It seems more probable, however, since the ballad identifies the wide variety of tasks and skills required in managing a home, that it is the husband who is forced to acknowledge that the running of a late medieval household required of any wife a high degree of domestic and business skill, not least of which is effective time management.

Having examined two very good wives, we turn now to Mrs Noah who, in the majority of the surviving cycle plays, demonstrates many of the vices of which wives were traditionally accused. Yet again, even as she is guilty of these vices, we hear her talking back to constructions of wifely misconduct and offering an indication of what absolute obedience to one's husband might cost in terms of other personal relationships with close friends and family.

The disobedient discourse of Noah's nameless spouse

Mrs Noah is known by the title that signals her possession by her husband. Genesis provides neither her nor her daughters-in-law (the wives of Shem, Ham and Japhet) with first names nor histories that predate their current married status. Genesis 6 informs that Noah is a righteous man but of his wife says nothing, accepting without question that she merits a place in the ark. Noah's wife is a blank canvas onto which successive centuries have painted as they have chosen fit.

In many medieval narrative poems Mrs Noah is patient, obedient and characterless as illustrated by her acquiescent silence in *Cursor Mundi* (*c.* 1300)[19] and in the assertion of the *Bible Moralisée* (*c.* 1235–45) that typologically she prefigures the Virgin Mary, and participates in her husband's salvific importance, '*Noe significant Christum, uxor eius beatam Mariam*' [Noah symbolises Christ, his wife the blessed Mary].[20] The dramatic portrayal of Mrs Noah, closest to that found in medieval poetry, is in the N-Town *Noah*. In a representation in which Mrs Noah possesses the spiritual awareness and maternal responsibility that will later characterise the Virgin Mary, the mother of the post-diluvial human race exemplifies spiritual perception, obedience and moral responsibility. In the N-Town *Noah* his wife has a clear understanding of the consequences of humanity's sin and of parents' joint responsibility to teach their children 'Synne to forsakyn, and werkys wronge' (43). She enters the ark without complaint, voicing pity at the volume of the water and offering thanks that the Noah family have been saved (217).

In their portrayal of Noah's spouse, the Chester, York and Towneley cycles suggest that their dramatists were influenced by two

---

19 *Cursor Mundi. (The cursor of the World). A Northumbrian poem of the fifteenth century in four versions*, ed., R. Morris, EETS OS 57, 99, 101 (volume I) and 59, 62 (volume 2) (London: Oxford University Press, 1874–93). The Flood narrative is found in volume one.

20 *The Parisian Bible Moralisée*, Oxford MS Bodley 270b, folio 9v as quoted in V. A. Kolve, *Chaucer and the Imagery of Narrative: The First Five Canterbury Tales* (London: Edward Arnold, 1984), p.199.

other traditions. The first derives from a lost apocryphal text, the *Book of Noria*. In this God commands Noah to build the ark in secret, the devil corrupts Mrs Noah to discover what is going on, giving her a potion to give to her husband so that he will reveal the secret after which the devil enters the ark by construing Noah's order to his reluctant wife to 'Come on you devil' as a personal invitation and leaves by boring a hole in its bottom.[21] This version of Mrs Noah as tempted by the Devil into betraying her husband, aligns her with Eve rather than Mary. The devil is depicted leaving the ark on the verso of the first of five leaves (now New York, Pierpont Morgan Library MS 302) of the *Ramsey Abbey Psalter* (late thirteenth-century), in the late fourteenth-century *Queen Mary's Psalter* (London, British Library MS Royal 2.B.vii, folios 6 and 7) and dramatised in the only surviving play of the Newcastle cycle, *Noah's Ark*, as performed by the Shipwrights.[22] This play concludes with Noah completing the ark and going to collect his family, so it is probable that, as at York, another guild was responsible for a second Noah pageant, since lost, that covered the events of the Flood and the release of the raven and dove.

The second tradition pays greater attention to the Noahs' marriage, presenting them as a couple set in quarrelsome ways. The violence between the Chester Noahs, and most especially the Towneley Noahs, is the subject of much critical discussion. In their presentation of the couple, Chester and Towneley recall the literature in which domestic squabbles arise when much older men take younger wives, and the violence that can erupt within the home, found depicted

---

21 Kolve, *Chaucer and the Imagery of Narrative*, p.201.
22 Both of the illustrations are described in detail by Adelaide Bennett, 'The Recalcitrant Wife in the Ramsey Abbey Psalter,' in *Equally in God's Image: Women in the Middle Ages*, ed. by Julia Bolton Holloway, Joan Bechtold and Constance S. Wright (New York: Peter Lang, 1990) and at http://www.umilta.net/equally.html. For a reproduction of the play as it survives in the book by Henry Bourne see *The History of Newcastle upon Tyne; or, the Ancient and Present State of that Town* (Newcastle, 1736), reproduced in *Non-Cycle Plays and Fragments*, ed. by Norman Davis, EETS Supplementary Text 1 (London: Oxford University Press, 1970), pp.19–31.

frequently on misericords where the housewife is shown attempting to bludgeon her husband.[23]

The Chester, York and Towneley playwrights portray Mrs Noah as the disobedient, garrulous shrew, warned against from pulpit and in conduct literature, who will not heed her husband's words. Her reluctance to enter the ark, only briefly mentioned in the *Book of Noria*, blossoms into full blown revolt characterised by obduracy, ill-temper, violence and a sharp tongue. She becomes a scold. Her behaviour endangers the safety of her family and causes the Towneley Noah to warn all prospective husbands – and those with young wives – 'Whyls thay ar yong, / [...] Chastice thare tong' (574, 576). Secular law supported Noah's attempts to chastise his wife for her ungoverned speech. The Borough ordinance of Hereford (1486), held scolds accountable for much urban discord,

> Also, concerning scolds, it was agreed that through such women many ills in the city arose, viz, quarrelling, beating, defamation, disturbing the peace of the night, discord frequently stirred between neighbours as well as opposing the bailiffs, officers, and others and abusing them in their own person [...] Consequently, whenever scolds shall be taken and convicted, they shall have their judgement of the cuckingstool without making any fine. And they shall stand there with bare feet and the hair of the head hanging loose for the whole time that they may be seen by all travelling on the road [...].[24]

In late medieval Hereford women who were violent, spoke in an unrestrained and indecorous fashion and flouted male authority were punished by the secular authorities: on a 'cuckingstool', placed usually before their own front door, upon which they sat and were pelted with filth by the mob.

23 Examples of brawling housewives can be found in Westminster Abbey as described in M. D. Anderson, *Misericords* (Harmondsworth: Penguin, 1954), plate 43; King Henry VII's Chapel in Lincoln Cathedral, M. D Anderson, *The Choir Stalls of Lincoln Minster* (The Friends of Lincoln Cathedral, 1967), p. 26, figure 21; Chester Cathedral as described in Brian T. N. Bennett, *The Choir Stalls of Chester Cathedral* (Chester: S. G. Mason, [n.d.]), pp.16–17; St Botolph's Church, Boston, Lincolnshire, John Orange and John Orange and Lorna Briggs, *St Botolph's Parish Church, Boston: The Misericords* (Much Wenlock: RJL Smith & Associates, [n.d.]), p.7.
24 Goldberg, *Women in England*, p.234.

The exploitation of familiarity with bad wifely stereotypes and the appeal of dramatising her reaction when presented with the sudden demand that she leave her friends and home, for an uncertain future immured with a menagerie on a bizarre craft, are reason enough to portray Mrs Noah as a shrew. So strong is the attraction of depicting Mrs Noah as a garrulous, disobedient wife that in the Waterleaders and Drawers of Dee's *De Deluvio Noe*, the Chester dramatist grafts this portrayal onto a Mrs Noah who commences the play prefiguring the Virgin Mary. The result is not a happy combination. Mrs Noah converts, suddenly and without psychological motivation, from the good wife who accepts the will of God and her husband and who carts timber in order to help Noah in his building (65), to a stubborn shrew who refuses to enter the ark and obey her spouse, and who 'will not doe after thy reade' (101). She exhibits characteristic female insubordination, 'Lord, that weomen bine crabbed aye, / and non are meeke, I dare well saye' (105–06). In the York Fishers and Mariners' *Flood* there is no attempt to combine both Marian and Eve-like traits. Mrs Noah's disobedience is obvious when she refuses to come at her husband's bidding '[...] telle hym I wol come no narre' (62). In the Towneley *Processus Noe cum filiis* Mrs Noah responds to her husband's greeting of 'God spede, dere wyf! / How fayre ye?' (274–75) with the terse 'Now, as euer myght I thryfe, / The wars I the see' (276–77) from which we are left in no doubt that she has always been the shrew 'full tethee, / For litill oft angré' (270–71) of which Noah warned.

Presenting Mrs Noah as a bad tempered, disobedient wife places a gendered spin on an opportunity for spiritual instruction. The audience is encouraged to read Mrs Noah allegorically and contrast her extra- and inter-ark behaviour. Rosemary Woolf suggests that when outside of the ark, Noah's wife represents 'the recalcitrant sinner, perhaps even the sinner on his deathbed, who refuses to enter the church'.[25] Mrs Noah is guilty of many of the branches of chiding or scolding, as identified in the *Book of Vices and Virtues*; encouraging strife, scolding, despising, evil speaking and reproving (fol.24b, pp.63–64). The dramatists render her sinfulness gender-specific, as Mrs Noah displays faults traditionally associated with bad wives;

25 Woolf, *English Mystery Plays*, p.139.

disobedience, garrulity and forwardness with the addition, in Chester and Towneley, of physical abuse of her husband.

Mrs Noah's manner, once inside, emphasises that the vessel, a prefiguring of the Church, is her salvation that transforms her from argumentative rebellion to obedience and chastens her tongue. When carried inside the ark by her sons, the Chester Mrs Noah takes a swipe at her husband before becoming submissive and, for the most part, silent for the remainder of the play, with the exception of her participation in the family's singing of Psalm 68. This psalm is highly appropriate for in it the psalmist requests God's help in extricating himself from the watery depths of sin, having been overwhelmed by a tempest. In the York *Flood* Mrs Noah's stubbornness transforms into acceptance of her situation and praise of God 'Loved be þat lord þat giffes alle grace, / Þat kyndly þus oure care wolde kele' (197–98). The transformation is at its most extreme in the Towneley *Processus Noe* where, on crossing the threshold, Mrs Noah shifts from a stubborn, violent refusal to do as her husband requests, to willing participation in the steering of the ark (625). She becomes an advisor to whom Noah defers in the choice of the first bird to leave the ark (683).

The violence between the Towneley Noahs has encouraged much critical debate. Quite how realistic of marital relationships this violence is meant to be is a matter for discussion in as much as any theatre can be said to be realistic, especially as Mrs Noah will have been performed by a man who may well have matched or even bettered the physique of Noah. The result of the couple's fight is a draw,

> *Noe.* Bot wife,
> In this hast let vs ho,
> For my bak is nere in two.
> *Vxor.* And I am bet so blo
> That I may not thryfe.
> (595–98)

The moment has potential for slapstick comedy. The transvestism of medieval theatre might provide a Mrs Noah who was bigger and stronger than 'her' husband, thus rendering the moment pantomimic in its violence. But to perceive it solely in this way is to read back onto medieval theatre a modern response to post-medieval pantomime dames. I suggest that the Noahs' abuse of each other, and their children's attempts to part and pacify their parents, is more troubling. It replicates what happens when men used their fists to assert their authority and wives fought back. The Towneley Noahs' domestic discord is shown to emanate from the same source as that described by Alisoun of Bath: a bullying husband's actions initiate wifely disobedience and her retaliation begins the cycle afresh. Here the subject is not sovereignty as in the *Wife of Bath's Prologue* and *Tale* but a matter of communication, or rather the lack of it. In Towneley Mrs Noah is presented with the incomprehensible. Having completed the ark in secret Noah goes to collect his wife and family, surprising her with the demand that 'Hens must vs fle, / All sam togeder, / In hast' (423–25) without offering any explanation for their removal. His wife's response is to accuse her husband of some malady, 'Whi, syr, what alis you?' (426). It is a reaction that might evoke sympathy among those in the audience whose spouse does not confide in them but presents them, all too frequently, with a *fait accomplis*. Noah's explanation is cryptic and unsatisfactory, 'Ther is garn on the reyll / Other, my dame' (430–31) and she has to force from her husband a complete explanation of God's plan (434–52).

In the York play too, Mrs Noah makes clear that she has she not been informed about, and so distrusts, the strange structure built by her husband and onto which he and their sons are so eager to drag her. She prefers dry and safe land to his 'toure deraye' (77). Her distrust is not without foundation since Noah admits in the Shipwrights' *Building of the Ark* that he is 'fulle olde and oute of qwarte [...] Of shippe-craft can I right noght' (50, 67). Mrs Noah's exclusion from the ark's planning and building is emphasised by the York cycle structure. The purpose of the ark, its dimensions and method of construction are revealed by God to Noah alone, in the Shipwrights' *Building of the Ark*, the pageant that precedes the Noah play. Noah's comment,

> It sall be cleyngked euerilka dele
> With nayles þat are both noble and newe,
> Þus sall I feste it fast to feele.
> (106–08)

indicates that the audience watch the construction of a medieval clinkered ship but Mrs Noah does not, since she is absent from this pageant. Mrs Noah is reliant on the ark made by her husband who has never before expressed interest in anything aquatic yet is excluded from any understanding of its making and the purpose of the Divine. It is of little surprise in the *Flood* that Mrs Noah accuses Noah of madness and complains that

> Erly and late þou wente þeroutte,
> And ay at home þou lete me sytte
> To loke þat nowhere were wele aboutte.
> (114–16)

Mrs Noah informs her husband how he should have fared in such a weighty matter, 'Thow shulde haue witte my wille, / Yf I wolde sente þertille' (123–24). Important subjects should be discussed between spouses. It is only at this point that Noah provides her with the detail that she needs to make an informed response.

Mrs Noah's reactions in Towneley and York reveal how wrangling and strife occur within the marital relationship, when wives are excluded from their husbands' lives and the decision-making process regarding the family's welfare. In as much as Mrs Noah is improved by her entry to the ark, a similar change appears in her husband, since both are willing to listen to their children's plea only when they have boarded and Noah agrees that 'We will no more be wroth' (Towneley *Noe*, 606). Female frowardness is shown transformed into the epitome of wifely obedience through the influence of the Church (symbolised in the ark) rather than by the exercise of male power through violence. In Noah's transformation the Church's influence is shown to be equally beneficial to the bullying husband. But this is theatre not real life. While the Church encouraged husbands and wives to live in accord, its court records provide evidence of domestic violence; in 1396 Thomas Nesfield is accused of throwing his wife to the ground, beating her with a club and breaking her arm.[26] One wonders how many wives, and husbands, were the victims of domestic violence that continued unnoticed, remaining covert through fear or shame.

26   Goldberg, *Women in England*, p.141.

As with so many of the wives included in this volume, so too in Mrs Noah's garrulous recalcitrance one can hear her talking back to the patriarchal social structure of the family that demands unquestioning obedience from its womenfolk. This was expected even when the husband made life-changing decisions about which the wife was neither informed nor consulted. Mrs Noah's disobedient discourse offers other truths about married life. Mrs Noah presents women's work as a valid and necessary complement to that carried out by the Noah males. In her concern for those who are drowned, she asserts the importance of an alternative social structure that coexists with the family and upon which it depends at moments of crisis: the female network of the gossips who attend men's and, particularly, women's lives from cradle to grave. As Jane Tolmie argues, Mrs Noah offers a voice 'not only for the dead but also for the living: all those women at the bottom of the hierarchy of discourse'.[27]

In the York *Flood* one reason that Mrs Noah gives for refusing to embark is that she has 'tolis to trusse' (110). Her concern for domestic utensils suggests that she remains concerned about the household economy, even if her husband has become obsessed by what she perceives to be a scheme detrimental to her family's wellbeing. In Towneley Mrs Noah's words reveal a wife's concern about the economics of daily living when the husband fails to provide for the family. Her actions suggest how a wife might attempt to remedy this. This motif is most fully developed in the Towneley *Processus Noe* in which Mrs Noah expresses her anger at Noah's unexplained absence and dereliction of the family's physical needs,

> Do tell me belife,
> Where has thou thus long be?
> To dede may we dryfe,
> Or lif, for the,
> For want.
> When we swete or swynk,
> Thou dos what thou thynk;
> Yit of mete and of drynk

---

27 J. Tolmie, 'Mrs Noah and Didactic Abuses', *Early Theatre*, 5.1 (2002), 11–35 (p.11).

> Haue we veray skant.
> (278–86)

Her criticism is clear: Noah has made no contribution to the most important task of putting food on the table. Unwilling to listen to her husband's explanation for his absence, she bemoans the obedience that men require of their wives after which violence erupts between the couple.

In ill temper Mrs Noah sends her husband away and busies herself with spinning, an archetypal female occupation and one that is capable of both positive and negative association. On the one hand, Mrs Noah's spinning aligns her with the first disobedient wife, Eve, and recalls the common belief, as stated in the N-Town *Fall of Man*, 'And wyff to spynne now must þou ffonde / Oure nakyd bodyes in cloth to wynde' (408–09), that in the postlapsarian world Adam was to dig and Eve to spin. Lurking behind the disobedient Mrs Noahs, and especially the spinning wife in Towneley, is the figure of the disobedient garrulous Eve. The Towneley Noah goes so far as to accuse his wife of being 'Begynnar of blunder!' (587), the initiator of sin and intellectual error, a charge brought against Eve in both the N-Town *Fall of Man*, 'Wyff, þi wytt is not wurth a rosch' (309) and the York *Expulsion*, 'Allas, what womans witte was light! / Þat was wele sene' (133–34). In Towneley the act of spinning is used as a delaying tactic of a stubborn wife. When encouraged by her husband and sons to enter the ark, Mrs Noah refuses until she has 'Spon a space / On my rok' (489–90) and then 'This spyndill [...] slip' (528). That is, she is determined to spin from her distaff enough prepared fibre to fill the spindle that she then intends to slip or empty onto a reel. This is a process that can be spun out by reluctant women to gain time, a tactic that Laura F. Hodges suggests would have been familiar to and caused amusement among husbands in the Wakefield audience, living as they did in a town dependent on the wool industry.[28]

Mrs Noah's spins out both her thread and her time on earth, in defiance of her husband's wishes and in contradiction to God's plan.

---

28   L. F. Hodges, 'Noe's Wife: Type of Eve and Wakefield Spinner', in Bolton, *Equally in God's Image* and at http://www.umilta.net/equally.html.

Her spinning is, nonetheless, work perceived as a virtuous, female activity. It is one of the merits of the *mulier fortis* and carried out by both anonymous wives in the *Wright's Chaste Wife* and *Ballad of a Tyrannical Husband*. A wife's spinning might clothe the family and provide income where the husband's contribution is precarious. This is suggested in the Towneley *Second Shepherds' Play* where Gyll moans at the loss of potential earning time when forced to get up from her spinning to answer the door to her errant husband, Mak,

> I am sett for to spyn;
> I hope not I myght
> Ryse a penny to wyn,
> I shrew them on hight!
> (430–33)

When her spinning is interrupted by the fight with her husband, Mrs Noah wishes that he was dead, 'Might I onys haue a measse / Of wedows coyll' (562–63) and acknowledges that other wives in the audience feel as she does (567–70). I suggest that her wish for her husband's death is spoken in frustration and expresses a desire, not so much for his actual death and her literal widowhood, but for the freedom to work when she chose as was the right of a *femme sole*. C. M. Barron reveals that some London wives did exercise such freedom and might choose to run their own businesses, rent shops, accumulate money (and debts), contribute to taxation and train their own apprentices.[29] The 1467 ordinances of Worcester indicate that wives in that city too enjoyed the same working conditions,

> Yf eny mans wyf becom dettor or plegge, or by or sylle eny chaffare or vitelle, or hyre eny house by hur lyf, she to answere to hym or hur that hath cause to sue, as a woman sole marchaunt; and that accion of dette be mayntend ayenst hur, to be conceyved aftr the custom of the seid cite, wtout nemyng hur housbond in the seid accyon.[30]

---

29 C. M. Barron, '"The Golden Age" of women in medieval London', in *Medieval Women in Southern England*, Reading Medieval Studies, 15 (1989), pp.35–85 (p.40).

30 *English Guilds*, ed. by T. Smith and L. T. Smith, EETS 40 (Oxford: Oxford University Press, 1870), p.382.

In wishing for Noah's demise, Mrs Noah suggests that, in economic terms, life lived as a *femme sole*, even with the legal responsibilities that this brought with it, was to be preferred to operating as a *couverte* legally subject to a husband who interrupted and curtailed her earning potential, without meeting the economic shortfall that this created himself. At its most productive, a woman's skill in spinning and weaving might lead to a career in cloth production, like that of the Wife of Bath. It is reasonable to infer, as does Laura F. Hodges, from her third daughter-in-law's comment 'If ye like ye may spin, / Moder, in the ship' (521–22) that Mrs Noah takes her spinning equipment into the ark.[31] Both Ruth Evans and Jane Tolmie concur that a power struggle is played out on stage in which the value of female work is contested.[32] In the *Processus Noe* Noah's bullying arises from his perception of his work as the more important, and of his wife's as serving only to delay its successful completion. His response to Mrs Noah, bearing in mind that she has already drawn attention to his failure as a provider, is to beat her. But Mrs Noah is not without an advocate. Her husband may fail to appreciate the value of spinning as a productive and affirmative female activity but God does not. In willingly making space for this spinner in his ark, the Lord signals that women's work will continue to have a place in the post-diluvial world, as it did for many families in the later Middle Ages.

In York and especially Chester, Mrs Noah expresses great concern for those who are left outside of the ark to drown. Doctrinally her concern is misplaced, in that it is for those who God has judged meritorious of such punishment. Mrs Noah does not forget the women with whom she has lived so closely. The York Mrs Noah requests that her gossips and relatives be permitted to join the family on the ark (144). During the flood Mrs Noah loses her peer group of gossips and extended family, those women who formed an informal but invaluable

---

31   Hodges, 'Noe's Wife', at http://www.umilta.net/equally.html. Gail McMurray Gibson suggests that Mrs Noah is in fact denied her distaff on entry into the ark, 'Scene and Obscene', p.15.
32   R. Evans, 'Feminist Re-Enactments: Gender and the Towneley Uxor Noe', in *A Wyf Ther Was: Essays in Honour of Paule Mertens-Fonck*, ed. by J. Dor (Liège: University of Liège, 1992), pp.141–54 (p.154) and Tolmie,' Mrs Noah', p.25.

support network for each other, complementary to that of a woman's immediate family. So strong is her attachment to her gossips that she wants to know where they are after the flood subsides (269–70). Her poignant query is brusquely dismissed by her husband, 'Dame, all ar drowned, late be thy dyne' (271), who fails to appreciate their importance. The Chester Mrs Noah values her gossips and their loyalty more than her own safety and that of her husband and family,

> But I have my gossips everyechone,
> one foote further I will not gone.
> They shall not drowne, by sayncte John,
> and I may save there life.
> The loved me full well, by Christe.
> But thou wilte lett them into thy chiste,
> elles rowe forthe, Noe, when thy liste
> and gett thee a newe wyfe.
> (201–08)

In this moment of crisis Mrs Noah calls on St John, the evangelist into whose safe keeping Christ handed over his mother at the Crucifixion. She requests St John's protection for the women whose job it is to care for all mothers. Their survival means more to her than that of her marriage. The Chester playwright alone permits the gossips a voice, in which can be heard their fear of the rising water and also their desire to share one last drink together,

> And lett us drinke or wee departe,
> for oftetymes wee have done soe.
> For at one draught thou drinke a quarte,
> and soe will I doe or I goe.
> Here is a pottel full of malnesaye good and stronge;
> yt will rejoyse both harte and tonge.
> Though Noe thinke us never soe longe,
> yett wee wyll drinke atyte.
> (229–36)

Although the speech is assigned to 'The Good Gossips', the use of the first person singular and the reference to Noah's impatience suggests that Mrs Noah is both speaking and standing with the chorus of gossips. Their speech indicates a habitual gathering of women for some serious drinking. Such gatherings in taverns were warned against in *How the Good Wijf Tauʒte hir Douʒtir*,

> And if þou be in place where good ale is on lofte,
> Wheþer þat þou serue þerof, or þat þou sitte softe,
> Mesurabli þou take þer-of þat þou falle in no blame,
> For if þou be ofte drunke, it falle þee schame;
> Þrift is from hem sunke […].
> (73–79)

Women should be sober as drunkenness led to shame, foolishness and unprofitable behaviour. The *Book of Vices and Virtues* identified the tavern as the Devil's schoolhouse in which men and women learned 'glotonye, lecherie, swere and forswere, to lye and mysseyn, to reneye God and his halewen, and euele rekenynge, gile, and many oþere manere synnes' (fol. 21b, pp.63–64). The gossips suggest that drinking serves another purpose: as a ludic safety-valve for the stresses made by the demands of marriage and life in general. Their celebratory drinking and chatter recalls the lyric in which the ten wives gather in a tavern, to denigrate the size and utility of their husbands' penises. Patriarchy regains control and disperses this subversive female community only by brute force, when her sons forcibly carry their mother onto the ark. Mrs Noah's gossips are left behind to meet their watery fate but their voices have been heard. For Gail McMurray Gibson 'the enclosing human solace of the gossips, though ruled out by biblical plot and official ideology, remains uneasily at issue in the Chester play.'[33] I suggest that in her repeated mention of her gossips, Mrs Noah impresses on the audience the value of female bonding and support. She has lost her gossips but all is not lost for women in the post-diluvian world. This gendered network will be reinstated by the wives of her sons, indeed, this much is hinted at in the offer of companionship made to Mrs Noah by her daughter-in-law in the York play. Mrs Noah's momentary subversion is closed down at the end of

---

33   Gibson, 'Scene and Obscene', p.15.

the play, since both scriptural authority and that of her husband demand the quelling of her disobedience and garrulity. This occurs only after we have heard, as Ruth Evans suggests, a character 'articulate grievances that were beyond those required simply by the allegorical framework [...] [and] begin to speak consciously from a gendered position'.[34]

The carpenter's chaste wife exposes the fraud of popular belief that women's insatiable desire for sex leads them into adultery as night follows day. Both she and the anonymous wife in the *Ballad of a Tyrannical Husband* epitomise those women who find God in their housekeeping. These wives demonstrate the hard work carried out by many women to keep their family fed, clothed and, if at all possible, in profit. The *Ballad of a Tyrannical Husband* reveals just how multi-skilled and hardworking women could be. Mrs Noah's spinning is both emblematic of her disobedience but, as significantly, is shown to be necessary in a family in which the father is a poor provider. Work is an issue for all three wives. Their portrayals reveal its gendered nature and both the wife of the tyrannical husband and Mrs Noah acknowledge women's resentment when men fail to recognise the skills required in carrying out women's work and its importance in keeping the family unit solvent. Mrs Noah's talking back teaches more directly than any sermon or conduct book how to encourage obedience in wives: women's disobedience is connected symbiotically to men's exclusion of them from their lives and the taking of life-changing decisions concerning the family. While many cultural texts reinforce that the husband is rightfully the head of the household, the Noah plays show how marriage fails if a wife is not given opportunity to participate fully.

---

34   Evans, 'Feminist Re-Enactments', p.151.

Conclusion

Having just experienced traumatic labour, Margery Kempe believed herself to be dying and called for a priest (*Book*, Chapter One). As Margery's act reveals, even in the hour of her death a wife remained subject to textual construction. In wishing to make a death-bed confession, Margery followed the prescription for dying well set out in fourteenth century works on the subject, that crystallise in the fifteenth into the *Ars Moriendi*.[1] Her reaction to what she perceived was her imminent demise merits quotation:

> Wherfor, aftyr that hir chyld was born, sche, not trostyng hir lyfe, sent for hir gostly fadyr, [...] in ful wyl to be schrevyn of alle hir lyfetym, as ner sche cowde. And whan sche cam to the poynt for to scyn that thing whech sche had so long conselyd, hir confessowr was a lytyl to hastye and gan scharply to undyrnemyn hir, er than sche had fully seyd hir entente, and so sche wold no mor seyn for nowt he mygth do. And anoon, for dreed sche had of dampnacyon on the to syde, and hys scharp reprevyng on that other syde, this creatur went owt of hir mende and was wondyrlye vexid and labowryd with spyrytys half yer, viii wekys and odde days.
> (*Book*, Chapter 1, 191–201)

Margery wished to follow the male text that defined a good death. This required her to answer, in the affirmative, seven questions asked of the dying by a confessor; if she believed in the articles of faith and holy scripture, knew and acknowledged the manner and frequency with

---

[1] Advice on making a good death appears in a number of guises in the fourteenth and fifteenth centuries. For an overview see P. Ariès, *The Hour of Our Death* (Harmondsworth: Penguin, 1981), pp.130–31; D. F. Duclow, 'Dying Well: The *Ars moriendi* and the Dormition of the Virgin', in *Death and Dying in the Middle Ages*, ed. by E. E. DuBruck and B. I. Gusick (New York: Peter Lang, 1999), pp.379–403 and Christopher Daniell, *Death and Burial in Medieval England 1066–1550* (London: Routledge, 1997), pp.37–38. For an edition of a fifteenth-century text in the *Ars moriendi* tradition see *The Boke of the Craft of Dying* in *Yorkshire Writers: Richard Rolle of Hampole and His Followers*, ed. by C. Horstmann (London: Swan Sonnenschein, 1895), pp.406–20.

which she had sinned, truly repented, had made amends and set aside all earthly things should she live longer, forgave all who had sinned against her and asked forgiveness of those against whom she had offended, forsook all worldly goods, believed that Christ died for her and that his Passion would save her (Myrc, *Instructions for Parish Priests*, fols 21b–22b). These questions were to be considered seriously as the pain of penance was believed more severe than the childbirth that Margery has just experienced (*The Art of Dieing* in the *Book Of Vices and Virtues*, p.73). But Margery failed. She discovered, at this moment of crisis, as in others throughout her life, that she could neither live up to, nor according to, masculine textual authority, since it did not speak to life, or death, as she experienced it. In what she presumed was her final hour, Margery believed that she had fallen short of the male text's expectation of what constituted a good death. Whatever sin it was to which she began to confess, and as stated earlier it is probable that this was some kind of sexual misdemeanour, her confessor anticipated such culpable behaviour from a woman. Pre-emptive in his criticism, he cut short her speech and truncated the completion of her confession. With her own text overwhelmed by male critique, Margery withdrew into silence 'and so sche wold no mor seyn for nowt he mygth do' and post-partum psychosis.

As Margery's *Book* demonstrates so eloquently, every moment lived as a wife was subject to textual construction and some women took this instruction seriously. Behind many of these texts lay the fear of woman's voracious sexuality, that was believed to impact upon her behaviour generally, and the assumption that, while it was not easy to tame women's sexuality, it required controlling. A second assumption was that women could be taught how to be a good wife and that this instruction began at her mother's knee and was perfected by her husband. This was done with the full support of the Church that paraded the holy housewifery and chaste, silent obedience of the Virgin Mary as the wifely exemplar *par excellence*.

Some literary wives marry *in facie ecclesiae*, the manner preferred and promoted by the Church but that, in this period, never entirely ousted clandestine, do-it-yourself affairs. Clandestine weddings continued to be contracted between those who did not have significant wealth to endow or with parents whose desires they wished to circumvent. The church weddings of Mary, Dame Ragnell, the Wife of Bath and May show how, for those who did marry in church, the witnessing of the event and its provision for making public a pre-nuptial agreement protected a bride against claims of the marriage's validity or against her dower rights.

Some literary wives exemplify the virtues of the *mulier fortis* of Proverbs. Griselda is obedience personified. Custance and the Virgin Mary are examples of selfless motherhood who produce the required son and heir. They exhibit the habitual good manners and demure personal conduct as recommended in conduct books. The Wright's wife is chaste and industrious, augmenting her husband's income through intelligent action. These wives are generally happy with their marriages, even Griselda, if we perceive her marriage through her eyes rather than our own. This was no more than the reality for many women. The Paston correspondence provides many examples of the quotidian living of married life in which spouses expressed their affection for each other. Margaret Paston (neè Mauteby), wrote to her husband, John I, to apologise for some matter of trifling importance that she worried had upset him. Written perhaps on 15 October 1453, the letter reiterated her continued commitment to being a dutiful wife, after thirteen years of marriage:

> Be my trowith it is not my will noþer to do ne sey that shuld cawse yow for to be displeased, and if I haue do I am sory ther-of [and will amend itt]; wherefore I beseche yow [to forgeve me and] þat ye bere none hevynesse in yowr hret ayens me, for yowr displeasans shuld be to hevy to me to indure wyth.[2]

This duty was demonstrated practically, in her attempt to source cloth for her husband's livery in the appropriate colour and at the right price, by watching over the running of the estate and keeping her husband informed of events in his absence. Testamentary evidence of their affection for their husbands is discovered in wives' requests to be buried with them. In her will Agnes Paston requested that, if she died in London, she was to be buried 'in the churche of the Blake Freeres by my husband John Haruy'.[3] Affection for a first husband might survive

---

2   Davis, *Paston Letters*, I, letter 148.
3   Davis, *Paston Letters*, II, letter 930.

subsequent marriages. In her will of 1498, Anne, Lady Scrope of Harling, widow of John, Lord Scrope of Bolton, requested that she be buried with her husband; not John, nor with her second, Sir Robert Wingfield, but with her first,

> in the chapelle of Seinte Anne, joined to the chauncell of the churche of the holy Appostellys of Seinte Peter and Paule in Estharlyng, in the tombe w^t my late worshipfull husband, Sir William Chamberleyn, accordyng to my promise made unto hym afore this tyme.[4]

Her fondness for her first husband and their life in East Harling remained with her until the end of her life. But she does not forget her other two spouses: she bequeaths monies for prayers for them all. When considered in relation to the behaviour of some of the literary wives included in this volume, and real women like Margaret and Margery Paston, the Merchant's ironic observation,

> For who kan be so buxom as a wyf?
> Who is so trewe, and eek so ententyf
> To kepe hym, syk and hool, as is his make?
> For wele or wo she wole hym not forsake;
> She nys nat wery hym to love and serve.
> (*Merchant's Tale*, 1287–91)

is a merited accolade.

Of the sex lives of wives who are modest paragons of virtue literature says little but the presumption is that theirs is a passive sexuality. This much is illustrated in the Man of Law's discussion of Custance and Alla's wedding night,

> They goon to bedde, as it were skile and right;
> For thogh that wyves be ful hooly thynges,
> They moste take in pacience at nyght
> Swiche manere necessaries as been plesynges
> To folk that han ywedded hem with rynges,
> And leye a lite hir hoolynesse aside
> As for the tyme – it may no bet bitide.
> (*Man of Law's Tale*, 708–14)

---

4   *Testamenta Eboracensia*, Publications of the Surtees Society, ed. by J. Raine, 53 (Durham: Andrew and Company, 1869), p.149.

The Man of Law presumes a modest reluctance on the part of a young wife, in honouring the marital debt promised in her vow to be 'bonoure and buxom'. He advocates that 'pacience' is the best response to the inevitable. In contrast, many other literary wives play out men's fear of unbridled female sexuality. Their recalcitrant behaviour appears to justify the male sovereignty advocated by culture and supported by both canon and secular law. The Wife of Bath perverts her marriage vow to be 'bonoure and buxom' and May commits adultery, possibly using contraceptive practices to help conceal this. In as much as these literary wives live up to stereotypical assumptions regarding women's voracious sexuality, their words and actions reveal that women have sexual desires of their own and that these are not always satisfied by their husbands. This is especially so when men are interested exclusively in their own sexual satisfaction, giving no thought to that of their spouse. Margery Kempe renounced sexual relations entirely, giving the lie to the assumption that what all women most desire is an erect male phallus.

Many literary wives behave in a manner frowned upon by society. The Wife of Bath and Margery spend their time wandering in public places, conducting themselves in a fashion that was far from the chaste, silent obedience that cultural texts suggested was required of wives. Mrs Noah nags and beats a husband whom she stubbornly refuses to obey. In the Chester play she prefers the company of her all-female drinking crew to that of her spouse and family. Real women did display such faults. The adultery and penchant for alcohol exhibited by May and Mrs Noah respectively, form an explosive combination in Elizabeth Calaber, who was successfully sued for divorce *a mensa et thoro* by her seemingly long-suffering husband, Roger, in the Church Court of the Archdeaconry of Buckingham in 1496.[5] What history does not reveal is why Elizabeth was driven to such behaviour in the first place.

These are the wives who are not happy with their lot and when they speak, their voices at are odds with the dominant discourses of approved wifely conduct. Alisoun's garrulity draws attention to the textual terrorism that sought to constrain and regulate being a wife.

5   Goldberg, *Women in England*, p.143.

Advocating that we listen to the perspective of the lion, Alisoun offers an explanation of women's anti-social behaviour that is so often absent from historical records. Alisoun reveals how women's misbehaviour is symbiotically related to their maltreatment by men that, in turn, stems from the misunderstanding and misrepresentation of women disseminated by patriarchal textual discourses. Mrs Noah's disobedient discourse exemplifies how this was the result of men's exclusion of their wives from their lives.

Mrs Noah's concern for her gossips, that directly contradicts her husband's order to enter the ark, draws attention to the existence and importance of a female network that supported a woman at moments of crisis and joy, from cradle to grave. The consequence of this network is demonstrated in texts other than the Noah plays. Midwives rush to Mary's aid in the Nativity plays and take part with other women in the celebration of Purification. Literature shows women uniting and supporting each other in the face of male aggression, as do the wives in the dénouement of *The Wright's Chaste Wife*. Mrs Noah and the overworked, desperate housewife in *The Ballad of the Tyrannical Husband* valorise women's work and its role in maintaining the family's welfare that was so undervalued by the men in these texts.

Real women found themselves undergoing trial by literature. Margery Kempe acknowledged the damage that a woman might sustain while endeavouring to live up to male textual expectations of wifely behaviour. Her *Book* reveals the inadequacy of the male text to address non-normative female sexuality and spirituality. Margery offers a glimpse of the way in which women's sexuality and sexual orientation might change over time. A desire for intercourse might be replaced by a desire for chastity. Margery reveals that the importance of a female support network is not merely literary convention. Repeatedly, Margery is found in female company, at home and abroad, and in many instances, it is women who respond to her unusual brand of piety. St Paul promised that the act of motherhood brought salvation but having successfully given birth, women were reminded of the post-partum impurity of their bodies in the ritual of the Churching of Women ceremony. Rather than boycott the ceremonies and face the opprobrium of the Church, women embraced their Churching, making it a largely female affair. Margery records how women reclaimed it as a celebration of the power of the female body to reproduce, detecting parallels between their own private ritual and the Virgin Mary's Purification. Where no text existed to validate the kind of wifehood that she wished for, Margery Kempe lived it, taking inspiration from the lives of married female saints. Towards the end of her life, with glorious irony, Margery had her dissonant voice recorded by a servant of the very patriarchal textual hegemony that caused her such grief and loss of self-esteem.

Today, most women who marry choose to do so and exercise the same freedom as men, in selecting a lifetime partner. If the marriage turns out unhappily, for twenty-first century women, unlike her medieval counterparts, divorce is relatively easy to obtain and the high divorce rate indicates that some women neither expect marriage to be 'until death do us part' nor for her first husband to be her last. Unlike her medieval sisters, modern women can control their biology, arresting starting a family or rejecting motherhood entirely, as they choose. Yet twenty-first century wives remain as constructed by patriarchal textual discourses, as their fourteenth and fifteenth century counterparts. The church and state continue to make legal requirements of one's eligibility to marry and the nature and location of the ceremony. Texts, overwhelming in their number and aimed at women, exist to advise future wives what is expected of being a wife and what they can expect from this life-changing event. The media of dissemination are different; glossy magazines, television programmes and the Internet have replaced the sermons, manuals of spiritual instruction and conduct books. The advice, however, remains remarkably similar. Magazine articles divulge how to find one's ideal man (usually dependent upon acquiring the normative body-beautiful espoused by men). Bridal journals recommend how to achieve the perfect wedding day, offering advice on the dress and reception. Once married, endless self-help books instruct a woman how to keep her husband (that is, how to satisfy his sexual needs) and maintain marital bliss while juggling children (many remain the primary child carer), paid work (that still often attracts less financial remuneration and kudos than that of their husbands) and running the home. Two impulses drive this phenomenal textual output. One is the presumption that being the perfect wife is a desirable goal for many women and their husbands, and the second is that such skills can be learned from the multiplicity of texts offering instruction. Undoubtedly, some women choose to ignore it but many others strive to follow this advice and become the textual fantasy, often at the expense of their self-esteem. It seems that the past is not always history, or even past.

Bibliography

Primary Sources

Baker, D. C., J. L. Murphy and L. B. Hall, eds., *The Late Medieval Religious Plays of Bodleian MSS Digby and E Museo* 160, EETS 283 (Oxford: Oxford University Press, 1982)

Barratt, A. ed., *The Knowing of Woman's Kind in Childing: A Middle English Version of Material Derived from the Trotula and Other Sources* (Brepols: Turnhout, 2001)

——, ed., *Women's Writing in Middle English* (London: Longman, 1992)

Beadle, R., ed., *The York Plays* (London: Arnold, 1982)

Benson, L. D., ed., *The Riverside Chaucer* (Oxford: Oxford University Press, 1987)

Brandeis, A., ed., *Jacob's Well: An Englisht treatise on the Cleansing on Man's Conscience*, EETS OS 115 (London: Kegan Paul, Trench, Trübner, 1900)

Clopper, L. M., ed., *REED: Chester* (Toronto, Buffalo: University of Toronto Press, 1979)

Carpenter, C., ed., *Kingsford's Stonor Letters and Papers 1290–1483* (Cambridge: Cambridge University Press, 1994)

Comper, F. M. M., ed., *Spiritual Songs from English MSS of the Fourteenth to Sixteenth Centuries* (London: Macmillan, 1936)

Craig, H., ed., *Two Coventry Corpus Christi Plays*, EETS ES 87 (London: Oxford University Press, 1957)

Davies, R. T., ed., *Medieval English Lyrics* (London: Faber & Faber, reprint 1981)

Davis, N., ed., *Non-Cycle Plays and Fragments*, EETS Supplementary Text 1 (London: Oxford University Press, 1970)

——, ed., *Paston Letters and Papers of the Fifteenth Century*, 2 Parts, EETS SS 20 and 21 (Oxford: Oxford University Press, 2004)

Delaney, P., 'Constantinus Africanus' *De Coitu*: A Translation', *Chaucer Review*, 4.1 (1969), 55–65

D'Evelyn, C., ed., *Peter Idley's Instructions to his Son*, Modern Language Association of America, Monograph Series 6 (Boston: D.C. Heath and Company, 1935)

Dickinson, F. H., ed., *Missale ad Usum Insignis et Praeclarae Ecclesiae Sarum* (Oxford and London: J. Parker & Soc., 1861–83, republished 1969)

Elliott, J. K., ed. and trans., *The Apocryphal New Testament: A Collection of Apocryphal Christian Literature in an English Translation* (Oxford: Clarendon Press, 1993)

Erbe, T. ed., *Mirk's Festial: a Collection of Homilies by Johannes Mirkus (John Mirk)*, Part 1, EETS ES 96 (London: Kegan Paul, Trench, Trübner, 1905)

Fleischhacker, R., ed., *Lanfrank's Science of Cirurgie, Part 1*, EETS OS 102 (London: Kegan Paul, Trench, Trübner, 1894)

Francis, W. N., ed., *The Book of Vices and Virtues: A Fourteenth century English Translation of the Somme Le Roi of Lorens d'Orleans*, EETS OS 217 (London: Oxford University Press, 1942, reprint 1968)

Furnivall, F. J., ed., *Robert Mannying of Brunne's Handlyng Synne*, EETS OS 119 (Washington DC: Microcard Editions, 1964)

——, ed., *The Babees Book*, EETS OS 32 (London: Trübner, 1868)

——, ed., *The Fifty Earliest English Wills in The Court of Probate, London, AD 1387–1439*, EETS OS 78 (London: Oxford University Press, 1882, reprint 1964)

——, ed., *The Wright's Chaste Wife*, EETS OS 12 (London: N. Trübner, 1865)

Gradon, P., ed., *Dan Michel's Ayenbite of Inwyt or Remorse of Conscience*, EETS OS 23 (London: Oxford University Press, 1866, reissued 1965)

Graesse, J. G. T., ed., *Jacobus de Voragine Legenda aurea vulgo historia lombardica dicta* (Leipzig: Arnold, 1846)

Gransden, A., ed., *The Letter-Book of William of Hoo Sacrist of Bury St Edmunds 1280–1294*, Suffolk Records Society, 5 (1963)

Hanna III, R. and T. Lawler, eds., *Jankyn's Book of Wikked Wyves. Volume I: The Primary Texts* (Athens: The University of Georgia Press, 1997)

Heath, T. R., trans., *Thomas Aquinas Summa Theologiae: Latin Text with English Translation, Our Lady*, 51 (London: Eyre & Spottiswode, 1969)

Horstmann, C., ed., *Yorkshire Writers: Richard Rolle of Hampole and His Followers* (London: Swan Sonnenschein, 1895)

Ingram, R. W., ed., *REED: Coventry* (Toronto, Buffalo: University of Toronto Press, 1981)

James, M. R., ed. and trans., *Walter Map De Nugis Curialium: Courtiers Trifles* (Oxford: Clarendon Press, 1983)

Konrath, M., ed., *The Poems of William of Shoreham. Part I. Preface, Introduction, Text and Notes*, EETS ES 86 (London: Kegan Paul, Trench, Trübner, 1902)

Littlehales, H., ed., *English Fragments from Latin Medieval Service-Books*, EETS ES 90 (London: Kegan Paul, Trench, Trübner, 1903)

Lumiansky, R. M. and D. Mills, eds., *The Chester Mystery Cycle*, Volume One: Text, EETS SS 3 (London: Oxford University Press, 1974)

Mayor, J. E. B., ed., *The English Works of John Fisher, Bishop of Rochester (1459–1535)*, Part I, EETS ES 27 (London: N. Trübner, 1876)

Meredith, P., ed., *The Mary Play From the N.town Manuscript* (London: Longman and New York, 1987)

Monfrin, J., ed., *Abélard: Historia Calamitatum* (Paris: Librarie Philosophique J. Vrin, 1959)

Morris, R., ed., *Cursor Mundi (The cursor of the World). A Northumbrian poem of the fifteenth century in four versions*, EETS OS 57, 99, 101 (Volume I) and 59, 62 (Volume 2) (London: Oxford University Press, 1874–93)

Ogden, M. S., ed., *The Cyrurgie of Guy de Chauliac*, EETS 265 (London: Oxford University Press, 1971)

Parker, R. E., ed., *The Middle English Stanzaic Versions of the Life of St Anne*, EETS OS 174 (London: Oxford University Press, 1928)

Peacock, E., ed., *Instructions for Parish Priests by John Myrc*, EETS 31 (London: Trübner, 1868)

Peltier, A. C., ed., *S.R.E. Cardinalis Bonaventura Opera Omnia*, 12 (Paris, [n.p.], 1868)

Perry, G. G., ed., *Religious Pieces in Prose and Verse*, EETS OS 26 (London: N. Trübner, 1917)

Radice, B., ed, and trans., *The Letters of Abelard and Heloise* (Harmondsworth: Penguin, 1973)

Raine, J., ed., *Testamenta Eboracensia*, Publications of the Surtees Society, 4 (Durham: Andrew and Company, 1869)

Robbins, R. H., ed., *Secular Lyrics of the XIVth and XVth Centuries* (Oxford: Clarendon Press, 1952, reprint 1961)

Rowland, B., trans., *Medieval Women's Guide to Health: The First English Gynecological Handbook* (Kent: The Kent State University Press, 1981)

Ryan, W. G., trans., *Jacobus de Voragine: The Golden Legend. Readings on the Saints*, 2 vols (Princeton, NJ: Princeton University Press, 1993)

Salisbury, E., ed., *The Trials and Joys of Marriage*, TEAMS Middle English Text Series (Kalamazoo, Michigan: Medieval Institute Publications, 2002)

Sands, D. B., ed., *Middle English Verse Romances* (Exeter: University of Exeter Press, 1986)

Sargent, M. G., ed., *Nicholas Love The Mirror of the Blessed Life of Jesus Christ: A Reading Text* (Exeter: Exeter University Press, 2004)

Sarjeantson, M., ed., *Legendys of Hooly Wummen*, EETS OS 206 (Oxford: Oxford University Press, 1938, reprint 1971)

Sherley-Price, L., ed. and trans., *Bede, A History of the English Church and People* (Harmondsworth: Penguin, 1955, reprint 1983)

Smith, T. and L. T. Smith, eds., *English Guilds*, EETS 40 (Oxford: Oxford University Press, 1870)

Spector, S., ed., *The N-Town Play: Cotton MS Vespasian D. 8.*, 2 vols, EETS SS 11 and 12 (Oxford: Oxford University Press, 1991)

Stevens, M. and A. C. Cawley, eds., *The Towneley Plays*, Volume One: Introduction and Text, EETS SS 13 (London: Oxford University Press, 1994)

Talbot, C. H., ed., *The Life of Christina of Markyate: A Twelfth Century Recluse* (Oxford: Clarendon Press, 1959)

Tanner, N. P., ed., *Decrees of the Ecumenical Councils. Volume I (Nicaeai–Lateran V)* (London: Sheed & Ward, Washington, Georgetown University Press, 1990)

The Publications of the Surtees Society, 63 (1874)

Tischendorf, C., ed., *Evangelia Apocrypha* (Avenarius et Mendessolin, 1853)

Tymms, S., *Wills and Inventories from the Registers of the Commissary of Bury St Edmunds and the Archdeacon of Sudbury*, Camden Society Series 1, 49 (London: J. B. Nicholls and Son, 1850)

Vinaver, E., ed., *Malory Works* (Oxford: Oxford University Press, 1983)

Warren, F., trans., *The Sarum Missal in English, Part II* (London: Alexander Moring Ltd. The De La More Press, 1911)

Weaver, F. W., ed., *Somerset Medieval Wills (Second Series) 1501–1530 with some Somerset Wills preserved at Lambeth*, Somerset Record Society, 19 (London: Printed for the Subscribers only, 1903)

Weber, R. et al., eds., *Biblia Sacra iuxta Vulgatam Versionem*, 2 vols (Stuttgart: Württembergische Bibelanstalt, 1969)

Windeatt, B. A., ed., *The Book of Margery Kempe* (London: Pearson Education, 2000)

Withrington, J., ed., *The Wedding of Sir Gawain and Dame Ragnell*, Lancaster Modern Spelling Texts, 2 (Lancaster: The University of Lancaster, 1991)

Wright, T., ed., *The Book of the Knight of La Tour-Landry*, EETS OS 33 (London: Kegan Paul, Trench, Trübner, 1868, revised edition, 1906)
——, collected and ed., *The Latin Poems commonly attributed to Walter Mapes* (London: The Camden Society, 1841)

Secondary Sources

Anderson, M. D, *Misericords* (Harmondsworth: Penguin, 1954)
——, *The Choir Stalls of Lincoln Minster* (The Friends of Lincoln Cathedral, 1967)
Ariès, P., *The Hour of Our Death*, trans. by Helen Weaver (Harmondsworth: Penguin, 1981)
Armstrong, N. and L. Tennenhouse, eds., *The Ideology of Conduct: Essays in Literature and the History of Sexuality* (London: Methuen, 1987)
Arnold, J. H. and K. J. Lewis, eds., *A Companion to the Book of Margery Kempe* (Cambridge: D. S. Brewer, 2004)
Ashley, K., 'Medieval Courtesy literature and dramatic mirrors of female conduct', in Armstrong and Tennenhouse, pp. 25–38
—— and P. Sheingorn, eds., *Interpreting Cultural Symbols: Saint Anne in Late Medieval Society* (Athens: The University of Georgia Press, 1990)
Atkinson, C., *The Oldest Vocation: Christian Motherhood in the Middle Ages* (Ithaca: Cornell University Press, 1991)
Axton, R., *European Drama of the Early Middle Ages* (London: Hutchinson University Library, 1974)
Baildon, W. P., 'The Trousseau of Princess Philippa, Wife of Eric, King of Denmark, Norway, and Sweden', *Archaeologia*, 67 (1915–16), 163–88
Barron, C. M., *Medieval Women in Southern England*, Reading Medieval Studies, 15 (1989)
Barron, C. M. and A. F. Sutton, eds., *Medieval London Widows 1300–1500* (London: Hambledon Press, 1994)
Beckwith, S., *Christ's Body: Identity, Culture and Society in Late Medieval Writings* (London: Routledge, 1993)
Beidler, P., ed., *Geoffrey Chaucer: The Wife of Bath* (Boston: Bedford Books, 1996)

Bennett, A., 'The Recalcitrant Wife in the Ramsey Abbey Psalter', at http://www.umilta.net/equally.html

Bennett, B. T. N., *The Choir Stalls of Chester Cathedral* (Chester: S. G. Mason, [n.d.])

Bennett, J. M., 'The tie that binds: peasant marriage and families in late medieval England', *Journal of Interdisciplinary History*, 15.1 (Summer, 1984), 111–29

Bernau, A., S. Salih and R. Evans eds., *Medieval Virginities* (Cardiff: University of Wales Press, 2003)

Biscoglio, F. M., *The Wives of the Canterbury Tales and The Tradition of the Valiant Woman of Proverbs 31: 10–31* (San Francisco: Mellen Research University Press, 1993)

Blake, N. F., *Middle English Prose* (London: Edward Arnold, 1972)

Blamires, A., *The Case for Women in Culture* (Oxford: Clarendon Press, 1997)

——, ed., *Woman Defamed and Woman Defended* (Oxford: Clarendon Press, 1992)

Blumenfeld-Kosinski, R., *Not of Woman Born: Representations of Caesarean Birth in Medieval and Renaissance Culture* (Ithaca: Cornell University Press, 1990)

Bronfman, J., *Chaucer's Clerk's Tale: The Griselda Story Received, Rewritten, Illustrated* (New York: Garland, 1994)

Brooke, C., *The Medieval Idea of Marriage* (Oxford: Clarendon Press, 1989)

Brown, P., *The Body and Society. Men, Women and Sexual Renunciation in Early Christianity* (New York: Columbia University Press, 1988)

Brown, S. and L. MacDonald, eds., *Life, Death and Art: the medieval stained glass of Fairford Parish Church* (Stroud: Sutton, 1997)

Brundage, J. A., *Law, Sex and Christian Society in Medieval Europe* (Chicago: University of Chicago Press, 1987)

——, *Medieval Canon Law* (London: Longman, 1995)

——, 'Sex and Canon Law', in Bullough and Brundage, *Handbook of Medieval Sexuality*, pp.33–50

Burns, E. J., *Bodytalk: When Women Speak in Old French Literature* (Philadelphia: University of Pennsylvania Press, 1993)

Bullough, V. and J. A. Brundage, eds., *Handbook of Medieval Sexuality* (New York and London: Garland, 1996)

—— and J. A. Brundage, eds., *Sexual Practices and the Medieval Church* (Buffalo, NY: Prometheus Books, 1982)

Cadden, J., 'It Takes all Kinds: Sexuality and Gender Differences in Hildegard of Bingen's Book of Compound Medicine', *Traditio*, 40 (1984), 149–74
——, *Meanings of Sex Difference in the Middle Ages: Medicine, Science, and Culture* (Cambridge: Cambridge University Press, 1993)
Carruthers, M., 'The Wife of Bath and the painting of lions', in Evans and Johnson, pp.22–38
Cartlidge, N., *Medieval Marriage: Literary Approaches, 1100–1300* (Cambridge: D. S. Brewer, 1997)
Catto, J. I. & R. Evans, eds., *The History of the University of Oxford, Volume II: Late Medieval Oxford* (Oxford: Clarendon Press, 1992)
Coletti, T., 'Genealogy, Sexuality, and Sacred Power: The Saint Anne Dedication of the Digby *Candelmas Day and the Killing of the Children of Israel*', *Journal of Medieval and Early Modern Studies*, 29.1 (Winter 1999), 25–59
——, 'Purity and Danger: The Paradox of Mary's Body and the Engendering of the infancy Narrative in the English Mystery Cycles', in Lomperis and Stanbury, pp.65–95
Cooper, H., *Oxford Guides to Chaucer: The Canterbury Tales* (Oxford: Oxford University Press, 1989)
Cosgrove, A., 'Consent, consummation and indissolubility: Some evidence from medieval ecclesiastical courts', *Downside Review*, 109 (1991), 94–104
Cosman, M. P., *Fabulous Feasts: Medieval Cookery and Ceremony* (New York: George Braziller, 1976)
Coss, P., *The Medieval Lady in England 1000–1500* (Stroud: Sutton, 1998)
Crawford, A., ed., *Letters of the Queens of England* (Stroud: Sutton, 1994)
Daniell, C., *Death and Burial in Medieval England 1066–1550* (London: Routledge, 1997)
Delany, S., trans., *A Legend of Holy Women: Osbern Bokenham Legends of Holy Women* (Notre Dame: University of Notre Dame Press, 1992)
——, 'Sexual economics, Chaucer's Wife of Bath and The Book of Margery Kempe', in Evans and Johnson, pp.72–87
Denny, N., ed., *Medieval Drama*, Stratford-Upon-Avon Studies, 16 (London: Edward Arnold, 1973)
Dickinson, J. C., *The Shrine of Our Lady of Walsingham* (Cambridge: Cambridge University Press, 1956)
Dillan, J., 'Holy Women and their Confessors or Confessors and the Holy Women? Margery Kempe and Continental Tradition', in Voaden, pp.115–40

Dinshaw, C. and D. Wallace, eds., *The Cambridge Companion to Medieval Women's Writing* (Cambridge: Cambridge University Press, 2003)

Donahue Jnr., C., 'Female Plaintiffs in Marriage Cases in the Court of York in the Later Middle Ages: What Can We Learn from the Number?' in Walker, pp.166-83

Dor, J., ed., *A Wyf Ther Was: Essays in Honour of Paule Mertens-Fonck* (Liège: University of Liège, 1992)

DuBruck, E. E. and B. I. Gusick, eds., *Death and Dying in the Middle Ages* (New York: Peter Lang, 1999)

Duclow, D. F., 'Dying Well: The Ars moriendi and the Dormition of the Virgin', in DuBruck and Gusick, pp.379-403

Duffy, E., 'Holy Maydens, Holy Wyfes: The Cult of Women Saints in Fifteenth- and Sixteenth-Century England', *Studies in Church History*, 27 (1990), 175-96

——, *The Stripping of the Altars. Traditional Religion in England 1400-1580* (New Haven: Yale University Press, 1992)

Egan, G. and F. Pritchard, *Dress Accessories c. 1150-c. 1450: Finds from Excavations in London* (London: HMSO, 1991)

Elliott, D., *Spiritual Marriage: Sexual Abstinence in Medieval Wedlock* (Princeton: Princeton University Press, 1993)

Ensler, E., *The Vagina Monologues* (London: Virago Press, 2001)

Evans, R., 'Feminist Re-Enactments: Gender and the Towneley Uxor Noe', in Dor, pp.141-54

—— and L. Johnson, eds., *Feminist Readings in Middle English Literature: The Wyf of Bath and all her Sect* (London: Routledge, 1994)

Fanous, S., 'Measuring the Pilgrim's Progress: Emphases in The Book of Margery Kempe', in Reveney and Whitehead, pp.157-76

Fleming, P., *Family and Household in Medieval England* (Basingstoke: Palgrave, 2001)

Fradenburg, L. & C. Freccero, eds., *Premodern Sexualities* (London: Routledge, 1996)

Franklin, M. J., '"Fyngres Heo Haþ Feir to Folde": Trothplight in some of the Love Lyrics of MS Harley 2253', *Medium Aevum*, 55.1 (1986), 176-87

French, R., et al, eds., *Medicine from the Black Death to the French Disease* (Aldershot: Ashgate, 1998)

Gibson, G. McMurray, 'Blessing from Sun and Moon: Churching as Women's Theater', in Hanawalt and Wallace, pp.139-54

——, 'Saint Anne and the Religion of Childbed: Some East Anglian Texts and Talismans', in Ashley and Sheingorn, pp.95-110

———, 'Scene and Obscene: Seeing and Performing Late Medieval Childbirth', *Journal of Medieval and Early Modern Studies*, 29:1 (Winter 1999), 7–24

———, *The Theater of Devotion: East Anglian Drama and Society in the Late Middle Ages* (Chicago: The University of Chicago Press, 1989)

Glasser, M., 'Marriage in Medieval Hagiography', *Studies in Medieval and Renaissance History*, 4 (1987), 3–34

Godfrey, W. H., *Transcripts of Sussex Wills*, 2, Sussex Records Society, 42 (1937)

Goldberg, P. J. P., trans. and ed., *Women in England c. 1275–1525: Documentary Sources* (Manchester: Manchester University Press, 1995)

Goodman, A., *Margery Kempe and Her World* (London: Pearson Education, 2002)

Graves, R., *Born to Procreate: Women and Childbirth in France from the Middle Ages to the Eighteenth Century* (New York: Peter Lang, 2001)

Green, M., 'Female Sexuality in the Medieval West', *Trends in History*, 4.4 (1990), 127–58

———, 'From "Diseases of Women" to "Secrets of Women": The Transformation of Gynecological Literature in the Later Middle Ages', *Journal of Medieval and Early Modern Studies*, 30.1 (Winter 2000), 5–39

———, 'Obstetrical and Gynecological Texts in Middle English', *Studies in the Age of Chaucer*, 14 (1992), 53–88

———, *The Trotula: A Medieval Compendium of Women's Medicine* (Penn, Philadephia: University of Pennsylvania Press, 2001)

———, *Women's Healthcare in the Medieval West: Texts and Contexts* (Aldershot: Ashgate Variorum, 2000)

———, 'Women's Medical Practice and Health Care in Medieval Europe', *Signs: Journal of Women in Culture and Society*, 14.2 (1989), 434–73

Hall, E., *The Arnolfi Bethrothal: Medieval Marriage and the Enigma of Van Eyck's Double Portrait* (Berkeley: University of California Press, 1994)

Hallissy, M., *Clean Maids, True Wives, Steadfast Widows: Chaucer's Women and Medieval Codes of Conduct* (Westport: Greenwood Press, 1993)

Hanawalt, B., 'Marriage as an Option for Urban and Rural Widows in Late Medieval England', in Walker, pp.141–64

———, *'Of Good and Ill Repute': Gender and Social Control in Medieval England* (Oxford: Oxford University Press, 1998)

———, *The Ties that Bound: Peasant Families in Medieval England* (Oxford: Oxford University Press, 1986)

—— and D. Wallace, eds., *Bodies and Disciplines: Intersections of Literature and History in Fifteenth-Century England* (Minneapolis: University of Minnesota Press, 1996)

Hansen, E. Tuttle, *Chaucer and the Fictions of Gender* (Oxford: University of Oxford Press, 1992)

Harding, W., 'Body into Text: The Book of Margery Kempe', in Lomperis and Stanbury, pp.168–87

Harford, G., M. Stevenson et al, eds., *The Prayer Book Dictionary* (London: The Waverley Book Company, 1912)

Hassig, D., ed., *The Mark of the Beast: The Medieval Bestiary in Art, Life, and Literature* (New York: Garland, 1999)

Helmholz, R. H., *Marriage Litigation in Medieval England* (Cambridge: Cambridge University Press, 1974)

Hodges, L. F., 'Noe's Wife: Type of Eve and Wakefield Spinner', at http://www.umilta.net/equally.html

Holloway, J., J Bolton, J. Bechtold, C. S. Wright, eds., *Equally in God's Image: Women in the Middle Ages* (New York: Peter Lang, 1990) and at http://www.umilta.net/equally.html

Howes, L. L., 'On the Birth of Margery Kempe's Last Child', *Modern Philology*, 90 (1992), 220–25

Hunt, T., *Popular Medicine in Thirteenth Century England: Introduction and Texts* (Woodbridge: D. S. Brewer, 1990)

Jacobs, K., *Marriage Contracts from Chaucer to the Renaissance Stage* (Gainesville: University Press of Florida, 2001)

Jacquart, D. and C. Thomasset, *Sexuality and Medicine in the Middle Ages* (Princeton: Princeton University Press, 1988)

Jewell, H., *Women in Medieval England* (Manchester: Manchester University Press, 1996)

Johnson, L., 'Reincarnations of Griselda: Contexts for the Clerk's Tale?', in Evans and Johnson, pp.195–220

Jones, P. M., 'Thomas Fayreford: An English Fifteenth-Century Medical Practitioner', in French, pp.156–83

Justman, S., 'Trade as Pudendum: Chaucer's Wife of Bath', *Chaucer Review*, 28.4 (1994), 434–52

Karras, R. Mazo, *Common Women: Prostitution and Sexuality in Medieval England* (Oxford: Oxford University Press, 1996)

Kelly, H. A., *Love and Marriage in the Age of Chaucer* (Ithaca, NY: Cornell University Press, 1975)

Kline, D. T., 'Female childhoods', in Dinshaw and Wallace, pp.13–20

Kolve, V. A., *Chaucer and the Imagery of Narrative: The First Five Canterbury Tales* (London: Edward Arnold, 1984)
Kunz, G. F., *Rings for the Finger* (Philadelphia: J. B. Lippincott Company, 1917)
Laqueur, T., *Making Sex: Body and Gender from the Greeks to Freud* (Cambridge, Mass: Harvard University Press, 1990)
Larson-Miller, L., ed., *Medieval Liturgy: A Book of Essays* (New York: Garland, 1997)
Laskaya, A., *Chaucer's Approach to Gender in the Canterbury Tales* (Cambridge: D. S. Brewer, 1995)
Lavezzo, K., 'Sobs and Sighs Between Women: The Homoerotics of Compassion in The Book of Margery Kempe', in Fradenburg and Freccero, pp.175–98
Lee, B. R., 'The Purification of Women After Childbirth: A Window Onto Medieval Perceptions of Women', *Florilegium*, 14 (1995–6), 43–55
Lemay, H. Rodnite, 'A Medieval Physician's Guide to Virginity', in Salisbury, *Sex in the Middle Ages*, pp.56–79
——, 'Some Thirteenth and Fourteenth Century Lectures on Female Sexuality', *International Journal of Women's Studies*, 1.4 (1978), 391–400
——, *Women's Secrets: A Translation of Pseudo-Albertus Magnus's 'De Secretis Mulierum' with 'Commentaries'* (Albany, NY: SUNY Press, 1992)
Leonard, J. K., 'Rites of Marriage in the Western Middle Ages', in Larson-Miller, pp.165–202
Lerner, G., *The Creation of Feminist Consciousness From the Middle Ages to Eighteen-Seventy* (Oxford: Oxford University Press, 1993)
Little Dunmow Priory. A Brief History and Guide to the Parish Church Today ([n.p.], [n.d.])
Llewellyn, R. H., '"The Wright's Chaste Wife" Disinterred', *Southern Folklore Quarterly*, 16 (1952), 251–54
Lochrie, K., 'The Book of Margery Kempe: The Marginal Woman's Quest for Literary Authority', *Journal of Medieval and Renaissance Studies*, 16 (Spring 1986), 35–55
Lomperis, L. and S. Stanbury, eds., *Feminist Approaches to the Body in Medieval Literature* (Philadelphia: University of Pennsylvania Press, 1993)
Mann, J., *Geoffrey Chaucer* (London: Harvester Wheatsheaf, 1991)
Marks, R. and P. Williamson, eds., *Gothic: Art for England 1400–1547* (London: V&A Publications, 2003)

Martin, P., *Chaucer's Women: Nuns, Wives and Amazons* (London: Macmillan, 1990, reprint 1996)

Maskell, J., *The Wedding-Ring: Its History, Literature, and the Superstitions Respecting It* (London: H. Parr, 1888)

Mate, M., *Daughters, Wives and Widows after the Black Death: Women in Sussex, 1350–1530* (Woodbridge: Suffolk, 1998)

——, *Women in Medieval English Society* (Cambridge: Cambridge University Press, 1999)

McAvoy, L. Herbert, *Authority and the Female Body in the Writings of Julian of Norwich and Margery Kempe* (Cambridge: D. S. Brewer, 2004)

McCarthy, C., ed., *Love, Sex and Marriage in the Middle Ages: A Sourcebook* (London: Routledge, 2004)

——, *Marriage in Medieval England: Law, Literature and Practice* (Woodbridge: The Boydell Press, 2004)

McGlynne, M. and R. J. Moll, 'Chaste Marriage in the Middle Ages: "It were to hire a greet Merite"', in Bullough and Brundage, *Handbook of Medieval Sexuality*, pp.103–22

McSheffrey, S., *Love and Marriage in Late Medieval London* (Kalamazoo, Michigan: Medieval Institute Publications, Western Michigan University, 1995)

Mulder-Bakker, A. B., ed., *Sanctity and Motherhood: Essays on Holy Mothers in the Middle Ages*, Garland Medieval Casebooks, 14 (New York: Garland, 1995)

Murray, J. and K. Eisenbichler, eds., *Desire and Discipline: Sex and Sexuality in the Premodern West* (Toronto: University of Toronto Press, 1996)

Muscatine, C., *The Old French Fabliaux* (New Haven and London: Yale University Press, 1986)

Nelson, A. H., *The Medieval English Stage* (Chicago: The University of Chicago Press, 1974)

Norri, J., *Names of Body Parts in English, 1400–1550* (Helsinki: Finnish Academy of Science and Letters, 1998)

O'Connor, E. D., ed., *The Dogma of the Immaculate Conception: History and Significance* (Notre Dame, Indiana: University of Notre Dame Press, 1958)

Orange, J. and L. Briggs, *St Botolph's Parish Church, Boston: The Misericords* (Much Wenlock: RJL Smith & Associates, [n.d.])

Owst, G. R., *Literature and Pulpit in Medieval England* (Oxford: Basil Blackwell, 1961)

Parsons, J. Carmi, ed., *Medieval Queenship* (Stroud: Sutton, 1994)

——, 'Mothers, Daughters, Marriage, Power: Some Plantagenet Evidence, 1150–1500', in Parsons, pp.63–78

Patterson, L., '"Experience woot well it is noght so": Marriage and the Pursuit of Happiness in the Wife of Bath's Prologue and Tale', in Beidler, pp.133–54

Payer, P. J., *The Bridling of Desire: Views of Sex in the Later Middle Ages* (Toronto, Buffalo: University of Toronto Press, 1993)

Pedersen, F., *Romeo and Juliet of Stonegate: a medieval marriage in crisis*, Paper 87 (York: Borthwick Institute of Historical Research, University of York, 1995)

Phillips, H., *An Introduction to The Canterbury Tales: reading, fiction, context* (Basingstoke: Macmillan Press, 2000)

Phillips, K. M., 'Margery Kempe and the Ages of Woman', in Arnold and Lewis, pp.17–34

——, *Medieval Maidens: Young Women and gender in England, 1270–1540* (Manchester: Manchester University Press, 2003)

Phillipps, T., 'Account of the Ceremonial of the Marriage of the Princess Margaret, sister of King Edward the Fourth, to Charles, Duke of Burgundy, in 1468', *Archaeologia*, 31 (1846), 326–38

Platt, C., *The Parish Churches of Medieval England* (London: Chancellor Press, 1995)

Pollock, F. and F. Maitland, *History of English Law Before the Time of Edward I*, 2nd ed, 1 (Cambridge: Cambridge University Press, 1911)

Poos, L. R., 'Sex, Lies and the Church Courts of Pre-Reformation England', *Journal of Interdisciplinary History*, 25.4 (Spring 1995), 585–607

Rastall, R., *The Heaven Singing: Music in Early English Religious Drama*, vol 1 (Cambridge: D. S. Brewer, 1996, reprint 1999)

Reuther, R. Radford, ed., *Religion and Sexism: Images of Women in the Jewish and Christian Traditions* (New York: Simon and Schuster, 1974)

Reveney, D. and C. Whitehead, eds., *Writing Religious Women: Female Spiritual and Textual Practices in Late Medieval England* (Cardiff: University of Wales Press, 2000)

Reynolds, P. Lyndon, *Marriage in the Western Church: The Christianisation of Marriage During the Patristic and Early Medieval Periods* (Leiden: E. J. Brill, 1994)

——, 'Marriage, Sacramental and Indissoluble: Sources of the Catholic Doctrine', *Downside Review*, 109 (1991), 105–50

Richards, M. P., 'A Middle English Prayer to Ease Childbirth', *Notes and Queries*, n.s. 27.3 (1980), 292

Riddle, J., *Contraception and Abortion from the Ancient World to the Renaissance* (Cambridge, Mass. and London: Harvard University Press, 1992)

——, 'Contraception and Early Abortion in the Middle Ages', in Bullough and Brundage, pp.261–77

Riddy, F., 'Mother Knows Best: Reading Social Change in a Courtesy Text', *Speculum*, 71 (1996) 66–86

Rigg, A. G., *A Glastonbury Miscellany of the Fifteenth Century: A Descriptive Index of Trinity College, Cambridge MS. O. 9. 38* (Oxford: Oxford University Press, 1968)

Rolleston, J., 'Penis Captivus: A Historical Note', in Salisbury, *Sex in the Middle Ages*, pp.232–36

Rosenthal, J. T., 'Fifteenth-Century Widows and Widowhood: Bereavement, Reintegration, and Life Choices', in Walker, pp.33–58

Salisbury, J., 'Gendered Sexuality', in Bullough and Brundage, *Handbook of Medieval Sexuality*, pp.81–102

——, ed., *Sex in the Middle Ages: A Book of Essays* (New York: Garland, 1991)

Saunders, C., *Rape and Ravishment in the Literature of Medieval England* (Woodbridge: D. S. Brewer, 2001)

Schaff, P., ed., *A Select Library of the Nicene and Post-Nicene Fathers of the Christian Church*, 2, St Augustine (Michigan: Wm. B. Eerdmans, reprint 1978)

Shahar, S., *Growing Old in the Middle Ages: Winter Clothes Us in Shadow and Pain* (London: Routledge, 1997)

Sheehan, M., 'The Formation and Stability of Marriage in Fourteenth-Century England: Evidence from an Ely Register', *Medieval Studies*, 33 (1971), 228–63

Sheingorn, P., 'Appropriating the Holy Kinship', in Ashley and Sheingorn, pp.169–98

Siraisi, N., *Medieval & Early Renaissance Medicine: An Introduction to Knowledge and Practice* (Chicago and London: The University of Chicago Press, 1990)

Stapleton, T., 'A brief Summary of the Wardrobe Accounts of the tenth, eleventh and fourteenth years of King Edward the Second', *Archaeologia*, 26 (1836), 318–45

Starr, R. W., *The Wedding Ring: Its History and Mystery* (London: S. W. Partridge, 1896)

Stevenson, K., *Nuptial Blessing: A Study of Christian Marriage Rites* (New York: Oxford University Press, 1983)

Straus, B. R., 'Freedom through Renunciation? Women's Voices, Women's Bodies, and the Phallic Order', in Murray and Eisenbichler, pp.245–64

Tatlock, J. S. P., 'The Marriage Service in Chaucer's Merchant's Tale', *Modern Language Notes*, 32 (1917), 373–74

Tavormina, M. T., *Kindly Similitude: Marriage and Family in Piers Plowman* (Woodbridge: D. S. Brewer, 1995)

Tolmie, J., 'Mrs Noah and Didactic Abuses,' *Early Theatre*, 5.1 (2002), 11–35

Tristram E. W. and M. R. James, 'Wall-paintings in Croughton Church, Northamptonshire', *Archaeologia*, 76 (1926–7), 179–204

Twycross, M., 'Beyond the Picture Theory: Image and Activity in Medieval Drama', *Word and Image*, 4 (1988), 589–617

Voaden, R., ed., *Prophets Abroad: The Reception of Continental Holy Women in Late-Medieval England* (Cambridge: D. S. Brewer, 1996)

Vriend, J., *The Blessed Virgin Mary in the Medieval Drama of England* (Purmerend: J. Muusses, 1928)

Walker, S. Sheridan, ed., *Wife and Widow in Medieval England* (Ann Arbor, Michigan: The University of Michigan Press, 1993)

Ward, J. C., *English Noblewomen in the Later Middle Ages* (London: Longman, 1992)

Warner, M., *Alone of All Her Sex: The Myth and Cult of the Virgin Mary* (London: Picador, 1976, reprint 1988)

——, *From the Beast to the Blonde: On Fairy Tales and Their Tellers* (London: Vintage, 1995)

Waterton, E., *Pietas Mariana Britannica: A History of English Devotion to the Most Blessed Virgin Marye Mother of God* (London: St Joseph's Catholic Library, 1879)

Wayment, H., *The Stained Glass of the Church of St Mary, Fairford, Gloucestershire*, The Society of Antiquaries of London, Occasional Paper n.s. 5 (London, 1984)

Whitehead, C., *Castles of the Mind: A Study of Medieval Architectural Allegory* (Cardiff: University of Wales Press, 2003)

Wilson, K. M. and E. M. Makowski, *Wykked Wyves and the Woes of Marriage: Misogamous Literature from Juvenal to Chaucer* (Albany, NY: State University of New York, 1990)

Wogan-Browne, J., 'The Virgin's Tale', in Evans and Johnson, pp.165–94

Woolf, R., *The English Mystery Plays* (Berkeley and Los Angeles, California: University of California Press, 1972, reprint 1980)

Index

A Feste for a Bryde 67–8, 142
Abbey of the Holy Ghost, The 135
abortion 103–4
ageism 122, 126
Adam of Cobsam, *The Wright's Chaste Wife* 27, 187–9, 193, 209, 216
adultery 19, 84, 86, 93, 96, 111, 115, 131, 138, 178, 181, 190–3, 206, 215
affinity 30–3, 43–4, 181
Albertus Magnus 96, 98, 113 n.73
Alice de Rouclif 103, 170
All Saint's Church, Croughton, Northamptonshire 26
Andreas Capellanus, *De Amore* 123–4
Anne, St 22, 24–6, 72, 110, 141, 144, 147, 167, 169, 172–3, 214 – see also Trinubium
Anne, Lady Scrope of Harling 214
Anne Stafford, Countess of Eu 48
annulment 33, 92
aphrodisiac 106
Aristotle 99
Ars Moriendi 212
Art of Dieing, The 212
Augustine, St 17, 18 n.18, 143
Avicenna, *Canon* 100

Ballad of a Tyrannical Husband, The 187, 193–4, 205, 209, 216
banns 45, 62, 81, 86, 88
baptism 30, 149, 152–3
Baret, John 43
Bede 149 n.24
Bedford Hours 147
Beidler, Peter 41
Bestiary (Aberdeen University MS 24) 108

Bible Moralisée 196
Bible, The: Old Testament: Genesis 15, 17 n.17, 130, 196; Leviticus 149; Proverbs 12, 16, 51, 54–5, 178, 185, 188, 213; Psalms 107, 144, 150–2, 200; Song of Solomon 107; New Testament: Colossians 134; Corinthians 16–17, 30 n.4; Timothy 141, 180
Biscoglio, Frances 12
Blamires, Alcuin 21–2
Boke of Nurture Folowing Englondis Gise, The 83
Boke of the Craft of Dying, The 211 n.1
Book of Noria, The 197–8
Book of Tobit, The 95
Book of Vices and Virtues, The 21, 117, 199, 208, 212
breastfeeding 146, 163
Brews, Elizabeth 38
Brews, Margery (wife of John Paston III) 37–8, 58
Bridget of Sweden, St *Revelations* 135, 141, 158, 160–1
Brooke, Christopher 65
Brown, Peter 16–17
Brundage, James 29, 31 n.29, 92
Burns, E. Jane 14–15, 116

Cadden, Joan 100
Calle, Richard 62
Candlemas Procession 165–8
Candlemes Day and the Kyllyng of þe Children of Israelle (MS Digby) 166–7, 174
canon law: marriage formation 12 n.3, 29–32, 47; sex 30, 31 n.9, 32–3, 91–6, 181

Carruthers, Mary 44
Chaucer, Geoffrey, *Canterbury Tales*:
  Clerk's Tale 42, 51–3, 55–6, 111, 186, 213; *Franklin's Tale* 127; *Man of Law's Tale* 26, 40, 42, 46–7, 51, 56–9, 186–7, 213–14; *Merchant's Tale* 41, 50, 53, 84–5, 106, 108, 111, 114–15, 117, 121, 186–7, 213–14; *Miller's Tale* 114, 118, 121, 188; *Parson's Tale* 133; *Second Nun's Tale* 23; *Wife of Bath's Prologue* 10, 13–14, 20, 26–7, 41–6, 48–51, 53, 55–9, 65–6, 68, 84, 88, 91, 114–28, 130, 139, 182, 184, 187, 189, 201, 210, 215–16; *Wife of Bath's Tale* 186
Chester Cycle: *De Deluvio Noe* 199; *Nativity* 156–9; *Purification* 166
childbirth: birth belts 144, 164–5 – *see also* Marian belts; birthing chamber 161, 164; death in 171; gifts 153, 164; linen 147; prayers 144–5; medical recipes 145–6
childcare 153–4
choice (of spouse) 32, 40–7, 51–9
Christina of Markyate 22–3, 135
church porch 65
church wedding ceremony (*in facie ecclesiae*) 61–2, 65, 69, 71–81, 84–5
Churching of Women, The 148–53, 165–71; fee 167–8 – *see also* Candlemas Procession
clandestine marriage 61, 63–4, 81–2, 212
coitus interruptus 104, 113
Coletti, Theresa 155, 165–6
conduct books 14, 27, 33, 86, 124, 178–86, 198, 209, 213, 217
consanguinity 30–1, 43–4, 181
consent 12 n.3, 29–32, 47, 50–1, 59, 61–2, 65, 72–3, 76
Constantine the African, *De Coitu* 106
contraception 103–5, 112–13, 139

Cooper, Helen 41
courting 34–5, 41, 49, 58
Coventry Cycle: *Shearmen and Tailors' Pageant* 156–60, 164
cuckingstool 198
Cursor Mundi 196

Dan Michel, *Ayenbite of Inwyte* 84
De Coniuge non Ducenda 19
De Secretis Mulierum 98
death in childbirth 171; of children 173–4
Delany, Sheila 48, 134
Denston, Katherine 171–2
digamy (remarriage) 30, 92, 116, 123
domestic violence 198, 200–1
dos/dotalium 36, 48, 65–6
dower 35–6, 39–40, 63, 65, 85, 88, 213
dowry 35, 38–9, 47, 49, 51, 53, 65, 189
Duffy, Eamon 25, 169
Dunmow Flitch 120, 184

Eleanor de Montfort 186
Eleanor of Castile 47, 50
eligibility to marry: *adolescentia* (age of puberty) 29 – *see also* affinity, consanguinity, consent
Elizabeth, St (Mother of John the Baptist) 25, 144
Ellen de Rouclif 145–7, 149, 153, 168
Elliott, Dyan 129, 132
Eros 92
Evangelium 69 n.25, 79 n.51, 80 n.55
Eve: garrulousness of 204; spinning of 204

fabliau 11, 106, 111, 114–15, 118, 188–90, 192
Fayreford, Thomas (Physician) 143
female sexual pleasure 98–101, 103, 105, 111, 115, 118–19, 121–5
femme couverte 206
femme sole 205
Fitzherbert, Anthony, *Boke of Husbandry* 194

Fleming, Peter 35, 42, 45
force (in marriage formation) 30–3
Fourth Lateran Council (1215) 21, 30, 62

Gaddesden, John, *Rosa Anglica* 100–1
Galen 99
Geoffrey de La Tour-Landry, *Book of the Knight of La Tour-Landry* 98–9, 142, 179, 181
Gibson, Gail McMurray 146, 150, 160, 165, 170, 172, 206 n.31, 208
Goldberg, P. J. P. 33 n.16
gossips (god-sibs) 149, 152, 170, 203, 206–8, 216
Gratian, *Decretum* 20, 30, 93 n.8
Green, Monica 101–2, 143, 146
Guy de Chauliac, *Cyrurgie* 99, 143

Hallissy, Margaret 113
handfasting 74–6, 91
Hanawalt, Barbara 34, 37, 188–9
Hansen, Elaine Tuttle 111
Heloise 18–21
Hildegard of Bingen 101, 109
How the Good Wijf Tauȝte hir Douȝtir 33, 49, 64, 154, 182, 185, 189, 208
How the Wise Man Tauȝt His Son 185–6
hymen 105, 109, 155, 162 – see also sophistication

Idley, Peter, *Instructions to his Son* 97–8, 119, 183–5, 187
impedimentum dirimens (marriage impediments) 31, 40, 44, 51, 61–2
impotence 31, 33, 121, 133, 177–8
Isidore of Seville, *Etymologiae* 97

Jacob's Well 94, 96, 108, 130
Jacobus de Voragine, *Legenda Aurea* 69 n.26
Jacquard, Danielle and Claude Thomasset 104

Jerome, St *Adversus Jovinianum* 17
Joan of Acre 50
jointure 36–9, 53, 59, 118

Kela, Thomas 38
Kempe, Margery, *Book* 27, 35, 86, 128–40, 161, 168–9, 175, 180, 211, 215–16
Knowing of Woman's Kind in Childing, The 102–4, 112 n.69, 143–4, 146, 156–7, 160, 171

Laqueur, Thomas 99
Lanfrank (Lanfranco of Milan), *Science of Cirurgie* 99
Laskaya, Anne 14, 110
lechery (effects on the body of) 95, 101, 108, 117
Liber Regie Capelle 168
Liber Trotuli (MS Additional 34111) 103
Love, Nicholas, *Mirror of the Blessed Life of Jesus Christ, The* 73 n.37
lyrics: 'A Forsaken Maiden's Lament' 34; 'A Midsummer Day's Dance' 34; 'Cherry Tree Carol' 156–7; 'Love in the Garden' 112; 'Old Hogyn's Adventure' 121; 'Our Sir John' 124; 'In Praise of Women' 22; 'Ten Wyves in the Tavern' 121; 'The Boar's Head Carol' 67 n.21; 'Too Much Sex' 108–9

magpie 108, 117
Malory, Thomas, *Book of Sir Tristram De Lyones* 171
Mann, Jill 47, 111, 116
Margaret Beaufort 132
Margaret, Princess (Sister of Edward IV) 82–3
Margaret, St 144
Marian birth belts 164–5
marriage: bed blessing 93–4, 106; ceremony blessings 77–81; chastity in

237

129, 132–8; contract 35–40 – *see also dos/dotalium*; liturgy 65–6, 69, 71–81 – *see also Sarum Missal*
married saints 23–6, 135–6
Martin, Priscilla 13, 41, 43, 66, 126
Mary Play, The (Cotton Vespasian D VIII) 27, 69–81; 155, 163
McCarthy, Conor 12, 77 n.46
Meditationes Vitae Christi 73
menstrual blood (toxicity of) 95
menstrual regulators 104–5
merchet 37–8, 51
Meredith, Peter 69, 71, 73
midwives 142–3, 159–62, 164, 167–8
misericords (domestic violence on) 198
misogamy 18–20
Mrs Noah 28, 196–209, 215–16
mulier fortis (Proverbs 31) 12, 22, 54–6, 59, 69, 178, 185, 188, 194, 205
Myrc, John *Festial* 24, 40, 54, 79, 110 n.61, 148; *Instructions for Parish Priests* 62–4, 95, 133, 148, 154

Newcastle Cycle: *Noah's Ark* 197
Nights of Tobias 109–10
N-Town Cycle: *Birth of Christ* 157–60, 162–3; *Fall of Man* 204; *Joseph's Return* 156; *Noah* 196; *Purification* 167; *Slaughter of the Innocents* 173; *Trial of Mary and Joseph* 97
nuptial mass 65, 71, 79 – *see also Sarum Missal*

Old Testament Wives: Rachel 80–1, 85; Rebecca 80–1, 85; Sara 80–1, 85
Osbern of Bokenham, *Vita S. Annae matris S. Mariae* 149–50, 170–1

Pastons: Agnes 32, 213; Edmund II 49; Elizabeth 32, 39, 42; John I 156; John III 36–9; Margaret 36–7, 62, 157; Margery 61–2 ; John II (Sir) 38; William III 49

penis captivus 98–9
Peter Lombard, *Sententiae* 61
Philippa, Princess, (Wife of Eric King of Denmark, Norway and Sweden) 82–3
Phillips, Helen 110, 116
Phillips, Kim 42, 128
postnatal care (of mother) 145–6
Priapus 107
prohibition (of sex) 92–3, 95
Protevangelion 69 n.25, 159
Pseudo-Matthew 69, 159

Queen Mary Psalter 25

rape 30, 32
Raymon de Penyafort 92
REED (*Records of Early English Drama*) Chester 70 n.30; Coventry 71 n.31
Riddy, Felicity 33 n.16
Robert Mannying of Brunne, *Handlyng Synne* 64, 97

Salisbury, Eve 12
Sarum Missal (*Ordo ad Faciendum Sponsalia*) 65, 71–81, 93, 106, 137, 150–1, 156 – *see also* nuptial mass
scolds 198
Scrope, Stephen 32–2, 39, 42
Sekenesse of Wymmen, The 145–6
senex amans 107, 109
separation (*a mensa et thoro*) 31, 177
sexual positions 93, 96, 107, 112–13
St Mary's, Fairford, Gloucestershire 74
sophistication 105
spinning (and allied procedures) 188, 191–3, 204–6, 209
sponsa Christi 131
swaddling 161

Theofrastus 20, 139
Thomas Aquinas, St *Summa Theologica* 29 n.21, 75–6, 94
Thomasine Bonaventure (digamist) 42

Towneley Cycle: *Annunciation* 155–6; *Processus Noe cum Filiis* 199–200, 203, 206; *Second Shepherds' Play* 161, 164
Trinubium (Holy Kinship) 24–5
Trotula ensemble (*Liber Sinthomatibus Mulierum, De Curis Mulierum, De Ornatu Mulierum*) 101
Twycross, Meg 87

Valerius 20
vagina 93, 98, 103–5, 112–14, 119–20, 127, 132, 139
vaginal constrictives 105
vaginismus 98–9 – *see also penis captivus*
verba de presenti (marriage formation) 62
virginity 13, 23, 25, 52, 105, 135–7, 155, 162, 164
Virgin Mary: childbearing of 155–63; churching of 165–7; motherhood of 163–4; wedding of 69–81

wedding: cake 68; dress 82–3; feast 83–5; ring 64–5, 76–9, 86–7; vows 65, 68–9, 73–6
Wedding of Sir Gawain and Dame Ragnell, The 81–4, 88, 186
wet nurse 146–7, 170
West, Eleanor 32–3
Whalley Abbey Orphrey 79
William of Hoo *Letter-Book, The* 87–8
William of Shoreham, *De Septem Sacramentis (De Matrimonio)* 31–3
women: anatomy (inversion of men's) 99; dress (as vanity) 180, 187; drinking in taverns 182, 208; wills (bequests in): birth belt 164, linen for childbirth 147, wedding rings 86–7; work 188–95, 205–6

York Cycle: *Building of the Ark* 201; *Expulsion* 204; *Flood* 199–200, 202–3; *Joseph's Trouble About Mary* 156; *Nativity* 157–8, 161; *Purification* 141, 166